Carol Altmann was born into a robust family of seven in Warrnambool, Victoria, in 1965. As a notorious classroom chatterbox, avid reader and writer, journalism became a natural career path and, in the last seventeen years, she has worked for country, metropolitan and national news-papers based in Warrnambool, Adelaide and Hobart. Carol is now a political reporter in Adelaide, where she lives by the beach with her partner, three exuberant dogs and one ageing cat. This is her first book.

After PORT ARTHUR

Personal stories of courage and resilience ten years on from the tragedy that shocked the nation

CAROL ALTMANN

ALLEN&UNWIN

First published in 2006

Allen & Unwin
83 Alexander Street
Crows Nest NSW 2065
Australia
Phone: (61 2) 8425 0100
Fax: (61 2) 9906 2218
Email: info@allenandunwin.com
Web: www.allenandunwin.com

National Library of Australia
Cataloguing-in-Publication entry:
Altmann, Carol, 1965-.
After Port Arthur : personal stories of courage and
resilience ten years on from the tragedy that shocked the
nation.

ISBN 1 74114 268 7.

1. Port Arthur Massacre, 1996 - Personal narratives. 2.
Victims of violent crimes - Tasmania - Port Arthur -
Biography. 3. Massacres - Tasmania - Port Arthur. I.
Title.

364.1523

Edited by Karen Ward
Text designed by Phil Campbell
Typeset by Michael Kuszla, J&M Typesetting
Map designed by Kerrie Denholm
Printed in Australia by Griffin Press

10 9 8 7 6 5 4 3 2 1

To those who were there at the beginning of this book,
and those who were there at the end.

CONTENTS

MAP OF THE
PORT ARTHUR REGION

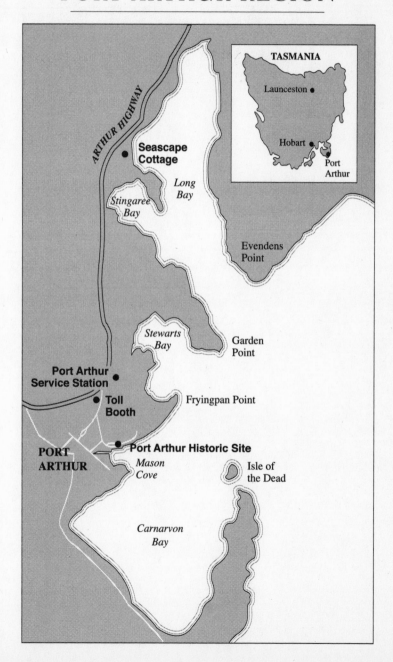

ARTHUR HIGHWAY

Seascape Cottage

Long Bay

Stingaree Bay

Evendens Point

Stewarts Bay

Garden Point

Port Arthur Service Station

Toll Booth

Fryingpan Point

PORT ARTHUR

Port Arthur Historic Site

Mason Cove

Isle of the Dead

Carnarvon Bay

TASMANIA

Launceston

Hobart

Port Arthur

PROLOGUE

Martin Bryant and his girlfriend, Petra Wilmott, awoke early to a gorgeous autumn morning on 28 April 1996. If Bryant was feeling the effects of a few drinks from the night before, he wasn't showing it. The pair had eaten dinner at Bryant's mother's house, just a few blocks from his own home at 30 Clare Street, New Town, then partied at Hobart's The Cadillac Club before heading home around midnight.

Bryant, a blond, lean 28 year old, had met the twenty-year-old Petra only a few weeks earlier, after she had answered his newspaper advertisement for a gardener. Bryant was Petra's first boyfriend and the two got along well. The sleepy-eyed young woman from Nicholls Rivulet, a rural locality nestled in the hills of southern Tasmania, was taken with his quiet, gentle ways. Despite the age difference, they liked to hang out together.

Petra had been with Bryant when he went shopping a fortnight earlier for a new sports bag which, he told her, would hold his Tai Chi gear. Petra remembers Bryant being quite specific about what sort of bag he wanted, even bringing a tape measure to the Myer department store in central Hobart to make sure the bag was long enough. He chose a large Prince tennis racquet bag: it was, he decided, just the right size.

Ten days later, the pair spent Anzac Day together, travelling to the historic tourist town of Richmond, about 30 minutes north of Hobart, where they took 'happy snaps' of each other. On the morning of 28 April, however, Bryant wanted to be alone. He had things to do, he told Petra, and they might catch up later in the day. After waking at 6 a.m., Petra left for home about two hours later. At precisely 9.47 a.m., Bryant set the electronic alarm on his rambling home and walked to his yellow Volvo 240GL sedan, which had a surfboard strapped to its roof-racks.

He threw the heavy Prince bag into the back seat, but this was to be no surfing trip. Zipped inside the bag was a Colt AR15 .223 semi-automatic rifle; a weapon capable of penetrating steel from half a kilometre away. Bryant also loaded another two weapons into the car that day; an SLR semi-automatic .308 calibre rifle and a semi-automatic Daewoo 12-gauge shotgun, plus numerous boxes of ammunition. Lastly, he packed two pairs of Smith and Wesson hand-cuffs, a long-blade hunting knife, a length of sash cord, firelighters and several containers of petrol. Satisfied with his preparations, Bryant climbed into the driver's seat and began the 90-minute journey from Hobart to the Port Arthur Historic Site on the Tasman Peninsula: a remote area made up of small farming and fishing towns and some of Australia's most breathtaking coastline.

Set amid the dry bush and black, ragged cliffs that dominate the Tasman Peninsula, the Port Arthur Historic Site appears, at first, incongruous. Hidden from the roadway, the site only comes into full view once visitors have left their cars, passed through the tourist centre and poured out near what was once a cricket oval. There, they are taken aback by the vastness of the grounds: a wide expanse of lush, well-tended lawns, punctuated by tall, leafy English oaks and pines. The sweep of green rolls to the edge of Mason Cove where, more likely than not, a fishing boat or two is retrieving cray-pots. Immaculately restored colonial cottages dot the landscape, the sun bouncing off their window panes and their gardens thick with the scent of lavender. It is an ethereal place of big, blue skies and fresh air: an English country town set down in the middle of nowhere. From a distance, the convict ruins – most roofless and missing great chunks from their walls – look more like the tumbled remains of Celtic castles than the remnants of a prison. The ruins are sprinkled across the 115 ha site, their sandstone walls absorbing and reflecting the sunlight, drawing visitors into what appears to be a place of comfort and warmth. More than 12,000 convicts passed through these buildings between 1830 and 1877 and it is their story which has made the site Tasmania's biggest tourist attraction.

Their lingering presence, however, makes Port Arthur a place of tormented beauty. Most people come away from Port Arthur with a sense of unease, knowing that this was a place of immense suffering.

It is as if, having walked through the remains of the penitentiary building, the asylum, the church and the Model Prison, something eerie and intensely sad is absorbed through your skin. There is a sense of treading on sacred ground, of being offered a sobering glimpse into the barbaric penal system upon which colonial Australia thrived. By the end of the day, many of the quaint English cottages don't have quite the same charm, and the convict ruins, with their gutted hearts, cast the longest shadows. For all of its aesthetic appeal, Port Arthur is a place with a cheerless soul.

By the time Martin Bryant set his security alarm, retired Adelaide funeral director Ron Neander was already on the road. He was travelling with his wife, Gwen, from the Mornington caravan park on Hobart's eastern shore down towards the historic site. The convict ruins were expected to be a highlight of their long-awaited Tasmanian holiday, which they had begun six days earlier.

Brigid Cook, the kitchen manager of the site's main eatery, the Broad Arrow Café, was anticipating a busy shift as she headed from her home at Highcroft, 7 km from nearby Nubeena. The café, housed in a rustic stone cottage, offered a relaxed, cafeteria-style lunch, after which people could wander through the adjacent souvenir shop and browse through the usual assortment of tourist knick-knacks. It was a popular spot in which to break up the long walk around the grounds and Brigid knew business would be brisk on such a fine day. The peak tourist season was winding down at Port Arthur, but the warm weather would still see more than 600 people pass through the gates on 28 April.

Nubeena chemist Walter Mikac was also determined to make the most of the sunshine, given the long Tasmanian winter that lay ahead. He set off early for a round of golf on the Tasman greens near the Port Arthur site. His wife, Nanette, and their two young daughters, Alannah and Madeline, would make their own fun that day with a ride on the Isle of the Dead ferry at Port Arthur, followed by a picnic lunch on the lawn. While Nanette was preparing the children for their outing, their grandfather, Keith Moulton, was sitting down at his kitchen table in nearby White Beach to pen a letter to family back on the mainland. Having lost his wife just weeks earlier, Keith found a new comfort in writing 'home'. One of Nanette's best friends, the local doctor Pam Ireland, was content to have a quiet day at home while her husband, Steve, also a GP, worked out in the paddocks of their Nubeena property. Pam was looking forward to a few easy hours stretched out on the couch with a copy of *The Weekend Australian* newspaper.

Back towards Hobart, Martin Bryant was a half-hour into his journey when he stopped at a newsagency in Midway Point and, despite being a non-smoker, bought a cigarette lighter. He left quickly, sharing none of the usual pleasantries with the owner, Angelo Kessarios, who once knew Bryant as a regular. This time, Bryant didn't even wait for his change.

Another fifteen minutes on and Bryant stopped again, at a supermarket in the town of Sorell where, inexplicably, he bought a bottle of tomato sauce. It was then on to the roadside shops of Forcett, where Bryant pulled over for a cup of coffee. He chatted briefly to the service station owner, Gary King, telling him he intended to go surfing at nearby Roaring Beach. Mr King thought this odd, given that the calm conditions would mean very few waves.

Bryant continued down the Arthur Highway to Taranna, where he made his third stop, this time to buy $15 worth of petrol. In doing so, he passed the home of Colin and Robyn Dell, who were busy preparing their wood pile for the coming winter. As they cut and stacked the timber, the volunteer ambulance vehicle sat idle in their yard. The Dells were volunteer officers, and it was Colin's turn to be on call for the Sunday. The Hobart *Mercury* newspaper photographer Leigh Winburn was using his rostered day off to help his brother-in-law chop firewood from a bush block. Come late autumn, most Tasmanians are consumed with the task of collecting firewood for the long stretch between May and September when the days are short and the frosts linger.

Not far from Taranna, Bryant pulled left off the Arthur Highway and into the grounds of the Seascape guest house. The two-storey, pink-and-white cottage was one of several buildings which made up the Seascape property tucked on the curve of Long Bay and enjoying one of the best views on the Tasman Peninsula. Having holidayed and later lived on the peninsula, Bryant knew the place and its elderly owners, David and Sally Martin, well.

This Sunday was David Martin's seventy-second birthday, but there was no time for a leisurely breakfast. Instead, the Martins were doing what they enjoyed most: entertaining travellers. A couple had just checked out of the guest house and, after waving them off shortly after 11.15 a.m., the Martins were setting about cleaning the cottage, when they were disturbed by a yellow Volvo crunching down the driveway.

Back in Hobart, Dr Bryan Walpole, the director of patient services and former head of emergency services at the Royal Hobart Hospital, was assessing the last of a group of interstate doctors who had attended a special trauma management training course that weekend. If he hadn't been otherwise occupied, chances are he might have joined a meeting scheduled that afternoon with his lawyer friend, Roland Browne, and other members of the Tasmanian Coalition for Gun Control. In the wake of the Dunblane massacre a few weeks earlier, the group was ramping up its push for tighter gun laws and was due to meet the state's police minister the following Wednesday. Hobart psychiatrist Dr Ian Sale was also caught up in a weekend think tank, having driven to Launceston for a briefing on workers compensation. He was looking forward to a relaxing drive back down the Midland Highway, listening to the football broadcast.

At about 12.30 p.m., a Victorian couple, Maureen and John Mason, pulled into the Seascape property, hoping to inquire about prices for a future holiday. It was Martin Bryant who came out of the house and met the Masons in the front yard. No, they couldn't come in and inspect the rooms, he explained, as 'my mother and father are out for ten minutes' and 'I've got my girlfriend inside'. While Mrs Mason would recall Bryant appeared agitated and talked strangely, he stood calmly by the front door of the cottage as they pulled away in their car.

Once the Masons were gone, Bryant locked the cottage, put

the house keys in the Volvo glove box and returned to the Arthur Highway. Only a short distance along, he stopped to talk to a couple of young women who were having car trouble. Seeing the surf-board, they asked Bryant if he was going surfing. 'No,' he replied quizzically, 'I'm going to the Isle of the Dead to get rid of some wasps'. WASPs is an acronym for white Anglo-Saxon Protestants. Bryant bought a small amount of cannabis from the pair and sug-gested they meet later at the Broad Arrow Café for coffee.

By 12.45 p.m., Bryant had passed the Tudor-style Fox and Hounds hotel and the Bush Mill tourist railway which signals the start of the Port Arthur area, before reaching the Jetty Road turnoff which marks the entrance to the Port Arthur Historic Site. Bryant, how-ever, continued straight past: there was more business to attend to. A couple of hundred metres from Jetty Road, he turned left onto Palmers Lookout Road which wraps around the southern edge of the historic site. Here Bryant visited Roger and Marian Larner, a long-time peninsula couple who had first met Bryant and his par-ents fifteen years earlier, when the Bryants owned a holiday house in the area. Bryant made small talk about buying some Murray Grey cattle from Mr Larner before mentioning that he 'wouldn't mind buying the Martins' place'. Mr Larner assumed he was referring to the land next door that was also owned by David and Sally Martin, who were a well-known and well-respected couple. Among their friends was the Tasman Peninsula mayor, Neil Noye, who on this particular Sunday was out fencing on his farm just a few kilometres from the Larner residence.

Before leaving the Larner property, Bryant asked if he might be able to visit Marian Larner up at the house. Mrs Larner had had previous dealings with Bryant. After a chance meeting in New Town in late 1993, Bryant had made a point of calling her regularly. The calls were frequent and annoying enough to prompt Mr Larner to encourage his wife to report it to police. She did. With this in mind, Mr Larner offered to accompany Bryant up to the house. Bryant's enthusiasm suddenly waned. He might come back later, he said, before returning to the Volvo and driving back towards the historic site.

The crowds might not have been at their summer strength, but still the Port Arthur Historic Site was humming by lunchtime. Information guide Wendy Scurr had just finished a tour on the Isle of the Dead ferry and was hoping to make it up to the Broad Arrow Café ahead of the ferry crowd. With only an hour for lunch, she didn't want to battle a long queue. Redline coach tour driver Ian McElwee had already returned to the sanctuary of his bus after enjoying a hot meal in the café. With his tour party out wandering the grounds, he could sit back and relax with the newspaper for a few hours.

Port Arthur information guide Ian Kingston had no such reprieve. He was still busy directing traffic when Bryant arrived at about 1.25 p.m. and argued about where he could park the Volvo. Bryant ignored Mr Kingston's direction to move away from the waterfront and parked there anyway. Bryant then grabbed his Prince sports bag and headed towards the Broad Arrow Café.

After ordering a large tray of food and a couple of fruit drinks, he joined those dining on the balcony. A Melbourne couple, Michael Beekman and Rebecca McKenna, were seated near Bryant and could hear him mumbling something about 'wasps' and there being few Japanese tourists at the site that day.

After eating his lunch, Bryant walked casually back into the café with his empty tray and the big, blue Prince bag hoisted over his shoulder. He found a vacant table in a far corner, placed the tennis bag down and coolly unzipped it.

1

THE MASSACRE

From the sports bag, Bryant pulled the Colt semi-automatic, loaded with about 26 live rounds in its 30-round magazine. Without uttering a word, he began shooting: precise, calculated, devastating shots that within 90 seconds would leave twenty people dead and another twelve severely injured.

Mo Yee (William) Ng and Sou Leng Chung, who were visiting Australia from Malaysia, were the first to fall. Death came so quickly to William that he was later found still clasping his dinner knife. Sou Leng was shot through the left ear, the bullet penetrating her brain. A third shot grazed the scalp of West Australian Mick Sargent, while a fourth entered the back of the head of his girlfriend, Kate Scott, killing the 21 year old instantly.

Bryant then began to move through the café, firing upon people at random. Victorian tourist Anthony Nightingale was heard to shout, 'No, no, not here' before taking a single, fatal shot to the neck. Anthony's body slumped against the café window, shocking those outside who, until that point, were still unsure if the gunfire was real or part of a re-enactment linked to the historic site.

Bryant next turned his gun on Victorians Kevin Sharp, his younger brother Ray and their close mate Wally Bennett, the last to arrive in a group of ten friends who were meeting for lunch in the café. Wally was shot at such close range that the bullet which passed through his neck held enough velocity to also kill Ray. Kevin was shot twice, including a fatal wound to the top of the head. Three of their friends, Gary Broome and Gaye and John Fidler, were wounded by the flying shrapnel. Nearby, Tony Kistan and Andrew Mills stood up as the shooting started and Tony, realising what was happening, quickly pushed his wife, Sarah, towards the door. Before he could follow, Bryant shot him through the back of the head.

Andrew Mills, an executive with a chemical firm, had only recently moved to Hobart from Sydney with his partner, David Capper. The pair had intended to open a guest house on the Tasman Peninsula. Andrew was killed instantly with a single shot to the head.

Sitting close to Mr Kistan and Mr Mills were two Camp Quality workers, Thelma Walker and Pamelia Law, who suffered shrapnel wounds before their friend, Peter Crosswell, who was also injured, dragged them from their chairs to the floor. Another tourist, Pat Barker, was also hit by shrapnel as she scrambled to hide under a table with eight of her ten friends lunching at the site that day. They remained huddled there as Bryant continued to shoot, this time turning his gun on a table occupied by Victorian man Graham Collyer, his friend Carolyn Loughton and her teenage daughter, Sarah. The three were hurrying to leave the table when Bryant fired at Graham, the bullet passing through his jaw, but not killing him. Graham slumped to the floor, conscious, but almost drowning on his own blood. He could see Sarah had been fatally wounded, despite her mother throwing herself on top of her to try to shield her from the gunfire. The bullet that hit Carolyn Loughton tore a 10-cm hole in her back and her eardrum was ruptured by the explosive noise of the bullet that killed her daughter. It would not be until Carolyn came out of surgery some 24 hours later that she would learn that Sarah, her only child, was dead.

From across the café, Ron Neander could see the skinny, blond-haired man shooting 'Rambo-style' from the hip. He watched as Bryant swivelled around from shooting Mr Collyer to take aim at Mervyn and Mary Howard. Mr Howard, a football administrator from the Victorian town of Dunnstown, died from a single shot to the head. The bullet which killed Mr Howard continued through the café window and past where Bryant had eaten lunch so calmly not minutes earlier. As Mr Howard slumped forward onto the table, Bryant shot Mrs Howard, but the injury was not fatal. Bryant moved closer, leaned over a vacant baby stroller owned by the Winter family, and shot Mrs Howard again at point-blank range.

Despite the unfolding carnage, the speed of the killings and a sense of disbelief that the gunshots could be real led to a strange calm in the café for the early part of Bryant's rampage. Once the enormity of what was happening began to sink in, however, those in the café began to push each other to safety or to scramble for cover.

Mr Neander was among them, hiding behind a rack of postcards and praying that his wife, Gwen, who had wandered off earlier to look at souvenirs, was safe.

Nearby, New Zealander Jo Winter crouched under a table with her father and her infant son, trying to quieten him and avoid attracting Bryant's attention. Her husband Jason, a talented young winemaker, was hiding elsewhere in the café with American tourists Dennis and Mary Olson. Bryant passed Jo Winter as he moved towards the souvenir shop. His attention was drawn elsewhere; this time to Robert Elliott who, perhaps in the hope of distracting the gunman and making a getaway, stood up from his table under which hid a group of other tourists. Bryant shot him twice: once in the arm and once in the head. Mr Elliott slumped against a fireplace where he lay badly injured, but alive.

Twelve people lay dead and another ten were wounded, some severely. It had taken seventeen shots in just fifteen seconds. Yet the killing was still not over.

Entering the souvenir shop, Bryant gunned down two local women working behind the counter; seventeen-year-old Nicole Burgess, who was shot in the head, and 26-year-old Elizabeth Howard, who was shot in the arm and chest. He then turned his rifle on Victorian tourist Dennis Lever who had seconds earlier pushed his wife, Coralee, and her friend, Vera Jary, behind a hessian screen used to display souvenir clothing. Before Mr Lever could hurry to his own hiding place, Bryant killed him with a single shot to the head.

Next Bryant aimed the gun at Gwen Neander who, separated from her husband, was trying to make it to an exit door when she was shot dead. Another four people, Peter and Carolyn Nash, Pauline Masters and Vera's husband Ron Jary, had rushed for the same exit: a glass door that, unbeknown to them, would not open. They pressed tightly against the glass doorway with an unidentified Asian man, all of them trapped and terrified, as Bryant momentarily returned to the café.

Here he spotted Jason Winter, who had recently moved to Hobart to take up a job with the Moorilla Estate winery. Mr Winter, hearing a lull in the gunfire after the shooting of Mrs Neander, thought Bryant had left the building. As he stood up from his hiding place, he saw Bryant and shouted, 'No, no' before a single shot penetrated his hand, neck and chest. A second bullet struck him in the head, killing him instantly. Shrapnel from his wounds sprayed into Dennis Olson, slicing his hand, scalp, eye and chest.

Somewhere within the turmoil, staff who had been serving customers at the café counter ran into the kitchen to warn their colleagues to get out. The kitchen manager, Brigid Cook, ran immediately out the back of the café and across to a group of tourists waiting to start a guided tour. She yelled at them not to go near the café, before running down into the car park to warn those who were milling around the tour buses.

Back inside the café, Bryant continued to prowl, this time moving back to the souvenir shop and the group pressed against the faulty glass exit door. They had nowhere to run. As Director of Public Prosecutions Damian Bugg, QC, would later tell the Tasmanian Supreme Court, people who survived the massacre would describe feelings of utter helplessness and 'almost a fatalistic acceptance that they were likely to be the next shot'.

As Bryant stood over the group crouched in the doorway, he first shot Ron Jary, then Pauline Masters and finally Peter Nash as he shielded his wife, Carolyn, who escaped unhurt. The Asian man huddling with them was to be next, but as Bryant took aim, his rifle ran out of bullets and didn't fire. The man, whose name remains unknown, was left unharmed as Bryant reloaded the rifle and, again without speaking a word, left the café.

Police estimated Bryant was in the café somewhere between 90 seconds and two minutes, yet the power of his weaponry allowed him to commit what Damian Bugg would describe as nothing less than slaughter. In that short burst of violence, Bryant had killed twenty people, almost murdered another five and severely wounded seven others.

Later the predictable and painful questions would come about whether something could have been done to stop Bryant as he moved through the café. As Damian Bugg was to tell the court, the defenceless tourists and café workers could do nothing. 'They had little or no opportunity to react…let alone escape; they certainly did not have any opportunity or means to retaliate.'

The speed of the killings did not abate as Bryant moved from the café on to the next part of his mission.

Standing on the café steps, Bryant began to take pot shots at the nearby information centre, the car park and across the cricket ground. With such a high-calibre weapon and full-metal jacket ammunition, he didn't need to get close to his intended victims.

As people began to flee, Bryant moved towards a string of buses parked near the waterfront. Raising the rifle to his shoulder, he fired at a group trying to run and struck Tigerline bus driver Royce Thompson square in the back. Mr Thompson crumpled to the ground with a fatal wound. Another group attempted to take cover behind the buses, but Bryant already had them in his sights. He fired at the group and struck Brigid Cook in the right leg. Winifred Aplin, who was holidaying from South Australia, was shot in the right side and died where she fell. Another bullet grazed the cheek of her friend, Yvonne Lockley, who managed to scramble onto a bus and to safety.

Janet Quin and her husband Neville, the owners of a wildlife park on Tasmania's east coast, were moving away from the buses towards the waterfront of Mason Cove until they heard Bryant was heading that way. They had begun to retrace their steps when Bryant fired and hit Janet. She collapsed near where Royce Thompson lay. The next shot struck the arm of another tourist, Doug Hutchinson, knocking him to the ground.

After Doug fell, Bryant lowered his rifle and walked calmly to his Volvo parked near the buses. There he switched firearms from the Colt AR15 to a .308 FN or SLR, another semi-automatic military-style weapon. Bryant then, inexplicably, sat for a moment in the driver's seat, perhaps contemplating his next move. Whatever his thoughts, Bryant soon left the Volvo and again began to take pot shots across the site, narrowly missing another four tourists, including two who had taken cover behind one of the site's glorious trees, which absorbed most of the bullet's power. He then walked back towards the buses until he reached the injured Janet Quin. Raising his rifle, he fired into her back. Her husband, Neville, who had become separated from his wife as people ran for cover, could hear the shooting from his hiding place on a nearby bus. Bryant climbed on board Ian McElwee's Redline coach but, finding it empty, began to shoot through the windows at passengers sitting in a Tigerline coach parked alongside. A South African tourist on board, Elva Gaylard, died instantly, while Adelaide visitor Gordon Francis was shot through the shoulder as he tried to close the coach door.

As the gunfire fell momentarily silent, Neville Quin moved from his hiding place to search for his wife, whom he found lying by the body of Royce Thompson. As he knelt by her side, clasping her hands, Bryant fired at him. The bullet missed, as did two more shots fired by Bryant as Mr Quin again dashed for the safety of the coach. Bryant followed him on board and, as Mr Quin crouched between two seats, raised his rifle, saying, 'No-one gets away from me'. Bryant fired, but a last-minute movement by Mr Quin saw the bullet miss its target and pass through the skin of his neck. He was badly wounded, but alive. Bryant, perhaps thinking Mr Quin was dead, moved on. Despite his own injury, Mr Quin managed to stagger back to his wife, only to have her die in his arms shortly later.

Bryant took a final shot before driving away from the car park. It was at American tourist James Balasko, who was scanning the scene with a video camera, trying to capture Bryant in action.

'There's somebody goin' crazy shooting people here,' Mr Balasko was able to mutter into his recorder as he watched Bryant move around the buses.

Although his hands were shaking, Mr Balasko kept the tape rolling as Bryant fired at him: and missed.

Video footage by a second tourist, Ian McLeod, would show a swarm of people moving up towards the toll booth at the top of Jetty Road to escape Bryant, who was also shown on the film driving towards the same area. Among those running up the hill was a group of mainland tourists, John and Caroline Boskovic and Peter and Pauline Grenfell, who had earlier shared a table with the Loughtons in the Broad Arrow Café.

Moving up Jetty Road, they caught up with Nanette Mikac and her two daughters, six-year-old Alannah and three-year-old Madeline. Nanette, carrying Madeline on her hip and with Alannah running beside her, tried to soothe the frightened children. 'We're safe now, Pumpkin,' she was heard to say to Alannah as they approached the toll booth. Bryant's Volvo came to a stop almost opposite Nanette who, thinking the driver might take them to safety, approached the vehicle. John Boskovic began to follow her, but stopped abruptly as Bryant stepped from the car, placed his hand on Nanette's shoulder and calmly told her three times to get down on her knees.

'Please don't hurt my babies,' Nanette pleaded.

Peter Grenfell, realising who the driver was, yelled, 'It's him' and sent the rest of the group scattering. The Mikac family was trapped. Bryant raised his rifle and killed Nanette with a single shot, before firing twice at Madeline. He then fired two shots at Alannah as she ran, terrified, to hide behind a gum tree off the roadside. Having missed, Bryant followed Alannah to her hiding place and, placing the rifle against her neck, fired a fatal shot. Amid the horror of what had already taken place, and what was yet to come, it was this brutal attack on a young family that Australians would come to consider as the defining act of a madman.

Since leaving the Broad Arrow Café, Bryant had murdered another seven people and severely injured five more. In all, 27 lives had now been lost in just a matter of minutes, with no hint of a reason. 'He clearly intended to cause maximum harm and there was no discrimination as to the choice of his victims,' Crown Prosecutor Damian Bugg was to later tell the court.

Bryant was now completely out of control. Whatever crazed plan he had held for blazing away at the Port Arthur Historic Site had been overtaken by events as they unfolded. He was now making it up as he went along. The swiftness of the shooting, the poor communications in the area and the geographic isolation of the site all combined to allow Bryant to run amok.

Perhaps not expecting to make it this far without being gunned down, Bryant decided to return to where he began: the Seascape guest house.

Having murdered the Mikacs, Bryant drove his Volvo to the toll booth and blocked a BMW that caught his eye. The burnished-gold coloured car was owned by Ken and Mary Rose Nixon, from Crabtree in Tasmania's Huon Valley. Behind the wheel was Jim Pollard, a retiree from New South Wales, who was enjoying a day out with Mrs Nixon and two other interstate friends, Robert and Helene Salzmann. Mr Pollard had been driving into the site when a tourist ran out on Jetty Road and warned them to turn back. While Mr Pollard managed to reverse the car back to the toll booth, it was to prove fruitless as, within minutes, all four occupants would be dead.

Bryant approached the BMW and asked the group to get out, prompting Mr Salzmann to leave the car to remonstrate with him. Bryant responded by returning to his Volvo, retrieving the .308 SLR, and shooting Mr Salzmann at point-blank range.

Despite the obvious danger, Mr Pollard climbed out of the driver's seat to confront Bryant and was also shot dead.

Other drivers in the area began to absorb the scene unfolding before their eyes and tried to reverse their cars as quickly as possible. As they did so, Bryant first pulled Mrs Salzmann and then Mrs Nixon from the BMW, fatally shot each of them and dumped their bodies on the roadway.

Bryant then transferred some of his belongings from the Volvo to the BMW, including the Colt rifle, extra ammunition, the two pairs of handcuffs and a can of petrol. He left behind his third rifle, a Daewoo semi-automatic, plus several more cans of fuel, fire-lighters and a cluster of keys marked Seascape. Before setting off towards the guest house, Bryant fired one more pot shot at a vehicle that was being driven by Graham Sutherland. As Mr Sutherland began to reverse his Magna at top speed, a bullet from Bryant's SLR shattered the windscreen, but failed to injure Mr Sutherland, his wife, or their two sons travelling in the back seat.

Bryant sped off towards the cluster of shops that constituted the main street of Port Arthur. Here, several of those who had escaped by reversing away from the toll booth had stopped outside the Port Arthur service station to warn others away from the site. One woman, Debra Rabe, had rushed into the photographic store across the road from the service station and urged its owner, Jim Laycock, to call the police.

Mr Laycock, who was to later die of cancer, described what happened next as 'the most frightening two minutes of my life'.

Bryant pulled into the service station, blocking the exit, just as former Tasmanian Glenn Pears and his girlfriend, Zoe Hall, were about to leave in their white Corolla. Mr Laycock watched help-lessly as Bryant tried to drag Ms Hall from the car and then, after Mr Pears intervened, marched Mr Pears away from the Corolla at gunpoint, forced him to kneel in the boot of the BMW and slammed it shut. A panic-stricken Ms Hall clambered from the pas-senger seat across to the driver's seat, but before she could grapple for the keys in the ignition, Bryant fired three quick shots through the windscreen, killing her instantly. Bryant then returned to the BMW and, with Mr Pears trapped inside, sped off to Seascape.

Exactly what had happened at the Seascape guest house that day remains known only to Bryant, but police believe the owners, David and Sally Martin, were murdered sometime between 11.45 a.m. and 12.40 p.m.: before he arrived at the Larners' and the historic site. Two residents reported hearing gunshots in the area – anywhere between two and twelve shots from a high-calibre rifle – at around lunchtime.

Autopsies would later reveal Mr Martin had a cloth gag tied around his mouth and chin and a gunshot wound below his right ear, with the wound tracking down the neck muscles into the chest. There was another bullet injury, an exit wound, just below the base of his neck.

DNA testing of Bryant's hunting knife would also reveal traces of Mr Martin's blood, indicating he had been stabbed.

Mrs Martin was found to have had five lacerations to the back of her head and a depressed skull fracture, as if she had been hit heavily with a blunt object. Her left shoulder also showed signs of a gunshot wound. It would be almost a full 24 hours, however, before their fate was discovered.

Having skidded to a halt at the entrance to Seascape, Bryant leapt from the BMW and began to shoot randomly at vehicles passing on the Arthur Highway, the single major road that links the peninsula to Hobart. His first bullets sailed past John Rooke, who was lumbering by in his Datsun sedan, pulling a fully laden trailer. Mr Rooke thought the bullets must have been blanks, but was stunned as he looked in his rear view mirror and saw the windows of a red Falcon shatter behind him.

A four-wheel-drive sat between Mr Rooke and the red Falcon. It was being driven by Melbourne woman, Linda White, who was travelling with her boyfriend, Michael Wanders. As Bryant peppered their vehicle, sending window glass flying, one of the bullets cut through Ms White's forearm and almost blew it away. Despite her massive injury, Ms White managed to steer the vehicle around the next bend, before it came to a halt, its throttle cable severed by the gunshots.

While Mr Wanders tried in vain to restart the four-wheel-drive, several more carloads of visitors drove unknowingly into Bryant's sights. The first driver, Doug Horne, suffered shrapnel wounds as a bullet pierced his windscreen but fortunately missed the other three occupants, including Neville Shilkin, who was sitting in the front passenger seat. Again, despite the damage to his chest, shoulder and arm, Mr Horne manoeuvred the car to where a distressed Ms White and Mr Wanders stood stranded. The young couple climbed into the Horne car and Mr Shilkin sped towards the safety of the nearby Fox and Hounds hotel.

Not long after the Horne vehicle was shot at, a red sedan rounded the bend towards Seascape. Its driver, Simon Williams, a Canadian embassy official based in Canberra, was touring Tasmania with his wife, Susan. The pair was startled to see a car reversing at high speed towards them but, within a few seconds, Mr Williams spotted Bryant and heard a shot. Mr Williams accelerated, hoping to speed past Bryant to safety, but a second shot punctured the car window, shattering Mrs Williams's left hand and spraying Mr Williams with shrapnel.

Although in pain, Mr Williams managed to guide his car to the refuge of the Fox and Hounds hotel. The driver of the reversing vehicle, Anne Wardle, also managed to make it to safety, despite a bullet hitting her car door as she passed Bryant. Once out of Bryant's sights, Mrs Wardle leapt from her car and waved down other vehicles that were driving into almost certain danger; a self-less act which may have spared lives.

As people learned that a gunman was shooting at random and the stream of passing cars dried up, Bryant turned his attention back to Seascape and his hostage, Glenn Pears. Parking the BMW close to the cottage, Bryant dragged Mr Pears into the house and secured his hands behind his back with the Smith and Wesson handcuffs. The second pair was tied to the first and then fastened to something solid within the house. Mr Pears could have done nothing but watch in fear as Bryant returned to the BMW, doused it with petrol and set it ablaze. At some point over the coming hours, Mr Pears would also be shot dead.

The two local constables who were first on the scene, Paul Hyland and Gary Whittle, arrived at Seascape to find the BMW in flames. It was about 2 p.m. Barely 30 minutes had passed since Bryant had removed the rifle from his Prince sports bag and begun shooting in the Broad Arrow Café, yet for those experiencing the drama, the world had become mad and misshapen.

Holed up in Seascape, Bryant had access to not only his own powerful weapons, but an unknown number of firearms and ammunition collected by the Martins and their two sons. He began firing at the two policemen, forcing them to take cover in a muddy ditch off the highway, where they would be forced to shelter for the next eight hours while Bryant continued to shoot sporadically.

Ambulance sirens began to wail as news of the shootings reached peninsula and Hobart emergency service workers. Volunteer ambulance workers Colin and Robyn Dell sped down a narrow back road towards the Fox and Hounds hotel after being flagged down by Anne Wardle and warned away from the more direct route along the Arthur Highway. The Dells' colleagues, Kaye Fox and Gary Alexander, headed to the toll booth area, while the Nubeena GPs, Pam and Steve Ireland, travelled straight to the Broad Arrow Café.

In Hobart, the Royal Hobart Hospital activated a Code Brown emergency; a disaster response plan that had only recently been updated and improved to deal with any large-scale trauma.

While the various medical teams worked frantically to help the injured, an enormous police operation was also moving into position on the peninsula. The response would eventually involve almost half of Tasmania's 1000-strong police force, plus officers from the Special Operations Group and reinforcements flown across from Victoria. A command post was set up at a Tasmanian devil tourist park in Taranna, from where police would spend the next eighteen hours locked in a tense stand-off with Bryant.

Tasmanian police negotiator Terry McCarthy, backed up by a team including police psychologist Mike Ryan and forensic psychiatrist Dr Ian Sale, tried to establish what sort of person they were dealing with, whether Bryant was acting alone and whether any of his hostages were still alive.

Sergeant McCarthy spoke by telephone to Bryant six times between 4.30 p.m. and 9.30 p.m., before the cordless phone at Seascape lost power and the line was lost. During this time, Bryant toyed with the negotiating team, calling himself 'Jamie' and, at various times, pretending to prepare meals and drinks for his hostages and to move them from room to room.

At one point he compared how he was feeling to being 'just like on a Hawaiian holiday' before Sergeant McCarthy asked him what he meant.

'I don't know myself, no,' Bryant responded, sounding confused.

He also was at pains to prove that he was apparently a man of significant means, saying he once missed out on buying a $95,000 helicopter advertised in the local newspaper.

'You can buy a helicopter. I've got the money, don't you understand, I've got the money,' Bryant said, his voice rising angrily.

His only demand was for a helicopter to fly him and one hostage, Sally Martin, to Hobart, where he intended to board a flight to Adelaide. What the police didn't know at that time was that Mrs Martin was already dead.

As the conversation trailed on, Bryant gave the first clue as to what, in his mind, prompted him to kill the Martins. He described Sally Martin as 'bad news' and explained that his father was going to buy the small farm the Martins owned at Palmers Lookout Road before Mrs Martin 'started causing trouble'.

Despite the devastation that he had caused that day, Bryant remained abnormally calm for most of his conversations with Sergeant McCarthy. His voice was high-pitched and almost singsong as he responded to questions about what had happened at Port Arthur.

'Was anyone hurt?' he asked in a childlike tone as Sergeant McCarthy talked about the shootings.

At other times he showed a sharp temper, warning Sergeant McCarthy he would 'blow this' if police marksmen attempted to move in on the cottage.

Not knowing if the hostages were still alive, the police Special Operations Group was unable to chance storming the cottage. Its broad, open gardens gave Bryant a perfect view of any rifle night sights or sudden movement. All the police could do was try to avoid the sniper shots that burst at random from the various windows of the cottage throughout the night. Except for a two-hour hiatus between 4 a.m. and 6 a.m., Bryant fired more than 250 shots from Seascape, using the wide variety of guns at his disposal. Not a single shot was fired by police in return, however, for fear of killing any of those they believed could still be alive inside.

As the siege entered its second day, there was a breakthrough. At 7.45 a.m., a police officer spotted smoke coming from the first floor of the cottage. Within ten minutes the fire had taken hold in the first and ground floors, causing ammunition to explode in the intense heat. Emergency services, unable to risk running into what sounded like gunfire, watched as the blaze continued to spread. Suddenly Bryant burst from the building, his clothes on fire, and disappeared around a corner.

A few seconds later he reappeared naked, having stripped himself of the flaming clothes, and dropped to his knees on the lawn. Police moved in swiftly, handcuffing his legs and wrists and dragging him to a waiting vehicle. The burning cottage continued to crackle and crumble behind them.

On 7 November 1996, after initially pleading not guilty to all charges, Martin Bryant changed his plea to one of guilty on all counts. In all, he faced 72 charges for what Tasmanian Chief Justice William Cox described as 'an unprecedented list of crimes': 35 counts of murder, twenty counts of attempted murder, three counts of grievous bodily harm, eight counts of wounding, four counts of aggravated assault, one count of unlawfully setting fire to property and one count of arson.

On 22 November, Justice Cox sentenced 29-year-old Bryant to 35 life terms; one term for each of the murders. On each of the remaining counts he was sentenced to 21 years imprisonment, to be served concurrently. There was to be no chance of parole.

The sentencing of Bryant closed a door on what, at the time of writing, remains the largest number of deaths perpetrated by a single civilian gunman anywhere in the world. For wider Australia, the case was over; justice had been done, although the question of why someone could commit such atrocities remained unanswered.

For those touched personally by the tragedy, however, the road to any form of recovery had barely begun.

2

SHADES OF BLUE:
WALTER AND KEITH

In the immediate aftermath of any major tragedy, the media inevitably homes in on one face; one story that appears to capture the essence of the catastrophe. After the 1997 collapse of a ski lodge at Thredbo, New South Wales, the remarkable rescue of Stuart Diver from beneath tonnes of rubble became the story that lingered long after other names and faces fell away from the news pages. Similarly, the Bali bombings of October 2002 became inextricably linked to the recovery of Australian Football League player Jason McCartney and the fortunes of the Coogee Dolphins rugby team, which lost six of its members.

The most recognised face of the Port Arthur tragedy was the then 34-year-old Walter Mikac. The dark-haired, boyish-faced pharmacist was the man Australians came to identify with the events of 28 April 1996 because Walter, if such things can ever be measured, was considered to have lost the most.

Walter was playing golf when, in a few, brutal seconds at the nearby Port Arthur Historic Site, his entire family was taken: his wife Nanette and his two daughters, Alannah, six, and Madeline, three. To Walter, they were Netty, Lani and Maddie. To wider Australia, their smiling faces captured the utter senselessness of the murders that day. The Mikacs had moved to the Tasman Peninsula from Walter's home city of Melbourne only eighteen months before the massacre to be closer to Nanette's retired parents, Keith and Grace. The young couple had set up the first permanent pharmacy in the town of Nubeena and quickly became well known and well loved by the small peninsula community.

Of all the horrible acts Bryant committed that day, it was the shooting of Nanette and Madeline, and then the stalking and killing of Alannah, that struck deep into the public heart. Nobody less than a monster, it was thought, could ever do such a thing.

Caught in the middle of that unthinkable scenario was Walter, whose grief and shock were palpable. The day after the shootings, Walter was photographed as he and his father-in-law, Keith Moulton, drove into the site to see the bodies of his family. As Bryant was still at large and the Port Arthur Historic Site remained part of an active crime scene, the bodies of those killed on Jetty Road remained there all night, with young police officers guarding them against carnivorous Tasmanian devils whose eerie cries could be heard from the surrounding bush.

The photograph of Walter driving to the scene is that of a broken man: his eyes swollen, his forehead cupped in his hand as he gazes out the window, unseeing. It was an image of despair that anyone who had ever suddenly lost a family member or close friend could understand. It was taken on Walter's thirty-fourth birthday.

At the Hobart memorial service held on 1 May for all those who died in the massacre, a photograph of Walter would again capture the sadness that had fallen across the nation like a heavy, black veil. Supported on either side by his grief-stricken brother, John, and his best friend, Chris McCann, a sobbing Walter was captured by the *Mercury* photographer Leigh Winburn as the three men made their way down the steps of St David's Cathedral. His hands clutch a spray of irises and Alannah's diary is pressed close to his heart. The girls' hair bands are wrapped tightly around his wrists.

The image captures the desperation of those left behind to cling to any small, human reminder of their loved one having been there; a scrap of handwriting, a familiar smell, a single hair.

The tenth anniversary of the massacre falls in a year in which Madeline and Alannah would have celebrated special birthdays: Madeline becoming a teenager and Alannah turning sixteen. They are remembered at the site, together with Nanette, by discreet bronze plaques marking the spots where they died.

Walter has since stepped back from public life and could not be contacted directly for this book. Instead I relied on the word of friends that he did not wish to participate. As it happened, one of those friends was my younger brother who told me 'Port Arthur' was not a topic he had ever discussed with Walter: it wasn't something his friends brought up as Walter tried to build his new life.

Others said Walter believed he had no desire to revisit his story in another book, having already told of his journey from immeasurable grief to an unshakeable belief in the future in his autobiography, *To Have and to Hold: A modern-day love story cut short*. His book, which he co-wrote with Tasmanian journalist Lindsay Simpson in the months after the massacre, deliberately avoids mentioning Bryant by name. This, the pair said, was in keeping with a decision taken by the families of victims of the 1996 Dunblane massacre who, in their book, *Dunblane: Our year of tears*, refused to name the gunman, Thomas Hamilton.

'This is a story of love and hope with no place for either of these creatures. They do not have a place in history, alongside their victims,' Walter and Lindsay wrote of their decision.

Walter's father-in-law, Keith Moulton, does speak about Martin Bryant. He talks openly and calmly about the man who murdered his daughter and two granddaughters, having spent many hours untangling his grief and refusing to become lost in bitterness and anger. It has been a long journey which began, as he describes it, with his 'blue days'.

In the months after the massacre, Keith would start each day by mentally colouring it a shade of blue. Sitting on the edge of his bed, in his home overlooking White Beach on the Tasman Peninsula, Keith would measure the dullness in his heart and gauge the tightness in his stomach and decide whether this day would be a shade of navy blue, a royal blue or, perhaps, a light baby blue. If it was a dark bruise of blue, Keith knew he would have to take it gently – just for today. If it felt royal blue, he knew, if only for today, he could enjoy feeling a bit better.

'I had a selection of about five blues. It sounds a bit ratty now, but it works, it works,' he says.

For Keith, the idea of colouring his days helped him prepare for each stage of grief in the wake of the murders of Nanette, Alannah and Madeline. Their deaths came just fifteen weeks after the loss of his wife of 42 years, Grace, whom Keith had nursed through most of the last two years of a debilitating respiratory condition.

The diagnosis of Grace's terminal illness was among the main reasons Nanette, who was the youngest of the Moultons' five children, Walter and the two girls moved to the Tasman Peninsula, so they could all spend more time with 'Nani'. The Moultons had retired to the area from Melbourne in 1992, but their plans for a quiet, relaxing life were not to be.

Grace died on 11 January 1996, but it was early April before Keith decided that he needed some extra support to cope with her loss and adjusting to living life alone. It began with a small public notice in the Hobart newspaper, *The Mercury*, advertising a grief counselling workshop to be held on 20 April at the Church of Christ complex in Hobart.

Keith was a Christian, but had not been actively involved in a church for some years. All the same, he decided to go along to see if he could learn anything of value.

Keith arrived at the workshop and immediately felt somewhat uncomfortable. It appeared everybody else in the room was a health professional looking to expand their knowledge rather than, like him, seeking solace for a personal crisis.

Despite feeling a little uneasy, he decided to stay, taking a seat at the back and listening in silence as the group was led through the reactions and symptoms that could be expected after a tragedy. By the end, Keith had compiled a thick sheaf of notes, detailing what sorts of emotions, thoughts and physical symptoms a person could expect to experience after a major trauma. After the crowd had filed out of the building, Keith hung back and talked to the woman counsellor who had hosted the session.

'I thanked her. I said, "My wife died fifteen weeks ago and I think I have got something here that might be able to help me".'

Keith reflected on what he had learned as he drove the 100 km of curving roads back to White Beach. The next day, he collated the hurried notes into a readable package and stored them in a drawer, knowing they were there if ever he needed to take stock of his feelings and to be reassured that he 'wasn't going around the bend'.

Just eight days later, these simple notes were to provide an anchor that Keith believes was given to him by his God in preparation for the devastating loss he was to suffer.

'To this day, I will never let anyone tell me it was a coincidence,' he says. 'I believe that God gave me these notes before [the tragedy] came and that's what gave me a kick-start to get back on my feet. I had someone that had already given me the pages of answers before the questions arose. Strangely enough, I felt as if a large rock had been pushed under my feet.'

It was late on the Sunday night of the Port Arthur massacre that Keith first learned his girls were among the dead. Another daughter, Bronwyn, had rung earlier in the afternoon from Melbourne to say there had been news flashes about some sort of shooting incident at Port Arthur. Knowing that Nanette often visited the site, Keith drove to her and Walter's house at nearby Nubeena twice that afternoon and on both occasions found it empty. While still hopeful that Nanette, as a nurse, had been caught up in helping some of those injured at the site, Keith was beginning to feel anxious.

He returned home, but having heard nothing from Nanette by about 6 p.m., he drove towards the site, only to be stopped at a roadblock set up on the road to Port Arthur. Nobody was being allowed through, for fear the gunman was still at large, so Keith could do nothing but join others who had also gathered in an anxious wait for news.

'Then a chap came up from the Port Arthur site in an SES [State Emergency Services] wagon. He knew me. He took me aside and he said, "I've got some bad news for you" and with that he started to cry. He was a big chap.

'He told me the girls had been shot. I remember saying that "I hope they're in good hands and getting looked after" and he said, "Keith, they're dead".'

Keith felt numb with disbelief. His first response was to try and get down to the site to find out more. 'I wasn't feeling agitated. I wasn't feeling peaceful. It's just a funny effect. I know now that it is shock. You just don't believe something like that has happened.'

Keith was desperate to find Walter and was able to convince those at the roadblock to let him drive through to the Port Arthur motel where many of those at the site were now holed up in darkness, unsure if the gunman was still at large. Keith remembers some of those gathered were still spattered with blood and body matter, their faces pale and wide-eyed. He began to feel intensely thirsty and unsteady on his legs as the shock set in, but he continued to search for Walter among the crowd.

Walter, he learned, was being cared for by friends, the two local GPs Pam and Steve Ireland, in the nearby youth hostel. Keith raced to the hostel to find Walter wrapped in blankets, shivering with deep shock. After speaking with police, he gathered Walter up and drove him back to his Nubeena home where they sat talking quietly with friends in the lounge until 2 a.m. The conversation went over and over the same ground: how could this have happened?

An exhausted Keith finally crawled first into Alannah's bed, only to find it soaked by a broken hot water bottle. He then tried Madeline's, bending his body into the small space and staring at the ceiling.

'I just laid there on my back, wondering what the ramifications for this would be, just sort of trying to think of the future a little bit.

'It's a funny state you go into. You're in a never-never land. Nothing seems real. You've got all the faculties, but they don't seem to twig together.'

Despite the shock he had suffered, or perhaps because of it, Keith had not yet shed a tear.

The following morning, remembering the words of the grief coun-selling session eight days before, Keith believed he had to see the girls where they had died. He wasn't sure why it was so important, he just knew that it was and that he had to get to the Port Arthur site as soon as possible.

Dr Pam Ireland, who was a close friend of Nanette, helped arrange for Keith and Walter to be let through the thick police cordon that surrounded the site on the Monday morning after the massacre. Martin Bryant had been taken into custody just hours ear-lier and the police tactical response unit was still packing up its firearms, which lay in canvas wraps across the road. 'I had to navi-gate those in the car. Looking out the side of the car, there was a whole swag of guns lying on the road,' Keith remembers.

Parking at the top of Jetty Road, leading into to the site, Keith was about to take the most difficult steps of his life. With Steve and Pam Ireland supporting Walter, Keith was joined by volunteer ambulance officer Kaye Fox.

'I remember [Kaye] saying, "Come on, mate" and she had a firm grip on my hand and she walked me down there.

'She had seen the girls the day before and she knew where she was going. She just hung onto my hand and she gave me a fantastic sense of inner strength, just walking down that hill. I felt that I was safe with her.'

In his book, Walter describes how he let out an 'animal-like shriek' as he saw the bodies of his family lying on the roadway and held Nanette and each of the girls for one last time:

I knelt closer, wrapping my arms around the stiffness of [Nanette's] body, trying to induce just one final cuddle. I told her how much I loved her between tears and sobbing, and that my love for her would never die.

When Keith saw Nanette, or Dit-Dit as she was known to her brothers and sisters, she was lying on her back, her head pointing downhill with a long line of blood trailing down the roadway. He picked up her lifeless hand and gently rubbed her skin. He stroked her face. As he did, he looked up at Madeline's body curled up nearby.

'I remember something started to well up in me and it came out like a bull roar. It was just a cry of – I suppose you would call it anguish. It was just a roar that started in my stomach. I remember some birds took off in the trees, so it must have been a good roar.'

Keith moved on to Madeline, again stroking her face gently for a minute, maybe two, before finally walking to Alannah's body, which was several metres away, hidden behind a tree. It appeared curious to Keith that her body was lying there and not next to Nanette. Even then, he had a dreadful sense that she was the last to be killed and had seen what had happened to her mother and sister. It was a fear that was to be confirmed later.

Keith returned to Nanette for a final goodbye before Kaye Fox gently asked, 'Is it time to go yet?'

'Yes,' Keith replied.

He never saw the girls again.

Very early on the Tuesday morning, Keith awoke in a breathless fright. He had suddenly realised with excruciating clarity that Alannah had been stalked by the gunman and had tried to take refuge behind the only hiding place she could see, one of the towering gum trees that lined Jetty Road. It was not nearly enough cover.

'The horror of that woke me up and I sat on the end of the bed and screamed. I remember having my legs over the side of the bed and the shock going through me in [waves of] crying and screaming. I don't know how long I was like that, but possibly up to an hour.'

Keith believes this outpouring of sorrow from seeing the girls' bodies as they were, before they were prepared for burial, helped him to accept their deaths more quickly. By absorbing the totality of what had happened, where it happened, the full force of his grief could be unleashed and his imagination kept in check.

'Seeing them where they fell, my imagination just flew out the door. From what I have seen since, imagination has made it harder for some people to recover, because they imagine what they think took place.

'If you confront a tragedy, you do away with all the "what-might-haves" and you're only faced with what *did* happen.'

Keith says that from the moment he left the girls, he accepted that they were not coming home. It didn't stop the waves of intense sadness and loss, but it did stop the torment of the unknown.

In the years since the massacre, spiritual faith was to become and remain an integral part of Keith's life. The circumstances which saw him receive the grief counselling notes before the massacre reignited his firm belief in God and provided a solid grounding at a time he needed it most. Rediscovering his faith, he says, was a bit like sitting in a sports car for a time, before finally turning the key.

'Until you put the key in the ignition and turn it on, you haven't got a clue where it will take you and you certainly haven't got a clue of the power available.

'That, in a sense, is what happened; the switch was turned and I began to experience what God would do for me.'

Keith, however, is not one to robustly push his religious beliefs onto others. Instead, the strength and comfort they provide are the silent forces behind his ability to reach out and help others. They are the secret behind what many see as Keith's unbreakable spirit.

Just four days after the massacre, he joined a public meeting on the peninsula where people were able to share their loss and find out more information about what would happen from there on.

Keith was one of the few in the room who had directly lost a relative. After the formalities were over, the group lingered, reluctant to leave the solace of each other's company. Suddenly one man, a big, 'rough-diamond' sort of guy, started to march determinedly towards Keith. He opened his arms, his eyes streaming with tears and embraced Keith in a long bear hug, saying over and over, 'I am so sorry'.

His actions broke the emotional restraint in the room. People began to hug each other and cry full, sobbing tears. 'What that tearful man did that night was a catalyst for starting real tears. There'd been a lot of tears shed before, but these were the deep tears that come from right down in your stomach.'

Since that night, Keith Moulton has helped many people cry many tears. He made a conscious decision to stay on the peninsula which, even though he no longer had any immediate family living there, had become his home. By deciding to stay, Keith gave the shattered community a much-needed reminder that none of what had happened at Port Arthur or Seascape was their fault.

In the months immediately after the massacre, it wasn't uncommon for locals to embrace Keith if they happened to meet him outside the Nubeena post office or supermarket. Keith recalls 'lots of hugs and tears' in public, and nobody giving the slightest heed to what others might have thought.

One afternoon shortly after the shootings, Keith was standing at the spot where the girls had been murdered. It had been transformed into a shrine of cards, flowers, teddy bears, books and children's toys. Keith was preparing to take photographs of the site for his eldest daughter, Bronwyn, when he noticed a young woman looking at the memorials that had been placed by the roadway. She was crying quietly.

Their paths crossed and Keith explained that he was taking photographs for Bronwyn: 'this girl's sister; that is my daughter there'. The young woman began to sob, saying she could not imagine, as the mother of a six year old, how it would be to lose a child in such a tragedy.

'Could I give you a hug?' she asked.

The pair hugged and cried openly together as the tourist cars continued to pass by, but there was no hint of embarrassment.

'I don't think I will ever forget the day I gave you a hug,' the woman said, before walking on. Keith still doesn't know her name, but will also never forget the 'warm glow' that came from her heartfelt sympathy, especially as she was a complete stranger. Life, he thought, is normally so buttoned down and controlled, with strangers reluctant to talk to each other, much less embrace.

In 1997, Keith decided to utilise his ability to inspire others by accepting an invitation to become a temporary minister at the Nubeena Church of Christ. It was a six-month position that was to last six years. During that time, he has, as he describes it, guided dozens of people over the first 'hump' of despair that looms so large with the death of someone you love.

'There is definitely a hump with [personal loss] and people feel that what they have to climb over is almost impossible. As a minister, it is my job to try and flatten that hump and calm the shock as much as possible.'

Having been through the Port Arthur massacre, Keith believes he has gained a deeper insight into human nature and come to understand the true meaning of compassion. By immersing himself in the community, and not fleeing from it, his smiling, round face remained an immense comfort to those living on the peninsula.

Keith also became an important contact for some of those who had lost loved ones in the massacre, but who did not live in Tasmania.

If he wasn't suffering a 'navy-blue' day, when his emotional strength was not quite as solid, Keith would agree to meet with relatives or friends of those killed who were either revisiting the site since the massacre, or seeing it for the first time. He would stand with them as they saw where their friend or family member had died and try to help them let go of their fear of the site.

He recalls, in particular, two young Brisbane women who needed to see the place where their father and their uncle had been killed. Bronwyn was visiting at the time, so with her help he arranged to take them through the skeletal remains of the Broad Arrow Café, where he held the elder sister tightly in his arms while she 'rattled' with tears. Keith cried with her until, after a few minutes, she lifted her head from his chest, looked around the building and remarked: 'Isn't it small? I thought it would be so much bigger.'

'As soon as she said that,' Keith recalls, 'I knew she had won her battle with it'.

Unlike his father-in-law, Walter Mikac could not stay on the Tasman Peninsula. He left to return to Melbourne in late 1996, before Bryant pleaded guilty to all charges.

He did this, he later explained, to escape from what he believed was a 'community that was disintegrating' in the wake of the massacre. It had, in Walter's eyes, shifted from being a haven, to a hellhole of 'rumours, innuendo, marital breakups and vicious gossip'. It was a view shared by others. With his former life irrevocably destroyed, Walter began to recreate himself as he attempted to carve out a new way of being. He left his hair longer, grew a goatee beard and traded the family four-wheel-drive for a sporty, red Mercedes.

'All of these things say I'm not as I was before. Physically, mentally or psychologically,' he wrote. There were also the questions that stretched out before him: would he return to the pharmacy, would he meet another partner, would he have more children? The questions came with a mix of hope, uncertainty and anguish. Underlying the tumultuous journey, however, was a profound strength and optimism that would go on to inspire thousands of others.

Being known around the world as 'the man who lost his family at Port Arthur' was physically and emotionally draining for Walter, but he did not shy away from the influence it offered. Walter was in a position to make real change, and he did. The Mikac name became an integral part of the push for gun law reform as Walter spoke at rallies across Australia in support of tighter laws.

Prime Minister John Howard, writing in the foreword to Walter's book, said the 'immense courage' shown by Walter in lobbying for stricter gun control helped to dissolve the political hurdles that normally confront any attempt to make a major change to the law.

> Walter's contribution to the debate helped the Commonwealth government achieve agreement with the states on national controls which, as I write, have reduced the number of dangerous weapons in Australia by half a million.

Shortly after his return to Melbourne, Walter also established a trust in the name of his two daughters – the Alannah and Madeline Foundation – which would raise funds to support child victims of violent crime. The foundation includes among its patrons Prime Minister Howard and America's Cup hero John Bertrand, and in October 2005, Her Royal Highness Crown Princess Mary of Denmark – who was born in Tasmania – became its international patron. Victorians Gaye and John Fidler, who survived the Port Arthur shootings, are also heavily involved. Walter also, for a time, joined the motivational speakers' circuit and became a patron of the Centre for Grief Education in Victoria, in the hope that his experiences could help others.

In keeping with this goal, in 1999 he wrote another, smaller book of inspirational thoughts that could be quickly drawn upon in times of sadness. The title of the book, *The Circle of Life: Replacing hardship with love* borrows from the hit theme song of *The Lion King*; a favourite movie of his two girls.

For his inspirational work after the massacre, Walter was named by the Australian National Trust in 2000 as one of Australia's 'Living National Treasures'. He is in fine company, sitting alongside the likes of former Olympic champion Dawn Fraser and High Court judge Justice Michael Kirby.

Today, however, Walter has consciously stepped away from the spotlight as he builds a new life separate to that shrouded by the massacre.

In researching this book, it became clear to me that Walter rarely, if ever, returned to the Tasman Peninsula or kept in touch with many of his friends from the area. It appeared he had made a clear and complete break from the place which had once seemed so full of opportunity. This moving on from the past has also meant Walter's relationship with Keith broke down after Walter returned to Melbourne. They no longer have any contact. Keith chooses not to talk about his relationship with Walter, other than to say he bears no animosity. He understands how grief can affect people in so many different ways.

Nobody, he says, can stand in judgment of another's reaction to such an immense loss.

For Keith, the Port Arthur site itself holds no fear. He remembered how much Nanette had loved the place and how she had told him it 'grows on you'. With this in mind, he willingly agreed in late 1996 to become a volunteer in an ongoing project to transcribe convict records. The project saw him work at the site once a week for seven years, during which he meticulously transcribed more than 2000 documents detailing the wretched lives of those once imprisoned there.

From his desk at Port Arthur, he could look down on the roadway where the girls were killed. Sometimes, particularly when it was one of the girls' birthdays, he would take his lunch over to the area and just 'chew on a sandwich' while he reminisced. Other times, as he drove past the spot, he would wish the girls 'good morning' or 'goodnight'. Keith believes it was again the decision to see the girls' bodies where they lay that enabled him to confront the site and see it as part of their lives, rather than a place to be forever avoided.

Part of Keith's coping mechanism has been a self-devised method he calls 'precompensation'; a word he would like to see installed in a dictionary some day. Put simply, it is to accept that, after a death, there will be 'humps' on the horizon – birthdays, anniversaries, Christmas – and to prepare for them in advance. Keith makes sure he spends those special days with friends, rather than alone. If it is a birthday, he organises to perhaps have lunch or coffee with someone.

'It's just a way of protecting yourself; helping yourself over a day that has a pretty good chance of having sad memories in it. Especially with the girls' birthdays, I'll go out or go visiting. Sometimes I have imposed myself on somebody else for the afternoon and not told them why I was there.'

Some things, however, cannot be planned for. The unexpected reminders of those he has lost produce the strongest emotions but, again, Keith has found comfort in embracing the shocks rather than pushing them away. He has, over the years, stumbled across personal items that belonged to Grace, Nanette or the girls – perhaps a note-book filled with familiar handwriting that had been forgotten in a drawer – and while the initial shock brought pain, he deliberately left them in place. Knowing the items were there became a source of pleasure rather than hurt and Keith often returned to look at them: holding these special mementos made him feel reconnected to those he had lost.

When I visited Keith, one wall of his neat brick home at White Beach was devoted to Nanette, including family photographs and, because Nanette worked as a ghost tour guide, a bravery award that was given to all 31 Port Arthur staff on site that day. Another photo frame contained a picture of the two girls, both wearing adult sun-glasses and smiling widely – two goofy grins – as they crowded the camera lens.

Personal items belonging to Alannah and Madeline are particu-larly precious. Among the few Keith has is a shawl. Keith recognised it instantly when the new owner of Walter's house discovered it and brought it to him one afternoon. It was the baby shawl Madeline was wrapped in the day she left the hospital. He holds it dear.

There is a letter Keith Moulton intends to write one day and it will be to Martin Bryant. It will not be a letter of hate. It will be a letter offering forgiveness.

After spending many hours contemplating his feelings towards Bryant, and drawing heavily on his faith, Keith feels ready to for-give, were Bryant ready to ask for such forgiveness. For most of us, it may be hard to comprehend ever forgiving someone who had committed such a crime, but for Keith, being prepared to forgive Bryant has brought an inner peace and contentment.

'If you get angry, it's like having a stomach full of battery acid. It will stew you up inside, give you stomach ulcers; it can shorten your life and make you miserable. The person who is angry gets knocked about and the person who the anger is against might never know a thing about it.'

Keith's path to releasing his anger towards Bryant began on the day of Bryant's sentencing. Keith sat just two people away from the slight, pale-faced Bryant as Justice William Cox, now the Governor of Tasmania, committed him to a life in prison. Instead of hatred, Keith felt pity towards the weak, long-haired young man who could only draw strength from a gun.

As they led Bryant from the docks to the cells, Keith turned and looked him in the eye. His thoughts were of how this pathetic young man would spend the rest of his days surrounded by concrete and bars, while Keith was about to step outside into the Hobart sunshine and share a coffee with his daughter, Bronwyn.

Yet the decision to offer absolution to Bryant was not one that came easily. Keith admits he spent a lot of time on his knees, praying for guidance. He came away from those moments of solitude and reflection with a belief that he could not be true to his God, or expect mercy from that God, unless he himself was prepared to forgive.

For Keith, the coming together of the wrongdoer and the wronged completes the circle that is necessary for true forgiveness. 'Forgiveness is very, very healing. It can start off a new relationship between two people that was not possible without the act of forgiveness, but then again it is sometimes not easy to do.'

The letter Keith expects to write one day will speak of the peace he has found by being prepared to forgive and, even though he has suffered enormous pain from losing a daughter and two granddaughters, he would grant Bryant forgiveness should he seek it. 'Whether that day comes, I don't know, but I have to be prepared for it.'

Although it may sound unbelievable to someone who watched the horror of Port Arthur from a distance, and incomprehensible to some of those who went through it, Keith says the experience was one he is glad he had.

It is an event he would not wish on anyone, but he considers himself a person who is living a richer, happier life than would have been possible had he not come through such an immense tragedy.

'I'm glad I have been through Port Arthur, because it has given me a life inwardly and outwardly that I never anticipated in my wildest dreams.

'I have tasted some extremes and I've tasted them well and I continually give thanks to God for the way He has, and is, helping me.'

When I met Keith, he was preparing to leave the Tasman Peninsula after eleven 'interesting' years to return to Victoria and be closer to his children and grandchildren. Just as he sat down with a pen and paper after the shootings and mapped out why he should stay on the peninsula and why he should go, Keith had made a decision that the time was right to leave. The real estate advertisement was appearing in the newspapers for the first time when we met and his waterfront house would sell amid Tasmania's property boom within a matter of weeks.

Keith had lived alone in his White Beach home for seven years and while he says he had never suffered loneliness, he did occasionally feel lonely. He explained the difference: 'Being lonely is when you miss someone to come home to and talk the matters of the day over…when you're closed away from everybody and there's no-one interested in you, that's loneliness, and I am not that'.

Working as a church minister in a close-knit community like that of the Tasman also came with its own challenges. Presiding over the funerals of family members of close friends was often the hardest part of the job. Who could he talk to at the end of the day, when he came home with his own memories of the person who had died and his own sadness at their loss?

His various community roles on the peninsula were also coming to a natural end and, while he knew he would miss the area deeply, including the native potoroos which he fed nightly on his back verandah, he felt it time to reconnect with his family. The grandchildren were growing up and some he had not seen for several years.

Having decided to leave, he experienced a strange thing. Just six or seven weeks before our interview, Keith was visiting Nanette and Walter's old home in Nubeena. It was only the second time he had been inside the house in six years, but his mind was on the job at hand – preparing a eulogy for a relative of the new owner – rather than on Nanette and the girls.

As he entered the lounge room, which had changed only slightly since the Mikacs had lived there, Keith suddenly heard Alannah and Madeline running through the room. Next, he glimpsed the two girls running past his left side before they disappeared. It all happened in a split second. Keith was momentarily stunned, but not frightened. He gripped the couch as the vision passed.

'I had been to the house before and that never happened. It didn't give me the horrors, it didn't worry me. It's a peculiar feeling and yet it is a lovely feeling to have, strangely enough.'

Despite his spiritual beliefs, Keith did not read too much into the experience, nor did he want to venture into theories that the house is haunted. Instead, he was happy to hold on to the 'lovely feeling' that, even once he left the peninsula, he would still be connected with the house that his girls called home.

The Tasman Peninsula community turned on a huge farewell party for one of its favourite citizens – even if he was still a few decades away from being a true 'local' – and people spoke openly of how much they would miss the man who had helped hold the place together after the massacre.

For Keith today there is still sadness, but the deep navy-blue days are behind him as he explores a new life in Albury, in country New South Wales. When I asked him what colour his days are now, Keith's eyes wrinkled behind his glasses as he broke into a warm smile: 'Bright golden, most of them.'

A year after the shootings, Walter Mikac met a television reporter, Kim Sporton, at a party thrown by Melbourne media identity Steve Vizard. The pair became engaged on New Year's Day 1999 and, in early 2000, they married in a low-key family ceremony in Brighton, near where they still live today.

Together, Walter and Kim maintained a commitment to the Alannah and Madeline Foundation, at one point raising $10,000 through a compilation book of uplifting quotes by prominent Australians, called *Reach for the Stars!*

Walter has since stepped down as a trustee of the foundation.

In his only interview at the time of his wedding, Walter told the weekly magazine *Woman's Day* that he was discovering new joys.

> I'm enjoying my life again and feeling happy, at peace, enjoying the moment...in spite of everything, I always believed I'd be happy again one day.
>
> I don't have a label attached to me saying I must always be a grief-stricken widower and it's very stifling that people expect me to behave like that.

Fourteen months after that interview, Walter again found himself in the news, this time to announce the birth of a baby girl, whose name was kept secret. Walter and Kim now have two daughters.

The family lives a quiet, private life in Melbourne's eastern suburbs, where Walter, who always thrived on physical activity, helps to coach a junior girls' soccer team and runs a gardening and lawn-mowing business.

Despite his decision to step back from the public eye, the Mikac legacy continues to inspire and comfort. When Australia mourned the loss of 88 lives in the terrorist bombings at the Sari nightclub in Bali in 2002, some church leaders chose to draw on the words of Walter Mikac to help people make sense of the killings.

A National Day of Mourning was held on 20 October 2002, during which Anglican Archbishop John Harrower stood before a packed St David's Cathedral, the spiritual home of Hobart where Walter and hundreds of Tasmanians had gathered six years earlier to grieve for those killed at Port Arthur.

Raising his arms, Archbishop Harrower called upon those before him to remember the commanding words that Walter Mikac had read during the funerals of Nanette, Alannah and Madeline.

'The power of love and creation will *always* triumph over the power of destruction and revenge.'

The words reverberated off the high sandstone walls of the century-old cathedral, where candles of remembrance still burn in a small shrine for victims of Port Arthur.

Walter Mikac not only penned a potent message, he remains in many minds as living proof of it.

3

JUMPING PUDDLES: BRIGID AND IAN

There are 704 steps to the elevator which sweeps to the top of the Eiffel Tower and, two years after Martin Bryant shot her through both legs, Brigid Cook climbed each one of them. It was a long haul and every step pushed a dull ache up through her legs, but Brigid was not about to turn back before reaching the top. This was a personal triumph. Bryant had robbed so many people of so much, but he couldn't touch the steely determination and plain, old-fashioned guts that makes up Brigid Cook.

Short, stocky and wearing rimless glasses, Brigid reminds you of a firm-but-kind schoolteacher. Her thick, dark hair is greying at the temples and her slightly guarded manner is that of a person reluctant to talk about herself. She only agrees to be interviewed because I have 'chased' her down. What could be perceived as aloofness, however, is actually a strong sense of self: of not having to prove anything to anyone.

It is a sense of being part of a bigger picture that comes from growing up as a Molloy in a bustling family of nine sisters and one brother. The Molloys can trace their roots back five generations in Brigid's native New Zealand, and to Scotland, Ireland, Germany and England before that. They are of tough stock. It takes a lot to knock a Molloy off their feet and even more to keep them down. They know, no matter what the trouble, they always have family. The events of 28 April, however, would see the Molloys muster like they had never done before, after Brigid was caught up in the madness of the Port Arthur massacre.

Brigid Cook remembers feeling pretty good about life as she drove to work on the morning of 28 April 1996. The autumn sun was shining, she had just celebrated her fortieth birthday with her family, who had flown across the Tasman for a huge party, and she was enjoying being a mum to her two children, Jessica, sixteen, and Izaac, eleven.

As kitchen manager of the Broad Arrow Café, Brigid began this Sunday like most others, preparing the scones, muffins, sandwiches and hot food for the hungry tourists that would descend later in the day. Sunday was also 'liver and bacon' day. The traditional English dish was a Sunday special and visitors couldn't get enough of the stuff. The café would move 5 kg an hour in busy periods, but this Sunday, thankfully, was proving less frantic than others. The Easter break had been and gone, and the Port Arthur Historic Site was winding down for winter, when visitor numbers would plummet from 1500 a day to about 100.

Brigid was bustling in the kitchen, keeping up with the flow of the lunch crowd, when she first heard the sound of something unusual happening in the café. Popping noises could be heard coming from the front counter. Brigid immediately thought there had been an electrical fault; perhaps one of the bain-maries had shorted. Suddenly a co-worker, Colleen Parker, burst into the kitchen, her face caught in a tortured expression.

'It was like she had seen the most horrific thing in her life, which obviously she had, and she was saying, "There's somebody shooting out there, there's somebody shooting".'

After a few seconds of disbelief, Brigid and her staff ran quickly out the back door of the kitchen and began to scramble their way to safety. As Brigid prepared to run up the hill behind the café, however, she spotted a group of tourists who were waiting for a guided tour. Not knowing the danger within, the group began to move towards the front of the café. Although she was still not entirely sure there *was* a gunman on the loose, Brigid decided to risk 'acting like a dick', and ran, not up the hill and out of danger, but back towards the crowd, yelling at them to move away.

The tour guide, Sue Burgess, whose own daughter, Nicole, was to be shot and killed while working in the souvenir shop, began to move the group on. Brigid, acting on instinct and with no regard for her own safety, continued to run along in front of the café, towards the car park, where more tourists were beginning to wander up from their buses towards the Broad Arrow.

In one of those moments of clarity amid growing chaos, Brigid remembers kicking off her clogs and carrying them as she ran, rather than risk stumbling. 'I remembered to take my shoes off, because I thought of those stupid TV shows where women are running around in high heels, falling at the feet of their attacker; it's not a good look.'

As she approached the tourists, she yelled that she thought there was a gunman in the café. The group turned back, not in a screaming rush, but 'like a group of birds or fish, they sort of moved as one'. It is impossible to know how many people were saved from entering Bryant's gun sight because of this single act of bravery, but Ian McElwee believes he was one of them.

A beanpole of a man with neat silver hair and a broad smile, Ian looks every bit the professional tour coach driver that he is. Ian was relaxing in his Redline bus reading the newspaper to help pass the time while his passengers roamed the Port Arthur grounds, when he suddenly heard a sharp, 'bang, bang, bang'. He dumped the newspaper, clambered down the steps of the coach and began to run towards the Broad Arrow Café, where he thought the sound was coming from.

As he ran, he saw Brigid heading towards the car park, screaming for people to move away. Ian immediately turned and started back towards his coach, running shoulder to shoulder with another bus driver, Royce Thompson, from the rival tour company,

Tigerline. The pair was racing to the shelter of the buses when Royce slumped to the ground, having been shot in the back. Ian, thinking Royce had lost his footing on the gravel, yelled, 'Are you right, mate?' as he saw him roll towards the undercarriage of one of the buses.

Ian found a hiding place behind another coach in the line. It was only when the firing had stopped that he was able to return to his friend, place a hand on his chest and realise he was dead.

As the tourists dispersed, Brigid also managed to take refuge near the buses. Bryant, having emerged from the café, was wandering towards the car park, taking pot shots as he moved. A voice shouted, 'There he is' and Brigid, again acting on instinct, looked out from behind the bulk of the buses. Her first, and only, glimpse of Bryant came as he raised the rifle and took aim. Wearing her brilliant white chefs shirt, Brigid was a clear target.

A single bullet burrowed through the top of her right leg and passed through into the left, where it remained lodged. The pain, she would later explain, was like having a star picket thrust into her leg. Torn flesh was poking out of her leg, but spurred by a mighty rush of adrenalin, Brigid made it to her feet. To stay put, she knew, was to remain in Bryant's line of fire as he made his way towards the buses. 'I wasn't hanging around. I wasn't ready to die there.'

Having completed an on-site first-aid course conducted by her co-worker Wendy Scurr only a few weeks before, Brigid knew she had to pad a serious wound as quickly as possible or risk bleeding to death. She ripped off her apron and pressed it tightly against her right leg – the worst of the two wounds – tying the ends in a bow rather than a knot. The bow was another of those seemingly minor details in daily life which suddenly become so important in a different context: 'I remember learning that a bow would be easier [for medical crews] to untie later'.

Pressing the makeshift pad to her leg, Brigid hobbled to the end of another bus, where she found a crouching Ian McElwee, his tall frame bent like a coathanger.

The pair, who were only acquaintances through the café, clutched each other behind the rubber bulk of the bus wheel, but soon realised that Bryant was trawling his way through the line-up of buses, shooting at random. Ian's coach was the last in the line; it would be only a matter of seconds before Bryant reached them.

'I could see a set of legs walking up the front of the coaches...he stopped firm in front of my coach...and then he walked back the other way, got into another coach and began firing through the windows. I didn't see it, but I could hear it,' Ian explains.

Ian would later learn that a colleague, Ken Howard, stood breathless and rigid in the toilet of his empty coach as Bryant climbed on board, fired several times through the bus windows, and left.

Even though Ian and Brigid risked being shot if they moved from their hiding place, they also knew that to stay behind the coach, with nowhere to run, could prove deadly if Bryant found them.

Mustering all of her remaining strength, Brigid stood and leaned on Ian and they staggered towards the only shelter they could see: a sentry box, no wider than a kitchen table, which stood near a wide open lawn sometimes used for cricket matches. They squeezed behind the box and remained there as Ian tried to help stem the flow of blood from Brigid's injuries. As they hid, Bryant left the buses, returned to his Volvo and drove away.

Ian recalls Bryant looking back at them, smirking, as he drove slowly up Jetty Road. 'I can't remember the exact words, but I think Brigid said something like, "Oh look at the bastard",' he says.

Brigid stayed behind the sentry box, unable to move as the adrenalin finally gave way to paralysing pain. Ian recalls her gripping his hand tightly, saying, with a dash of black humour, that the pain was 'worse than having a baby'.

Ian soon heard the chilling sound of more shots coming from the top of Jetty Road. Although Ian was not entirely sure if it was Bryant who had left in the Volvo, or if there was more than one gunman, he decided to take a chance on briefly leaving Brigid and 'running like a rabbit' to the nearby Information Centre where he tried to phone for help. In the stuff of nightmares, Ian repeatedly dialled 000, but there was no connection. He then tried to dial a zero to get a line out, but his call was picked up by a woman – he is still unsure who it was – who said she was 'up the top' and asked, 'What's going on?' Ian yelled at her: 'There's a bloke heading your way and he's been shooting everyone down here. Get out, get out.' The phone line went dead.

Ian grabbed a nearby worker who helped dial out to the police who by now were receiving a number of calls about 'a shooting at Port Arthur'. Before leaving the Information Centre, he grabbed some blankets folded neatly on a first-aid couch and ran back down to the coaches where he found the injured Janet and Neville Quin. There was nothing that could be done for Janet and Ian could only try to comfort Neville, who was sitting on a nearby fence in a state of severe shock. Ian then returned to where Brigid lay near the sentry box and stayed with her until it was safe for her to be moved.

A group of young Port Arthur workers, terrified by what they had seen, had run down from the café to gather around Brigid for comfort and Brigid, despite her own pain, spoke to them calmly, gently explaining where they could find tea towels, biscuits and sweets in the kitchen to help care for the shocked and wounded.

Ian is still amazed by her resilience. 'She was a tower of strength to those girls. These girls were only sixteen, seventeen years of age or even younger…and she was trying to talk to them and reassure them.'

Brigid, unable to walk, was carried from the sentry box to the verandah of the Broad Arrow Café, where local doctors Pam and Steve Ireland were administering shots of morphine to the wounded. Brigid still recalls the enormous relief from that first hit of the drug: 'It was just lovely'.

Ian ventured into the café to again try to find a working telephone but, eyeing the devastation within, decided not to stay. Others, he could see, were already working on the injured inside.

By this time, contract builder Mark Kirby, who could see the shootings from his cherry picker high above the penitentiary building, had sprinted to the café to try to help. He asked Brigid if she wanted him to do anything.

'Phone my kids,' she said. 'I want them to know I am still alive.'

Brigid was among those loaded onto one of the medivac

helicopters that were shuttling between the site and the Royal Hobart Hospital. It was a tense flight, not only because of her wounds, but also as a result of a warning from the pilot that she must not lean too heavily on the helicopter door: it could swing open. The possibility of plummeting to the ground from a medical helicopter after living through a massacre would have bordered on the absurd, if it hadn't been so serious.

'I was very uptight the whole trip,' Brigid recalls. 'I really wasn't sure if he was kidding or not.'

As Brigid was being airlifted to hospital, Ian McElwee was loading up his bus with other traumatised, but less severely injured victims to drive them back to Hobart.

Ian can't remember how many he carried that day. Three paramedics helped care for the wounded as they began what would seem an interminably long drive back to the city.

As they pulled up and out of Jetty Road, Ian saw the bodies of Nanette Mikac and her two daughters and, even though he had briefly stepped inside the Broad Arrow Café earlier, the enormity of what had happened began to fully sink in. Ian tried to ease his bus between several bodies that still lay along the road, but the large bus wheels began to sink into the storm drain. One of the paramedics climbed out of the coach and gently rolled each body to one side to let Ian drive through, before placing them back where they lay. Ian could not comprehend what his eyes were seeing. Feeling completely numb, he could do nothing but drive.

With Bryant still shooting from the Seascape cottage on the main road out of Port Arthur, Ian had no choice but to use the narrow, winding back roads. The 95 km journey to Hobart felt the longest in his life and every car that flew past him, travelling in the opposite direction, was a police car.

As he arrived on the city fringe, a police escort guided him the last few kilometres into the Royal Hobart Hospital in Argyle Street, where he parked the bus in the cordoned-off street and the wounded passengers began to make their way inside.

After watching the sad procession in silence, Ian pulled out a packet of cigarettes and a lighter that someone had given him that afternoon and, leaning against a fence outside the hospital, he took his first smoke in three years.

Ian was soon briefly assessed himself by a doctor, but all he wanted to do was get home to Marg, his wife of 30 years. First he returned the bus to the depot in downtown Hobart but, upon arriving there, he suddenly felt a driving thirst. Ian decided to duck into the pub next door for a quick beer with a few off-duty work-mates in the hope it would settle his nerves. As the front bar television blared with news flashes from the Port Arthur site, Ian ordered and gulped down a 10 oz glass. By the time he made it to his car parked out the front of the pub, the beer had made a violent return. Ian still struggles to hold a beer down today: the taste brings back terrible memories. It is the same with hot chips. Having seen one of the bodies in the Broad Arrow Café slumped into a bowl of chips, he can no longer eat them.

Another symptom of shock came upon him as he drove the handful of kilometres from the depot to his home overlooking the sweep of the River Derwent. He began to feel incredibly cold; a shivering, deep cold that rattled his frame. Ian finally arrived home, pale and shaking, at about 9 p.m. and, unable to eat or drink, just talked for hours with Marg. Even then, the events of the day were not quite over, with Ian taking a phone call late that night from a 'very polite' police officer seeking a statement. Ian made a time to meet in the morning and, exhausted, finally fell asleep.

In the first twelve months after the massacre, Brigid Cook was rarely alone. One, if not more, of her nine sisters was always there. At one stage, shortly after the shooting, five of them arrived at once. Then her parents, Patrick and Julia, both strong, open-hearted people, arrived from Dunedin. When one family member had to return home, another would drop into the void.

'They came immediately. I think for a period of probably a bit more than a year, there was a sister with me all the time. It was amazing. They just sort of put their lives on hold.'

It was a support network that had been established from birth. In such a large family, each older sibling was 'delegated' a younger sister to look after and that sister would, in turn, look after another. As the second eldest, Brigid had done a lot of caring. She originally moved to Australia as a 21 year old to help look after her younger sister Felicity, a dancer, who was living in Melbourne. There were the normal fights and squabbles among the Molloys, but this was a family that stuck together.

'I had total support and it was unconditional. You could say anything, or say nothing. You didn't have to be anything, didn't have to put on a show at all. [Without that support] I wouldn't be doing what I am now. I'd be some gibbering mess sitting in a quiet room somewhere.'

Buffered by her family, her two children and a tight circle of friends, the feisty New Zealander didn't feel the need for professional counsellors or psychologists. It wasn't until two years after the massacre that Brigid began to realise she might need outside help to cope with the fallout from what she had experienced. 'I was determined, you know, that no bastard is going to tell me what I should be doing with my life…but it was all churned up. It's like an infection; if you take the top off it, it heals, if you don't it festers.'

Several survivors have spoken of the counsellors who were bussed into the site in the hours after the massacre to help people debrief, but while their intentions were good, many of those at Port Arthur resented being forced to talk immediately and intimately to a group of strangers.

'There were so many counsellors and people around the site initially, which I felt was quite odd, because you felt like you were going to be the project for somebody's thesis.

'It was quite needy, which was weird. You would have these people coming up to you and saying, "How *are* you?" It was like they wanted to make it part of their experience.'

After holding firmly onto the belief that she was a strong person and could cope with just about anything, Brigid began to notice the signs that all wasn't well. Her approach to managing her physical injuries had been one thing; even while in hospital, Brigid began walking up and down the fire escape steps to rebuild her strength and was, apart from a few 'wobbles', able to walk normally by the September after the shootings. Her state of mind, however, was less manageable. Brigid became teary at work and felt like she was losing control. Her teenage daughter, Jessica, began to take on the role of mother in the house.

'I wasn't able to work properly and my children were really unhappy: not unhappy, but really uncomfortable,' Brigid says. 'I came to the realisation that if I was a car, I would go to a mechanic for a tune-up. The way I see it is the body is a machine and you need to [treat] it properly.'

Brigid remained in professional counselling in Hobart for almost three years, where she just 'talked it out'. Her counsellor was a straight-up-and-down kind of woman, who wouldn't let her get away with avoiding difficult subjects. Brigid felt a comfortable, if not immediate, connection. 'She was completely pragmatic and really clear and honest and wouldn't let me divert.'

During her time in counselling she also came to process and finally accept her role in saving potentially dozens of lives by warning others away from the Broad Arrow Café. Some of those who escaped that day tracked her down to thank her for her bravery, but Brigid herself found it difficult to accept any notion of being a 'hero'. 'I felt I hadn't done anything much, but then – it took about four years before I could say, yes, that's quite a good thing to do, really.'

She maintains, however, that she did nothing more than anyone else would have under the same circumstances.

Running alongside Brigid's emotional recovery were the demands of the workers compensation system. It was a bureaucratic nightmare that dragged on for more than six years as she haggled with authorities over the amount paid to supplement her income while working part-time, and the expense of various treatments for her injuries.

'I had to justify every single point of treatment. I went to New Zealand once and my wages were cut off. I'd told people verbally that, you know, "I am falling in a bit of a heap here and I need my family", but they saw it as me being on holidays. I came back to bounced cheques.'

A bullet fired from a Colt AR15 semi-automatic rifle not only penetrates flesh at lightning speed, but churns like a Mixmaster blade as it passes through. The bullet that hit Brigid chewed up two fistfuls of muscle as it spun at high velocity through her right leg, before lodging in her left. Most of the impact was absorbed by the fatty tissue in her right leg, leaving a 10 cm scar which has thickened. The scar has created a dam that disrupts the lymphatic system – which removes toxins from the blood – in a condition called lymphedema. The left leg, by contrast, bears only an entry-point scar not much wider than a twenty-cent piece: the damage was already done. Brigid's lymphedema made her leg balloon by 10 cm in diameter and needed what she described as an unsightly and uncomfortable 'industrial strength' crepe bandage to keep the swelling down. The bandage is now used only rarely, but the condition still requires weekly physiotherapy, plus regular laser treatment and massage to 'move' the toxins that would otherwise poison her.

Despite her injury, Brigid returned to part-time work at the Broad Arrow Café in the June after the shootings and became a full-time employee again later that year. The site itself never bothered her; the continued use of the Broad Arrow Café did. When the site reopened later in 1996, a temporary kitchen and café had been built, but the Broad Arrow Café kitchen was still being used for food preparation. Brigid was among the catering staff who found the reuse of the café hard to tolerate.

'It was washed but it was, you know, dark and we used to walk through the café to get to the kitchen. The kitchen was in use for a long time afterwards: too long. It shouldn't have been used at all.'

The then Port Arthur site manager Craig Coombs asked all staff who entered the café area and kitchen to sign a release form saying they had entered of their own free will and, by implication, could not later sue the site. Brigid recalls there was 'no way' she was going to sign the letter and her co-workers were equally disturbed by the document. The café team held a meeting and decided not to sign, a decision which was backed by their union. A meeting of Port Arthur staff shortly later saw a long and heated discussion about the letter, after which it was withdrawn.

Special Commissioner Max Doyle, who in 1997 was asked by the Tasmanian Parliament to look into the issues surrounding the Port Arthur massacre, received one submission that summed up the feelings around the decision to use the kitchen:

> Those girls should never have been sent back to the Broad Arrow Café – they became stressed – some had to stay for up to two hours a day in that awful area. When the girls got a break, they went behind the buildings and cried.

In his report, Doyle said he was 'amazed' that a site manager could be concerned about the importance of a legal release form, but not the trauma and stress on those staff who were 'required to enter and work in that unhappy place'.

Apart from having to relive the nightmare by entering the café, catering staff were also subjected to the ghoulish fascination of tourists who would wander through the area, looking for bullet holes. Others would bluntly question staff about what they had seen. Brigid would always give them a little bit more information than perhaps they were expecting: that usually quietened the questions.

Given the constant reminder the Broad Arrow represented, it was not surprising that Brigid, among others, wanted it pulled down. At one point, Brigid and a colleague seriously considered leaving the gas lines open in the kitchen so the building would blow up. They never went through with it, but the thought showed their antipathy towards the place. Brigid occasionally returns to the site, which she still enjoys, but not to the remnants of the café: even as a shell, it is too confronting.

In late 1998, Brigid received $10,000 from Martin Bryant's estate which she used to pay for a European holiday for herself and her son, Izaac. The pair visited London, Scotland (meeting with families from the Dunblane shootings), Ireland and France, where they scaled the Eiffel Tower.

Keith Moulton, father of Nanette Mikac, at his home in White Beach, Tasmania, shortly before he left the Tasman Peninsula.

To many Australians, Walter Mikac became the face of the Port Arthur tragedy after he lost his entire family in the massacre.

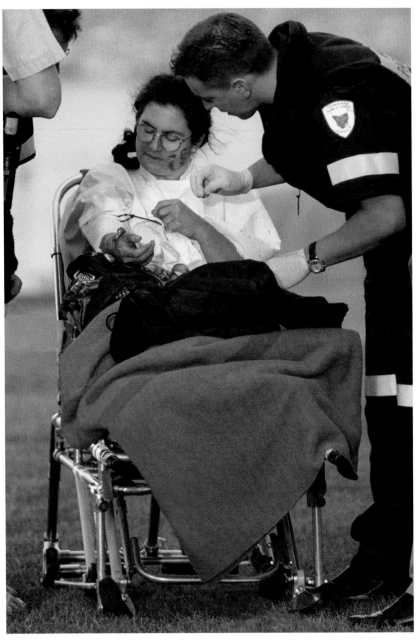

Brigid Cook, the then kitchen manager of the Broad Arrow Café, was airlifted from the Port Arthur Historic Site after a single shot penetrated both her legs.

Today Brigid Cook refuses to let the fallout from the massacre dominate her life and continues to embrace new challenges: 'You have got to jump puddles every now and then, leap the tall buildings and do what you can'.

After narrowly escaping being shot, Tasmanian tour bus driver Ian McElwee helped transport the wounded to Hobart on his bus.

Ron and Gwen Neander, photographed in 1992. Gwen was among those shot dead during Martin Bryant's rampage in the Broad Arrow Café.

Ron Neander and Lily Kernahan were still grieving over the loss of their long-time partners when they met in 2001. Their shared experience led to a deep connection as they rediscovered happiness together.

Former Port Arthur Historic Site colleagues Wendy Scurr, second from left, and Brigid Cook, second from right, photographed in 1996 as they left the Tasmanian Supreme Court after hearing Martin Bryant initially plead not guilty to all charges.

Wendy Scurr is convinced Martin Bryant is an innocent man and she is still seeking answers as to what really happened at Port Arthur on 28 April 1996.

More than 25 years experience as a newspaper photographer wasn't enough to prepare Leigh Winburn for the impact of covering the Port Arthur massacre.

Former Nubeena GP Dr Pam Fenerty was among the first on the scene after the massacre, but it was the fallout from the event that proved the most devastating for her.

As mayor of the Tasman Peninsula, Neil Noye became the voice of the community in the wake of the massacre and remembers the immense outpouring of sympathy from people around the world.

Former volunteer ambulance officers Colin and Robyn Dell were part of the huge emergency service response to the massacre.

Tasmanian psychiatrist Dr Ian Sale was immersed in several different roles after the massacre, including interviewing Martin Bryant in prison.

Dr Bryan Walpole managed many of the dead and wounded taken to the Royal Hobart Hospital in the aftermath of the massacre.

Prime Minister John Howard embraces Dr Bryan Walpole outside the Port Arthur memorial service held in Hobart. After this image was published around Australia, Walpole found himself in demand to speak at gun control rallies.

An aerial view of the Port Arthur Historic Site on the day of the massacre. Despite its picturesque location, the site has a history steeped in violence.

The Broad Arrow Café, where twenty people were shot dead and another twelve were severely wounded within the space of just two minutes.

The husk of the Broad Arrow Café as it stands today, forming part of a memorial garden dedicated to the victims of the massacre.

Upon each anniversary of the Port Arthur massacre, mourners gather before the Huon pine cross at the site in quiet remembrance.

Martin Bryant as he appeared during his trial for the murder of 35 people and the attempted murder of twenty others. He was sentenced to 35 life terms, one for each of the murders, and 21 years for each of another 37 charges.

For Brigid it was important to spend Bryant's money on something enjoyable and impermanent, rather than on bricks and mortar which would forever remind her of the gunman. 'I wasn't going to use it to pay off the mortgage. I just wanted to spend the money and have a bloody good time.'

Brigid, having stared death in the face, knows the value of embracing life. She has never been a particularly nervous person, but now she lives with an even deeper commitment to not letting fear stand in her way. 'I have always worked on the principle that you should do things even if you are frightened of the consequences, if you think it is the right thing to do,' she says. 'You have got to jump puddles every now and then, leap the tall buildings and do what you can.'

To live in anticipation of disaster, she says, is to not live at all, or, at the very least, to have a very dull life indeed.

While Bryant's actions have had an impact on some of the choices Brigid can make in her life, she rarely thinks of him. She considers him an inanimate object, someone born without the ability to feel empathy or compassion. When he shot at people, she believes, he didn't see humans, but moving targets for which he had no feeling.

'I think the whole thing for him was a game. He just wanted to see what it felt like. He had seen it in the movies and he was fairly into that sort of thing, so I think he thought he would run his own little show.'

Brigid doesn't particularly care whether Bryant lives or dies, but she does worry that somebody will eventually take sympathy on him, believe he is truly sorry for his crimes and lobby for his release from prison. 'I don't think anything will have changed for him. I don't think his mind works that way. I don't think he is able to show regret, or sorrow, or anxiousness.'

For now, she says, there is no way she is going to let an 'arsehole' like that dominate her life. 'I live my life the way that I want to. It is not constrained; there are no locked doors or anything like that. I mean, if that is the worst thing that is going to happen to me, oh well, I am not dead.'

The swelling and pain associated with the lymphedema ended Brigid's professional cooking career; something which she misses greatly. Dreams of taking a year off and 'cooking' her way around Australia had to be put aside, but she still caters for weddings and relishes any opportunity to mess about in a kitchen.

Despite the pain, she can still dance, and often does, down in an old courtyard behind Salamanca Place, where people in Hobart gather each Friday to hear salsa and share wine.

Her daughter, Jessica, also works in hospitality and is a talented tattoo artist. The pair lunch regularly and are best friends. Son Izaac is the adventurer, the free spirit who loves to backpack around the world. Family remains very important and, at the time we meet, Brigid is preparing for a Christmas reunion with her sisters in Dunedin.

After leaving the Port Arthur Historic Site in 2000, Brigid moved from the Tasman Peninsula to Hobart, where she lives on-campus at a TAFE college and manages the student residence and café.

It is a job she loves, including keeping a keen eye on the shenanigans of the students and campus security via a closed-circuit TV screen attached to the wall of her townhouse. Brigid has her own mental video of 28 April which still runs through her head. She can see Colleen's stricken face, the scramble in the kitchen, people running out doors and herself running towards the buses, yelling at Ian and his passengers not to go in the café.

It is not a nightmare, but a series of uncomfortable images. Sometimes there are still tears, particularly if there is a news item about the shootings, or someone recognises her and wants to talk about the day.

Brigid used to hold a tight rein on her thoughts, allowing herself to only process images for a certain period of time before mentally shutting them down. Now she lets the thoughts come as they need to. 'I learned to just let it happen; it's got to flow.'

Insomnia had been a problem, with Brigid becoming accustomed to living off three to four hours' sleep a night. She would devour books to pass the hours, often reading twelve to fifteen books a week. At the time we meet, her sleeping patterns are beginning to return to normal. While sleeping was difficult, she rarely suffered nightmares about the shootings. The only weird dream came during her time in hospital, when she dreamed of Martin Bryant. He was standing in front of his yellow Volvo, which rolled slowly forward, trapping him underneath. He was pinned, but not hurt. In the dream, people came out of their hiding places from among the trees and shrubs and buildings and walked up to him, each saying, 'You shouldn't have done that'.

Brigid's on-campus townhouse is decorated with bright splashes of her favourite colour, orange, and, on the day of our meeting, the music of US country singer Alison Krauss flows in and out of the rooms. The townhouse is full of light and air and, on this day, the rich, herb smells of a risotto Brigid has made for lunch. In her bright orange shoes, she moves about the kitchen with flair and ease, a woman who is very comfortable in her space.

The experience of Port Arthur has torn away any need to pretend, or any reluctance by Brigid to be anything but herself. 'It consolidated things and allowed me to be…it gave me permission to be the person I wanted to be. I used to be quite reserved and shy…I would think about things to say, but wasn't confident enough to say them. Now I do.'

On the back of the toilet door in Brigid's townhouse are dozens of colourful postcards, the eye-catching and clever type usually given away in cafés as advertising. Right in the middle is one with a simple, but poignant statement:

What is the meaning of your life?

I ask her how she would answer such a question. 'As far as possible, to be the most that I can.'

Ian McElwee first revisited the Port Arthur site the week after the massacre. His manager at the time insisted upon it as some sort of get-back-on-the-horse therapy. It didn't quite work. Ian arrived early at the site with a group of American tourists with whom he had drunk wine the night before at the Fox and Hounds. They had somehow learned of his involvement with the massacre, although he didn't tell them. When the bus pulled up near the café, Ian was overwhelmed to see it surrounded by a sea of flowers. He got out and walked around the locked building, where the only physical sign of the utter devastation from just a week before was a single pane of shattered glass.

His group, who were scheduled to spend a day at the historic site, looked at Ian and made a collective decision to return to Hobart. 'Come on, let's go,' one said. Their paid tour was truncated but, months later, Ian was still receiving letters thanking him for making the effort to remain the professional tour driver, despite the personal significance the site had for him. Ian was given the next three weeks off on full pay, during which time Redline also provided external counselling that he describes as 'fantastic'. Ian is still with the company, although now as an operations manager. The largely deskbound job didn't sit easily at first with a man who loves nothing more than the open road, but, he jokes, he now gets to do the bossing around.

Not having lost any loved ones in the tragedy, or been physically injured, Ian feels awkward when talking about the impact Port Arthur had on his life. How can he talk about his suffering when there are those who went through such personal loss? There is no comparison, but nor need there be. Everyone who was at Port Arthur that day, or had some connection with it, has a story.

'A lot of people have said to me that I have dealt with it very well, but it is such an individual thing. It is how you feel inside; how strong you feel inside. You hurt in here and in here,' he says, pointing to his head and his heart, 'but people can't see that hurt'.

In the months after the massacre, Ian remained jittery. An exploding tyre at a service station near his bus depot was enough to send him flat to the pavement. Ian's family also bore the brunt of his anguish over the years and, at times, he feels he must have been a bastard to live with: moody, unable to eat and often kicking off the bedclothes in tormented sleep. If he did doze for an hour or two, he would usually wake up Marg with his yelling. His powerful dreams were not full of horrific images, but the torment of imagining what he could have done to prevent what happened. It was a persistent, useless guilt which all but drove him mad.

'I used to dream that I could have done this and I could have done that. It was guilt, I felt guilt, but you know, when you think about it, there was nothing else you could have done. What could you have done?'

Crown Prosecutor Damian Bugg was acutely aware of the sense of overwhelming helplessness felt by many of those who survived the massacre, and the nagging sense that perhaps they could have stopped Bryant.

In his address to the Supreme Court during Bryant's hearing, Mr Bugg made specific reference to speculation about why someone didn't try to stop the rampage. Perhaps to ease the torment of those who lived with such a question daily, Mr Bugg pointed out the reality of the situation:

> When you look at the time span of what occurred in that café, and take a 15 second gap to achieve the carnage that he did, it's quite understandable that there was no violent physical reaction to curtail what he was doing, the time just wasn't there, the opportunity wasn't there, and there was nothing available to those people to defend themselves or take any step to stop him.

The question still nags at Ian, although far less than it used to. In those moments when it does stir his stomach, he forcibly reminds himself: 'I'd rather be alive and kicking than a dead hero.'

He still harbours an intense anger towards Martin Bryant and can understand why those who lost loved ones could find it impossible to ever forgive. 'Nobody can imagine how they feel for losing somebody like that. They must feel absolute hatred and devastation towards him. They've probably formed their own views, but personally I feel very angry that someone could go there and do that.'

The views are expansive from Ian's home high on the hills of Hobart. The River Derwent opens blue and wide below, the mustard-yellows and purples of the Tasman Peninsula lie in the distance. It is calming, peaceful. Ian has been drawn to the water many times since the day of the massacre. Sometimes, if he feels the knot of stress or sadness looming, he stands on the shoreline near his home, or on the cliffs high above Clifton Beach, south of the city, where he can watch the surf rush against the rocks.

'I would ask myself, why do I feel this way? I shouldn't feel this way, because I am still here. I wouldn't be eating; I would be just feeling down.'

These moments by the water became Ian's personal debriefing sessions and, without fail, he always felt lighter as he left the shoreline. It's perhaps not surprising, then, that one of the earliest shifts in his coping with the aftermath of the shootings came by the water at the Port Arthur site.

It was in the spring of 1996 and Ian had a load of schoolchildren on board who were booked for an after-dark ghost tour. Ian parked his coach in the same area as that which had been under siege on 28 April and just metres from where Royce Thompson had been shot that day.

As dusk fell, Ian sat by the waterfront, enjoying the serenity of the unusually mild night. A local fisherman putted around the bay in his dinghy, a single light bobbing from his vessel. Ian watched and, suddenly, an exhilarating, goose-pimple chill ran through his body. As the shiver left, he felt as if an enormous weight had been lifted from his shoulders and replaced with a lightness of being that he still finds hard to describe.

'I don't know; it was like something had left me and I just felt absolutely marvellous. It is amazing, but it sounds rather silly.'

Today, people and time have much greater importance to Ian than they did before. Like Keith Moulton, Ian has learnt to hug, to touch people when he feels they may need it and to talk openly and honestly, without the waffle.

'You know, if you meet somebody, never be afraid to talk to them, never be afraid to take their hand, never be afraid to put your hand on their shoulder…and never be afraid to give them a hug either, there is absolutely no harm in it.'

Ian has also learnt to listen. He was, he admits, someone who probably used to butt in, who couldn't wait for the other person to finish their story before he began his own. Now, he can actually *listen* and hear that person's story with compassion and empathy.

He has been listened to many times, by his counsellor and by his family, and he knows the value of having someone who does not pretend to be able to fix things, but who just listens.

Within his newfound openness, however, there remains a sliver of shyness. It is what has prevented him from making contact with the one person connected with Port Arthur that he would perhaps most like to see, Brigid Cook. He visited her in hospital in the days after the shootings, taking a small teddy bear that, he thought at the time, would last longer than flowers: blame the Scot in him, he says. They talked and Brigid asked him how his hands had recovered from her bone-crushing squeezes behind the sentry box. It was a brief reunion, a closeness born from catastrophe that, perhaps inevitably, was to fade as both returned to their daily lives.

Having been connected with Brigid through tragedy, Ian has had mixed feelings about tracking her down. She has, he figured, got her own life, her own friends and 'every time she sees this bloody ugly looking Redline driver, it is going to bring back memories'. He still thinks of her occasionally, and tried, unsuccessfully, to have her awarded a citation for bravery from Rotary. In his mind, however, he still owes her his life.

'She is a lovely lass and sometime I would just like to see her and say, "Hey, how are you?" In my mind, she saved my life. Not only mine, but others' too. It's something that I shan't ever forget.'

4

A DIFFERENT MAN:
RON NEANDER

The soft, floral bag bulges with newspaper and magazine clippings, letters and cards: so many cards. For Ron Neander, this is his 'Port Arthur bag'; a personal collection of memorabilia that documents the day and the aftermath of losing his wife, Gwen. It is not a neat file, but Ron knows everything in it. His hands reach in and pluck out a red plastic travel pouch, the type issued by travel agents to hold tickets and itineraries. 'Tassie Temptations Holidays' it reads on the front. Ron unfolds it and reveals the paperwork for a two-week, self-drive holiday around Tasmania from 22 April to 3 May 1996. 'This was the trip we were going to do.'

Between raising a family of three girls and three boys, and Ron's often erratic work hours as a funeral director at Blackwell Funerals in Adelaide, there was not a lot of time for travelling. The trip to Tasmania was to be the Neanders' first serious holiday in 44 years of a solid, loving marriage, in which Gwen was the grounded soul from which her family blossomed. The pair had planned to visit the island in November of 1993, partly to offset the grief of losing their youngest son, Trevor, two years earlier in a car accident. A back operation, however, kept Ron off his feet and unable to handle the ferry journey across Bass Strait. Another two years would pass before the travel plans could be revived. This time, although Gwen walked with the help of a walking stick, there were no physical impediments to their great escape. Ron had retired by January 1996 and earlier that month the couple had celebrated the marriage of their youngest daughter, Pat. The Neanders, both aged in their sixties, were themselves as carefree as two young honey-mooners as they boarded the *Spirit of Tasmania* ferry in Melbourne on 22 April 1996.

The first three days of their long-awaited holiday were spent driving through the rural heart of Tasmania; first Ulverstone, on the edge of the rugged north-west coast, then down the west coast to Queenstown with its rolling hills stripped bare by decades of copper mining. By Friday, the pair had arrived in Hobart, where they crossed the Tasman Bridge to the eastern shore to check in at the no-fuss Cosy Cabins in suburban Mornington. 'That was our way of life. We're not those people who like to stay in rich hotels.'

The weekend began as it does for so many thousands of visitors to Tasmania, with a stroll through the bustling Salamanca Markets on Hobart's waterfront, where Ron and Gwen browsed through the woodwork, sheepskins and second-hand books on sale. Ron recalls they spent the rest of the afternoon wandering through the historic city itself, absorbed by the early colonial and convict-built architecture that was so different to that in their home city of Adelaide. It was early to bed on Saturday night, knowing the day ahead was to be a tiring one with a day-long visit to Tasmania's most popular and famous tourist attraction: the Port Arthur Historic Site.

The first thing Ron noticed about the strange man in Port Arthur's Broad Arrow Café was the bulky sports bag he was carrying. It was a large tennis bag; not the sort of thing, Ron thought, you would want to be lugging around all day. Ron and Gwen were sitting opposite each other on a two-seat table in the café, enjoying a lunch of lasagne and salad before setting out to tour the vast Port Arthur grounds. The thin, blond-haired man Ron would later know as Martin Bryant walked past them with the sports bag hoisted over his right shoulder.

'I said to Gwen at the time, "Gee, if that bag was full, he would not be able to carry it".'

As Bryant approached the servery, the bag slipped from his shoulder and caught on his elbow. Ron saw Bryant wince briefly with pain before he adjusted the bag back onto his shoulder. He then moved around a corner in the café and out of sight. Ron thought no more of it as he and Gwen moved from their table into the adjacent souvenir shop to peruse the postcards and tourist trinkets.

Within minutes, the shooting started.

Ron and Gwen had their back to the café area, but they could hear the sound of rapid gunfire.

'I turned and saw him standing in the middle of the café itself and – I use the term Rambo-style – firing at each and all of the patrons in there.'

As Bryant stood firing his Colt AR15 from the hip, Ron watched in astonishment. Like many caught up in the shootings that day, he thought the former penal colony must have been staging some sort of re-enactment and the bullets could not possibly be real.

Disbelief quickly gave way to revulsion when he saw a bullet pass through the temple of Victorian tourist Mary Howard; blood spurting as she fell to the ground. Ron dropped to the floor, scrambling behind a rack of postcards for cover as the shooting continued around him.

Only when the café fell quiet did Ron feel safe enough to raise his head from his hiding place. Less than 2 metres away, he could see his wife lying on the floor near a glass exit door. She wasn't moving. Gwen was lying on her back, having been facing Bryant as he fired. She hadn't stood a chance as the bullet struck the left side of her face. Ron knew from the extent of her wounds that his wife of so many years, the once-flaming redhead who first caught his eye on a Collingwood street all those years ago, was dead. She was 67. Like others who lost loved ones that day, Ron says his first reaction was to 'shut down' after realising his wife had been murdered. 'I just went numb and I couldn't care what happened.'

From the café window, Ron could see Bryant continuing to run riot. First, returning to his Volvo to exchange his weapon for another semi-automatic and then shooting across the grounds at random before aiming his sights on another visitor, Neville Quin. Ron looked on helplessly as Bryant followed Quin onto one of the buses, firing as he walked.

Standing by his wife's body, Ron watched as Bryant drove away from the car park. Despite being numb with shock, Ron had the clarity of thought to try to remember the number plate. With his long-range eyesight a little patchy, he asked a man nearby if he could help decipher the plate and they managed to make out what they thought were the first two letters – DC. Bryant's number plate actually began with CG, although a search for his vehicle proved unnecessary after he dumped it at the top of Jetty Road.

After spending several minutes with other victims, trying their best to comfort each other, Ron left the café and crossed the car park to his hire car. People were warning that the gunman could still be on the loose. Ron didn't care anymore. Right then he couldn't care much about anything. He collected his coat from the car and walked down to the waterfront where the ferries and fishing boats were moored. As he stood alone, looking out over a peaceful Mason Cove that stood in such stark contrast to the bloodshed he had just witnessed, Ron wondered how he could go on without the person with whom he had shared most of his life.

As a funeral director, Ron Neander had seen death up close many times. He'd spent a career absorbing other people's grief; a dependable, stoic figure in the maelstrom of loss. Working with death, Ron says, perhaps helped him accept more quickly that Gwen was physically gone.

'It's a pretty crude industry; the fact that we get to see death in its natural form, albeit through violence or an accident. I had seen it in the past, so it helped me to accept the fact that Gwen was deceased. The appearance was horrific, but I was able to accept it.'

The intense feelings of loss, however, were something for which he could never prepare. 'As a funeral director, I would often stand with the bereaved and gently place a hand on their arm or shoulder as a gesture that I understood what they were going through. Pig's bum I knew! You can never know unless you go through it yourself.'

A month after the shootings, while still absorbing the shock of Gwen's death, Ron faced one of his most emotionally challenging moments. It began with a call from a reporter seeking comment for a story. Ron, who had built a good relationship with the media since the tragedy, was normally happy to oblige, but this time he was unprepared for the impact of the question.

Prominent historian Professor Geoffrey Blainey, according to the reporter, had made comments at a Melbourne book launch about there being no acts of 'conspicuous bravery' during the Port Arthur massacre.

The Adelaide *Advertiser* was to quote the Professor as saying: 'If, by chance, at Port Arthur, in the face of those terrible obstacles, somebody had managed to jump forward and disarm the man – even if the rescuer lost his life – in the end they would have half redeemed the episode, having the act of conspicuous bravery alongside the act of villainy.'

What, the reporter asked, did Ron think about that?

According to the report at the time, Professor Blainey acknowledged there were 'quiet acts of bravery' and that no-one had much chance to overpower Bryant, but argued that he was trying to make a point about the declining value placed on bravery, courage and valour in modern Australia compared to earlier generations. Ron saw it as a grossly insensitive attack on already wounded hearts.

Was, Ron thought, someone seriously suggesting that the husbands, wives, friends and loved ones of those shot dead would not have done everything humanly possible to stop the slaughter? There was nothing possible in the face of such firepower. 'We were holiday-makers and not in a position to have weapons. We didn't have a hope in hell trying to overpower him – he fired fifteen to seventeen shots in seconds – what hope did we have?'

Ron's fingers form a ball and his voice becomes thin with anger as he explains how the Blainey comment, even today, was in some ways more hurtful than what Martin Bryant had done. Bryant was to him unhinged; a madman. Esteemed thinkers like Professor Blainey, he reasoned, should know better. 'That really hurt and it still hurts to this day.'

While Ron battled to keep a rein on his feelings, his five adult children were fighting their own war against a range of emotions after their mother was so brutally removed from their lives. 'The stress that occurred in my family was horrific. It has caused broken marriages, divorces and, well, depression.'

Pat, the youngest daughter who was married just four months before her mother's death, still, according to Ron, struggles to accept that Gwen is gone. Her marriage was one of three among the children to either become almost unbearably strained, or to break down completely during the next four years.

Ron still feels immense guilt that he may have contributed to the depression suffered by one of his sons, Alan. As the eldest boy, Alan was the first person Ron called from Hobart to tell him that his mother had been murdered.

'This caught him off guard. I wanted him to tell the rest of the family, because I had only one call. One call sounds like a movie, but there were others who had to make calls. That is the part where I feel guilty, because I was quite forceful. I pressured him.'

Alan today remains distant and Ron is yet to sit down and discuss his feelings of guilt with his son, despite the pair living together for a time after Alan's marriage broke down. The eldest in the family, Cheryle, also moved back into the family home at Parafield Gardens after her marriage became strained. Three grieving adults under one roof caused a tension and strain of its own and Ron, describing himself as 'stressed out', decided to break the chain. He bought a transportable home at nearby Virginia and, for the next two years, lived alone.

As the husband of a victim of the Port Arthur shootings, Ron was automatically entitled to compensation through the Tasmanian *Criminal Injuries Compensation Act*. He received the maximum payable, which was $20,000: '$20,000 was the value they put on a person's life'.

(The death of Andrew Mills in the massacre would later contribute to the Labor Government's push for long overdue law reforms in Tasmania which recognised same-sex partners, after it was discovered Andrew's partner, David Capper, was not automatically entitled to compensation. A raft of reforms which gave same-sex couples the same legal rights as all de facto couples was enacted in Tasmania on 1 January 2003. The laws were considered the most progressive in Australia.)

The Port Arthur Appeal – which raised $3.6 million from around Australia – paid for Gwen's funeral and, upon Ron submitting a claim to the committee that was allocating the funds, gave the Neander family a further $15,000. The seizure and sale of Martin Bryant's assets, valued at more than $1 million, saw the family eventually receive another $12,000. 'The only thing I used that money for was the comforting of my children,' says Ron. 'They had outstanding accounts which were paid. We shared the compensation.'

Some of the money also helped pay for ongoing counselling bills, although Ron decided against the formal counselling that several of his children used. Instead, he found solace in talking to 'anyone and everyone'. He kept in touch for more than a year with the Tasmanian parents of Nicole Burgess, the seventeen year old shot dead in the souvenir shop attached to the Broad Arrow Café. Ron also made himself freely available to the media, where he left an indelible impression with his gentle voice, selflessness and grace.

In describing his wife just days after her death, he told cub reporter Danielle Wood, from Hobart's *Mercury*: 'She was getting on a bit, getting a touch of arthritis, and like me getting a bit bigger around the girth, but she was ours and we loved her.'

A decade on, Wood, now a Vogel award winning author, can repeat the quote almost verbatim and will never forget Ron's politeness to a young, frightened reporter sent to interview a man who had just endured the most shocking of experiences.

For Ron, talking about the nightmare helped him to accept it: 'There was nothing that we had done that caused the situation. It was something that happened. I do feel it was the best therapy; talking about it.'

Port Arthur often seemed a million miles away for Ron after he returned from Tasmania to the outer suburbs of Adelaide. The monthly newsletters, *Port Arthur Update*, produced by the Port Arthur Incident Recovery Centre, became a lifeline and the only way to keep up to date with details on the arrangements for Bryant's trial and other issues, such as the controversial debate around deciding upon an official memorial for the massacre.

Despite the pain it represented, Ron spent the first two years after Gwen's death immersing himself in the discussion about how the massacre should be memorialised. 'I suppose I was doing it for myself, but more so for my family. I wanted somewhere where they could go and see the memorial of their mother.'

The entire Neander family returned to Port Arthur on 19 May 1996 for an ecumenical service in memory of the 35 lives cut down just weeks earlier. It was, Ron says, a 'crunch' moment. The family arrived to see a memorial cross made of Tasmania's Huon pine erected by the water's edge: the shores of Mason Cove where Ron had retreated for a moment's solace from the madness of 28 April. The power of the memorial lay in its simplicity. A rough-hewn, honey-coloured cross cut from the most beautiful of pines, standing tall in the name of peace.

As two pipers played 'Amazing Grace', the Neanders joined dozens of other victims and their families in the shadow of the cross to watch the release of 35 white doves. The birds burst from their confines and soared. It was, says Ron, 'the biggest tear-jerker' he had ever experienced.

Ron has returned to the site every year since to join the memorial service on 28 April, but it was his fifth visit, in 2001, which proved a turning point.

This was the year Ron and his youngest daughter, Pat, arrived to find the memorial cross had been moved. It was no longer at the water's edge, but placed at the back of landscaped gardens that surround the remains of the demolished Broad Arrow Café. Its backdrop was now a wall of dark stone, rather than the calming waters of Mason Cove. Ron was bitterly disappointed and driven to pen an angry letter to the *Mercury* newspaper, demanding to know why it had been shifted. He received no reply. It still riles him that the cross was moved virtually out of sight and away from such a tranquil and peaceful setting. There was, however, to be another significant shift that day.

As Ron and Pat wandered through the remains of the demolished Broad Arrow Café, Pat made a passing remark about the native plants that were beginning to grow where the souvenir shop had once been.

The timber partitions of the shop had been dismantled and the tile floor where Gwen and four others had been gunned down had been pulled up and landscaped. Where human blood had been spilled, tiny plants now lifted their heads. 'This is new life coming on,' Pat remarked to her dad.

Up until that point, Ron says, Gwen had 'remained' at the site: in the timber, in the stone, in the tiles. Now, with the 'new life coming on', he could release her. He walked away from the Broad Arrow Café knowing it was time to move on. His darling wife was no longer in this place.

Lily Kernahan was a mess the day she walked into the Salisbury Library to meet with a Justice of the Peace. It was May 2001 and just a couple of months since Bob, her soul mate and husband of 30 years, had lost a three-and-a-half-year battle with cancer. Armed with legal documents, Lily was intending to ask the duty Justice of the Peace to witness some of the myriad paperwork that needed attending to after Bob's death. Instead, she found herself weeping at the JP's desk; great, wracking sobs that she had been holding back for the sake of 'being strong' for the family.

The gentle, blue-eyed man behind the desk reached out his hands to firmly clasp hers and said softly, 'You will be fine'.

To Ron Neander, the shattered woman across the desk was someone in need: he knew what that felt like. He knew the loneliness and isolation after losing a much-loved partner and the sense that, despite the genuinely sympathetic gestures of others, nobody could quite understand what you were going through. Rather than feel empathy, but do nothing about it, Ron decided to keep in touch with this Lily Kernahan to see if he could help brighten the darkness of a loss he knew so well.

Lily appreciated the friendship and help that Ron offered. They began by catching up for coffee and then made casual appointments for Ron to come over and fix Lily's leaking roof, to mend a broken chair or attend to any of the dozens of other jobs that were seemingly piling up since her husband's death.

Ron finally moved things along by inviting Lily home for dinner as, for the first time in the five years since Gwen's death, he felt he might be ready to meet a new partner. 'I had no thought about moving in with anybody or associating with anybody, until such a time a sweet person came into the library one day full of sorrow, and I felt compassion for her.'

Perhaps what Ron didn't expect was that Lily would unlock something in him. As they talked, sharing each other's stories, Ron came to realise that he had never really cried in front of other people. Not even his children. He looked back on the death of his youngest son, Trevor, and remembered that while he and Gwen were utterly devastated, he had held back his tears. He was, after all, a funeral director and trained to keep his emotions in check. As a young boy, Ron had been taught to be seen and not heard and, as a man, he had taken on the responsibility of holding the family together at times of crisis. He was the head of the household and men don't cry, do they? 'I couldn't show emotions: I grieved inside.'

Ron also came to realise that, for all the talking he had done after Gwen's death, he had never really opened up the fullness of his heart: he was able to clinically discuss his grief, but not share it. It was the same with compassion towards others. Ron believed he was a compassionate man, yet he was unable to show it. 'I would feel for people and I would often say something, but I wouldn't be able to share it emotionally, because that just wasn't the done thing, you know?'

Lily, the vivacious, curly-haired Pom who had come into his life, had no such reservations. She had learned the value of a good cry and couldn't fathom going through what Ron had experienced and not being able to weep about it.

Gently and slowly, she unravelled the tight ball of pain that had sat inside Ron for more than five years. They talked for hours, sharing stories about their partners: the good times and the challenges. Ron spoke of the woman Gwen was; her limitless love for her children, her larger-than-life presence in their family and her unwavering support for Ron during his often-demanding career. For the first time in his life, Ron allowed himself to collapse and cry in the arms of another. He felt safe. He knew Lily understood.

'We brought Gwen into our lives and we brought Bob into our lives. We could talk about them openly and have them with us,' Lily said.

Within the tears came laughter and a growing intimacy as the friendship developed into a relationship. They decided to sell their homes and, in March 2002, bought a rundown townhouse in Salisbury, in Adelaide's northern suburbs, which they have since renovated to make it their own.

When asked what has been the greatest change in Ron during their years together, Lily gives what seems to be, at first, an unusual answer: his haircut.

When they first met, Ron was as he appeared in the media coverage that followed Port Arthur: a buttoned-down, grandfatherly figure who felt comfortable in cardigans. His steel-grey hair was slicked down and parted to the side, much, as Lily explained, 'like my father would do it'.

'He had long hair and a couple of times he would take me out to dinner and he would keep on pulling these long ends down the back of his hair and I would think, oh my goodness, how awful,' Lily says with a robust laugh.

A turning point came after Ron was fixing a trailer at Lily's house and returned to the kitchen with long strands of hair flopped over his face. 'How about I cut those off?' Lily suggested. 'Go on then,' was Ron's unexpected response.

Seizing the moment, Lily grabbed the scissors, pulled the offending ends into a cockatoo crest and – snip! – sliced straight through. 'There,' she said, 'now you have to go to the hairdresser'.

Ron returned with a half-inch buzz cut all over. In retrospect, this moment was about far more than the haircut. It was the symbolic beginning of the 'second' Ron. He looks, and is, a changed man.

The conservative cardigans and dark trousers have been replaced by crisp, white shirts and khaki pants. He is much slimmer and more tanned. He smiles broadly and often. He cries, too, although he is yet to completely let his guard down in front of his children. 'I haven't cried outwardly [with them], but, yes, I get watery eyes.'

With the luxury of retirement and time, Ron and Lily travel frequently. In 2003, they visited Port Arthur for the first time together. For Ron, it was the first time since the 1996 massacre that he began to feel comfortable enough to again indulge in the tourist attractions of the area, rather than consider the trip a pilgrimage. He and Lily took the guided tour of the penitentiary area and enjoyed it.

Lily was, at first, wary that Ron would feel overwhelmed by emotion as they toured the site together. Instead, they were drawn closer as Ron honoured the memory of Gwen and together they saw the place where her life had ended.

'The whole idea was for me to see where this had happened to Gwen,' Lily says. 'I felt sadness. The cross was the thing that really got to me: we had to search for where it was. Something like that needs to shout to the world that this must not happen again, but it was tucked in a corner as far as I was concerned.'

Sitting with Lily in their bright, airy kitchen, sharing a plate of sandwiches, Ron says he is a different person to the one he was in those first years after Gwen's death.

'I have learned more compassion in my life and more under-standing for human beings. I am happy that something like that has come about from such sadness.'

Does that compassion extend to Martin Bryant?

'He is there forever, but I won't let him get on top of me,' he says.

The word Ron uses to describe Bryant is 'unfortunate'.

'I have some empathy for the fact that he wasn't quite 100 per cent in the mind. But what he did was cowardly, it was premedi-tated and nobody can say that he wasn't intending to do what he did.'

Ron doesn't allow himself to be consumed by revenge, but he is also not at the point of forgiveness. He may never be. 'What he did is not a forgivable offence. I will never forgive the man for doing what he did, because he's taken my partner away. I do think justice has been done, but I only regret that he came out of that Seascape fire.'

Gwen remains very much a part of Ron Neander – 44 years of marriage will never be put to one side and forgotten – but he has come to accept that he cannot bring her back and return to a life that was. He now cherishes Gwen's memory, while looking ahead to a rich life with Lily. 'I appreciate life so much more. Lily has turned my life around. I am happy in the situation I am living. I hope it extends forever,' Ron says.

Before they moved in together, Ron asked Lily to marry him. 'I believe in vows. I made a vow to Gwen 44 years before her death and she was the only woman in my life.'

Lily, at first, turned him down. She worried that some of her eight children (including four stepchildren from her late husband Bob's first marriage), might have felt she was abandoning them or the memory of their father.

After three years of persistent proposals, however, Lily finally agreed. 'Ron said he was wearing out the knees of his pants from asking me,' she says.

The pair married on 17 August 2005 in a civil ceremony that was kept so quiet, most of their family and friends didn't know until after the event. They didn't want a fuss, they said, or any presents.

With Ron placing a simple gold band on Lily's finger, they pledged honesty and loyalty to each other.

For them, that is more than enough.

5

THE TRUTH IS OUT THERE:
WENDY SCURR

Sitting in her weathered home in Kempton, a historic hamlet about 45 km north of Hobart, Wendy Scurr appears tiny and tired. To Wendy, Martin Bryant is an innocent man and her pursuit of what she perceives as justice for Bryant and his victims both drives and exhausts her.

Today, with her small shoulders and pale eyes, she strikes a very different figure to the one photographed leaving the Tasmanian Supreme Court after hearing Bryant's first pleadings of not guilty to all charges. That image, which appeared on 1 October 1996, shows a robust woman, firm of mouth and gaze, striding out alongside her former colleague Brigid Cook. Wendy and Brigid now walk to the beat of very different drums. While Brigid rarely permits Martin Bryant to cross her mind, Wendy remains immersed in an obsessive quest for the 'truth' behind and around the events of 28 April 1996.

Part of that truth for Wendy is that Bryant was the victim of a complex, government-sanctioned conspiracy that saw him lured into a trap. Instead of being an emotionally disturbed mass murderer, Bryant is nothing more than a simpleton who, through mind control, became the patsy for someone else's crimes. That person –

or persons – is still at large and, according to those who subscribe to the same views, living freely without fear of being arrested.

The elimination of a full trial after Bryant later pleaded guilty to all counts only added momentum to the so-called Port Arthur conspiracy movement. On one hand, witnesses to the event were spared having to relive their experiences in forensic detail, but on the other, the absence of such testimony meant that the chaotic events of the day were open to a multitude of interpretations, and sparked limitless gossip and innuendo. Stories that could have been openly shared and compared instead became mired in a confusing and painful mass of conflicting versions of the same event. The flames of conspiracy theory were further fuelled by good old-fashioned coincidence and the natural links between people living on a small island where the theoretical six degrees of separation are often reduced to two.

Wendy, who was working at the site on the day of the shootings, has been an important and enthusiastic part of the movement that believes the state and federal governments conspired to create the massacre. She has devoted hundreds of hours to collecting and distributing reams of information on what she believes really happened that day and has continued to lobby vigorously for a royal commission – or at least a full coronial inquiry – to finally settle the many unanswered questions which continue to plague her today.

As an articulate, respected worker at the historic site, Wendy's views were given a wide airing by the media in the immediate aftermath of the massacre, when the entire nation was still trying to come to grips with the enormity of what had happened. These days, people are less willing to listen and any public discussion of conspiracy theories is considered distasteful and disrespectful to those who have suffered so much. Yet for those like Wendy Scurr, the truth is still out there and, irrespective of whether her theories appear plausible or completely outrageous, it is an unresolved anguish with which she lives daily.

Wendy closes her eyes and pulls on a cigarette as she explains why she believes there was something askew at Port Arthur in the two months before the shootings.

It began with the tourist who suffered a fatal heart attack on 3 March as he returned to his car after the Beating Retreat event, a special one-off military-style performance. Wendy, who worked at the site as an information officer, first-aid instructor and tour guide, did not know of a similar fatality in all the years the tourist site had been open.

Then the trees began to fall down. First a massive limb from an oak tree, which crashed on the very spot where a large group of people were due to gather twenty minutes later and under which a couple had walked not seconds earlier. Several weeks later, a towering macrocarpa pine tree came plummeting down, roots and all, again just metres from a tour group. It was enough to give Wendy the creeps − it was 'as if we were being prepared for something' − and to inspire her to organise a mock emergency to test the first-aid skills of those staff she had previously trained on site.

The training drill, organised without the knowledge of general staff, was to have been held on Port Arthur's Isle of the Dead, partly to test the ferry-to-shore radio system on the tourist ferry. The radio system was apparently unreliable and Wendy hoped that exposing its inadequacies through a mock emergency would fast-track its replacement.

Just before the drill was to start, however, rough seas forced its relocation to the Commandant's House. It was the Tuesday before Easter 1996 − three weeks before Bryant's rampage. The reliability of the ferry-to-shore radio system could have proved critical had Bryant carried out his original plans for the day. On his way to the site, Bryant had mentioned to some tourists that he met on the Arthur Highway that he was going to travel to the Isle of the Dead to kill some 'wasps'.

On the day of the shootings, Wendy, who had only become a permanent employee at the site that March, was working as a guide on the ferry. She remembers the morning well, as among the many faces on board were three that stood out for their familiarity: Nanette, Alannah and Madeline Mikac.

Nanette, who, like Wendy, had worked as a ghost tour guide, explained that she and the girls were going to enjoy a picnic at the site. Wendy remembers giving each of the children an Isle of the Dead postcard which they were carrying when she later saw them at the Broad Arrow Café buying sandwiches for lunch. They had come off the 1 p.m. Isle of the Dead tour and had beaten Wendy, who was delayed on the ferry selling souvenir books, to the long line in the café. The two women again chatted, with Nanette confirming she would be taking a first-aid course scheduled with Wendy for the following morning. It was the last time Wendy saw Nanette or the girls alive.

Wendy had also noticed another face at the Broad Arrow Café that lunchtime, one which seemed like it should be familiar, but wasn't. He was a man with long blond hair, seated in the sun on the balcony. As Wendy passed by, he stared at her and nodded. She nodded in return, thinking he must be a surfing mate of one of her two sons. Wendy believes this man may have been the blond-haired gunman, but not Bryant, whose face was to later stare out from the front page of newspapers around Australia as the man responsible for killing 35 people that day.

All of this was yet to unfold as Wendy, armed with a bowl of hot potato wedges, made her way to the nearby Information Centre, just a short walk from the Broad Arrow Café, to share lunch with some fellow workers. It was about 1.28 p.m., by her reckoning, when the first of a series of rapid shots began to fire out. Believing, like many others, that it was gas bottles exploding, Wendy ran out towards the café and was about twelve paces away from the side door when a piece of metal – she is still not sure if it was a bullet or shrapnel – 'whizzed' past her shoulder. At about the same time, a person – she can't remember if it was a man or a woman – came tearing out of the café screaming that someone was shooting everyone inside and to run.

From that moment, life for Wendy Scurr, as for so many others that day, was to change irrevocably. Amid the chaos unleashed by Bryant's actions was a series of personal shocks and sustained trauma for which anyone would be ill prepared, even those like Wendy, who was well versed in dealing with the front line of human trauma. She began to learn first aid in 1970 while living in Launceston and went on to become an instructor and a St John's Ambulance volunteer.

Wendy remained a volunteer for the service after moving to the Tasman Peninsula in 1986, yet no amount of personal skill or training could have readied her for the overwhelming scenario into which she was thrust on that last Sunday in April 1996. 'I had seen lots of trauma as an ambulance officer, like opening a car door after an accident and having a man's head roll out, but nothing, nothing compared to what happened at Port Arthur.'

The personal nightmare for Wendy began after she helped herd some of the approaching tourists away from the danger in the café and then ran back to the Information Centre to call the police. Two colleagues, Sue Burgess and Steve Howard, were already making calls on the internal phone system to warn other staff about the shootings. Standing just metres from a window through which she expected the gunman to fire any minute, Wendy dialled 000, somehow managed to give her name and address and then, her heart racing with anxiety, tried to convince the sceptical police officer on the end of the line that she was telling the truth.

'I took the receiver and put it out the door and let him hear the shots that were still going on.

'I went back in and said, "Do you believe me now?" and he said, "Look, I need your contact phone number" and I said "Don't ring me, I won't be here. I've got to go. Please believe me – there are people here getting murdered".'

Wendy's call was the first logged by police that day about the mayhem unfolding on the Tasman Peninsula, where major incidents were usually limited to car crashes and farming accidents.

Knowing they would be trapped in the Information Centre if the gunman arrived, Wendy, Sue and Steve decided to make a run for the safety of the thick scrub behind the Broad Arrow Café. In one of those lucid, yet irrational moments in the middle of chaos, Wendy remembers Sue worrying about leaving the contents of the till behind.

'Fuck the till,' was all Wendy could suggest as they raced out the door. Sue, however, did grab a hand-held radio.

The trio, their skin hot and prickling with adrenalin, made the dash from the office to a nearby toilet block, then into the bush behind the café, all with the sound of gunfire popping around them. Wendy could hear the shots, but never saw the gunman.

Already hiding in the scrub was a terrified café worker who had run from the shooting. Wendy recalls the young woman was physically unharmed, but 'as white as a ghost'. Just at that point, a call came over Sue's radio from their colleague, Ian Kingston, warning that the gunman's car was still in the car park and that he was still at large on the site. 'It was the most frightening thing for us all to hear, but especially for that young girl.'

Wendy pushed the young woman deep into the bushes with two men who had also managed to escape from the café after being wounded by shrapnel. They were in severe pain, but their wounds were not life-threatening.

Wendy did her best to reassure them they would all be safe if they remained hidden in the dense scrub, before bracing herself to enter a back door of the café and check on those inside. She expected the worst, given the number of shots that had been fired in quick succession, but her anticipation of the bloodshed within was compounded by a simple question from Sue: 'I wonder if the girls got out?'

'What girls?' Wendy asked.

Sue explained that her teenage daughter, Nicole, and Steven's wife, Elizabeth, were rostered on that day in the souvenir shop. Wendy suddenly realised that people she knew, friends and colleagues, could be among the dead and injured inside.

'I was all braced up for a terrible sight, because I knew what was going to be in there, but that news [about the girls] came as a terrible shock, because I didn't even know they were working that day, and to think of them in there. It was a terrible, terrible shock.'

The three pushed open the café door and entered a scene that Wendy can only describe as 'a butcher shop'. Pools of blood lay thick on the floor and human remains were spattered around the walls and ceiling.

'It was absolutely silent inside. Not a sound. It was the most eerie feeling. You couldn't cry; you were in too much shock to cry. You just felt helpless.'

Nicole and Elizabeth were lying side by side behind the counter in the gift shop and Wendy could tell immediately by the blood loss and their injuries that they were dead. As Sue and Steven looked on, she crouched down and tried in vain to find a pulse: she thought by just going through the motions she could hold back, if only for a moment, the heartbreaking truth.

As she 'worked' on the bodies, Wendy's mind was searching for what to say to her two colleagues who had just lost a child and a young wife. 'I got on very well with the two girls personally, but to have two of my workmates run with me right through that and to be confronted with that, it was probably the hardest thing I have ever had to do, ever, in my entire life.'

Sue asked if there was anything Wendy could do to help the girls. Her reply had to be blunt.

'All I could say was, "No, they are dead". My very next thought was, what do I do now? I remembered from my training that the best thing you can do with someone who has suffered a casualty like that is to give them something to do, so I told Sue to leave the café, that she would be needed elsewhere, and for Steve to find some blankets. I asked them to get out of there.'

Knowing there was nothing more she could do for the girls, Wendy began to pick her way through the café to see if there was anybody alive. As she stepped through the crumpled bodies, it was brutally obvious – without the need for touch – who was dead. In one corner, Wendy could see someone was already working on a badly injured Graham Collyer, who had taken a bullet through the neck. The woman, who was later identified as a Melbourne nurse known only as Lynne, was using a straw to remove the blood pooling in his throat. His friend, Carolyn Loughton, sat in agony nearby, her back torn open and her eardrum shattered by the gun-shot that had killed her fifteen-year-old daughter, Sarah. For those like Wendy who had entered the café after the shootings, it was a sustained assault on all the senses.

'I had to confront the whole damn thing and go right through that café on my own. There were other visitors, but it wasn't their responsibility, as a first-aid officer it was mine. Horrific is not a good enough word for it.'

She recalls, in particular, how she decided at one point that she had to make sure an ambulance, and not just the police, had been called and so went in search of a telephone. As she did, she heard a crunch beneath her foot and looked down to find she had stepped on part of a woman's skull, the long hair still attached and flowing along the ground.

'I will never forget the crackling under my feet,' she says.

Part of the woman's brain had fallen into a bowl of chips on the table at which she sat. Wendy could do nothing but find a tea towel and cover the mess.

Blood and bits of human remains had also attached themselves to Wendy's hair, feet and shoes as she moved through the café. She still smarts as she describes brushing the sticky body matter from her shoulders and using a sink in the back of the café to wash her bloodied legs and feet.

As the Special Commissioner for Port Arthur, Max Doyle, was to write in his 1997 report for the Tasmanian Parliament on the Port Arthur shootings, nobody but the staff on duty that Sunday, and those tourists and emergency workers caught up in the massacre, could ever hope to fully understand the extent of the experience:

> It is perhaps impossible for other than those 31 people…plus the visitors present, to fully understand the amazement of the happening and the fright, hopelessness, bravery, heroism, stress, trauma and the wonderful acts of thinking of others, of planning, of sharing and of loss and sadness that all took place in the space of that first 30–60 minutes of the shootings.

As he explained, because the entire Port Arthur senior management team was at a conference in Swansea that day, it was left to the 'rank and file' staff to shoulder the full burden of responsibility in the immediate aftermath of the shootings.

Let there be no doubt that what happened during the first
hour after 1.30 p.m. on April 28 saw all these acts of heroism,
love and care take place – but at a terrible toll on the lives of
those who were then, and have been since, affected by these
events.

It was well past midnight before Wendy finally left the Port Arthur
site. Once the ambulance crews and the two local GPs, Steve and
Pam Ireland, arrived and began treating the injured in the café,
Wendy triaged the walking wounded outside, including Brigid
Cook, who was sitting on the verandah with her bleeding leg
wrapped in her apron.

As she attended to the injured, Wendy kept waiting for the
police to arrive and began to wonder if her first call had been taken
seriously. The first police helicopter did arrive within the hour, but
it was a medical rescue rather than a swarm of armed officers as
expected by those on the ground. It would be another five hours
before the police arrived at the site in force.

The police operation, unbeknown to most at the site, was centred on the Seascape cottage, about 2 km from the Port Arthur site,
where Bryant had fled after his rampage. Those still trapped at the
site, however, had no idea of knowing where Bryant was, or if there
was more than one gunman at large. The absence of any large-scale
police presence after such a major incident only added to their
sense of vulnerability.

Aside from the anxiety of not knowing where the gunman
was, Wendy and other Port Arthur staff had the added burden of
dealing with the raw grief and trauma of those caught up in
the gunfire. With no uniformed police on site, the navy blue
Port Arthur staff uniform became a symbol of authority to those
desperate to know the fate of their missing relative, or to retrieve
personal items from the bodies – 'Which I couldn't do,' says
Wendy.

Once the senior management team arrived back from Swansea,
Wendy was given the task of helping identify the bereaved and

taking them to the manager's cottage, 'Clougha', for a quiet space and a cup of coffee.

'I'd have to walk up to a group of people and say, "Have you had someone die here today? Well, if you have, come with me." '

It was at this point a frantic Walter Mikac approached her and asked if she had seen Nanette and the girls. Nanette's car was still in the car park, he explained. Word had filtered down through the staff that a woman and two children had been killed up Jetty Road, but only then did Wendy realise it must have been Nanette and the girls.

'Nanette was a registered nurse and I knew if she had still been at the site, she would have been down there in that café helping out. I knew then she was dead, but I couldn't tell Walter.

'I looked him in the eye and said I didn't know where she was, because I knew he would want me to take him up there, and that would have done me in…I contacted him much later and apologised for not being able to tell him.'

By now it was close to 6 p.m., more than four hours after the shootings, and still there was no certainty on where the gunman was, or any visible police presence. Wendy was among those still tending to the shocked and wounded while suppressing her own emotions: her own feelings would have to wait.

Wendy was eventually directed up to a motel which shared a boundary with the historic site and to where many had run for safety. Inside, she found dozens of stunned and frightened people, including a grief-stricken Mick Sargent, who sat and swayed as he grappled with how he would tell the parents of his fiancée, Kate, that she had been shot dead. There was a man suffering severe chest pains and a woman trying to find a fresh nappy for her baby; all slivers of stress that added to the chaotic scene inside.

The only figure of authority Wendy could see among the crowd was a single policeman who was trying valiantly to gather names and addresses. As dusk fell, the ongoing nightmare shifted again as shots were heard close to 'Clougha', sparking fear among the grieving friends and relatives sheltering in the cottage that the gunman had returned. Like those in 'Clougha', the people gathered in the motel were told to close the curtains, shut off the lights and

keep quiet, but Wendy recalls she refused to plunge frightened, traumatised people into darkness.

'If I had turned the lights out on those people, they would have
been blown out of their brains, so I made an executive decision to
leave them on. I was panicking, but I had been panicking all day. I
was calm on the outside, but inside I was just shot to pieces.'

About an hour after the gunshot scare, believed to have been caused
by an unsuspecting rabbit hunter, a swarm of heavily armed police
descended on the motel. It was 7 p.m. and, for the first time since
the shooting began, those huddled inside began to feel safe. The
police were closely followed by a group of counsellors and social
workers bussed down from Hobart to hold a debriefing at the
nearby youth hostel. Wendy wasn't interested; she felt physically and
emotionally exhausted, hungry and resentful of 'well-meaning
young things' trying to pick away at her feelings.

'They tried to make us relive it all again, for God's sake. The
trauma had been going on and on, so nothing they were saying was
going in. It was the worst thing they could have done to us. The
nicest thing they could have done was just let us go our own way
and be together [with our families] on our own.'

One of the most humiliating aspects, as Wendy remembers it,
was a communal water bowl and ladle set in the middle of the room
from which people could drink, rather than being offered individual glasses. At one stage, the pet dog of the Isle of the Dead ferry
owner wandered up and slurped from the same bowl. 'We were
treated like dogs then and we have been treated like dogs since. We
were treated like animals, not even given our own drinking vessel.'

After a 90-minute debriefing session, Wendy wandered to the
hotel bar for a stiff drink. It was close to 1 a.m. by the time a staff
car shuttle ferried her home the 10 km to White Beach. There
she collapsed into the arms of her husband of 34 years, Graeme,
and wept.

Despite her exhaustion, Wendy was unable to sleep as the emotions from the day ran through her. There was also the lingering fear

that the gunman was still roaming the peninsula, with conflicting reports on whether he was contained in Seascape. Wendy begged Graeme to drive the short distance to the nursing home in Nubeena to see if they had a sleeping tablet to calm her nerves. He obliged.

While he was gone, she sat rigid on the edge of their bed, Graeme's .308 rifle across her knees.

For those who have experienced such sustained trauma and anxiety, it is wellnigh impossible to know which parts have left the deepest scars, but a significant part of Wendy's personal anguish today centres on a simple glass exit door that failed to function.

Its significance emerged after Wendy left Nicole and Elizabeth in the gift shop and walked towards a pile of bodies against a nearby glass exit door. The door provided the only way out of the gift shop that did not lead back through the café.

Wendy tried to lift three of the bodies off to see if one trapped underneath, a man, was still alive, but their dead weight proved too much. Outside the glass door she spotted a tourist who she decided to ask for help, but as she pulled the door handle down, she realised, with a sudden rush of panic, that the door would not open. The handle rattled up and down, but failed to catch the lock.

In a frightening, bone-numbing flash, she realised that anyone in the gift shop who had tried to run to safety had been trapped and, if the gunman was to return, so was she. She turned and ran back into the café.

'I went into a blind panic and left. I felt terror, absolute terror.'

Wendy would spend months trying to reconcile her guilt over leaving a man who may have been alive in order to preserve herself; a mental burden which was eased only slightly after it was later revealed all of those killed in the café died instantly.

Her anguish surrounding the door, however, continues to churn through her mind as a serious safety breach for which someone must be held accountable. Wendy is convinced that the seven people killed in the gift shop, including Elizabeth and Nicole

– who most likely knew the door was broken so instead hid behind the counter – would have survived if it was operable.

'Those seven only had to get out of that door, do a left, go around the corner and they were in the bush. They had about twenty metres to get under the cover of bush, but they couldn't get out...so they waited, they waited to be shot.'

One of the survivors of the shootings, Carolyn Nash, was among those who did try to escape through the door, only to find it locked. A police statement tells of how Ms Nash and her husband, Peter, attempted to make a run for it through the door, but found themselves trapped. All Peter could do was crouch over his wife and attempt to shield her body as Bryant took aim and fired. Peter was fatally wounded.

The report by Commissioner Max Doyle into the shootings confirmed the Port Arthur Historic Site Management Authority was aware the door was faulty and intended to have it repaired, although this had not been done prior to the shootings.

More than twenty people expressed their concern to Doyle about the door, prompting him to recommend an independent investigation into the issue to help resolve their unanswered questions about why it had not been repaired, and therefore help with their healing and recovery process. Doyle urged that the investigation consider, among other things, who held legal responsibility for maintenance of the door, whether it had been inspected by government or council safety officers and 'the accuracy of comments' that had been made about the door in a blunt staff memo issued after the shootings.

The staff memo, distributed on 20 February 1997, was a dreadful attempt to try to discount media coverage of speculation that the broken door may have added to the death toll in the Broad Arrow Café. In what Doyle described as a document of 'bad taste', the two-page memo was a cold, clinical assessment of what the site management considered to be the 'facts' surrounding the door and the futility of pondering what may or may not have happened if it had been working that day.

It read in part:

If the door was operable, would it have saved lives? Perhaps. Perhaps not – the deceased may have simply got two steps outside before they were gunned down in a similar manner. To dwell on this question is likely to be far more destructive than constructive, at best an exercise in futility.

To debate conflicting opinions and views between ourselves has the potential to open a whole range of wounds and perhaps bring us all down in the end.

The memorandum then goes on to criticise the media for its apparent sensationalist reporting of the issue and to warn that 'our role in all this is to ensure we don't add fuel to the fire – by getting drawn into a volatile, emotional debate and that we don't bring each other down by discussing "what if" scenarios until we all become manic depressives'. It ends with a glib, 'Can we please support each other through these difficult times. Thank you.'

Given the memo was issued to staff less than twelve months after the massacre, it is little wonder Doyle was moved to describe some of its comments as 'amazing' and, in his view, confirmation of concerns around 'the lack of quality and professionalism of some of the management staff'.

Port Arthur Authority Board chairman, Michael Mazengarb, and the site's general manager, Craig Coombs, resigned in the wake of the Doyle report, which was considered so damaging to the site at the time that it was not expected to be publicly released.

What Doyle exposed amongst the mire of rumour and innuendo in the aftermath of the massacre was a deep seam of genuine concern that the full story around the killings had not been told, including the truth around the issue of the malfunctioning door. His report also revealed that some of the Port Arthur staff, including Steve Howard, who lost his wife, and contractor Mark Kirby, who was working on the penitentiary building that day, had been treated appallingly by their employer and had become locked in lengthy and bitter disputes over their entitlements.

Indeed, some of the damages claims lodged by staff and visitors who were at the site that day were still being fought through the courts in early 2004. Others who had begun fighting for compensation had either lost patience or become exhausted by the process and withdrawn their applications.

The release of the Doyle report prompted swift action by a state parliamentary group which assigned the then Director of Public Prosecutions, Damian Bugg, QC, to follow up the recommendations.

Bugg, who had led the prosecution against Bryant, released his report in late July 1997. In it, he attempted to settle many of the burning questions that remained over what happened in the massacre, such as how long Bryant was shooting in the café, exactly what weapons he had used and, perhaps the most troubling, whether anyone could be deemed responsible for failing to repair the gift shop door.

Bugg confirmed that the door was not working that day and that the site authority had been made aware that it was not functioning about two weeks before the shootings. A request to have it repaired, however, appeared to have been made only verbally and not in writing. There was, Bugg found, no sense of urgency about having it repaired because it was used rarely by staff and not at all by the public. Nobody, of course, could have foreseen how important the door would become.

Bugg made it clear in his report that the search for somebody to blame was causing pain and stress to many of the Port Arthur staff and that, hopefully, his report would go some way towards ending hurtful speculation. During the prosecution, Bugg had become highly respected by many of Bryant's victims and their families for his personal approach – he was applauded at the end of the trial – and no doubt knew what sort of impact continual questions about the massacre were having on these same people.

For Wendy though, the matter will not and cannot rest until there is a full coronial inquiry. She sees the faulty door as part of a wider cover-up. 'I'll never get closure until I get some answers and the only way I can get those answers is through a coronial inquiry which we should have had. Why can't we have one? Why can't they give us some closure? They say the healing process began right after the massacre, but for a lot of us, we are still waiting for it to start.'

The broken door is one of a string of issues that continue to trouble her and fuel an obsessive quest to unearth what Wendy perceives as the truth. That truth includes her belief that there were two gunmen shooting at the site that day; that Martin Bryant was brainwashed to make sure he was at Seascape, but that he did not commit the atrocities for which he pleaded guilty; and that the state's health and law enforcement officials were not only prepared for such a massacre, but expecting it. It was, the theory goes, a government-sanctioned act of terror. Wendy is unable to explain why the government would wish to commit such a crime, or what it possibly stood to gain, but considers the massacre the ultimate act of a government that cannot be trusted.

They are shocking allegations, but for Wendy, they are real and an indication of the depth of her stress.

'For the first twelve months after the massacre, I thought it was Bryant...then I read the full court transcript and I saw the lies in it. I know what's right and wrong, because I was there.'

She and her supporters, including former Victorian policeman Andrew MacGregor and retired New South Wales gunsmith Stewart Beattie, have devoted hundreds of hours to uncovering what they believe is the greatest conspiracy in Australian history. They have contacted every state and federal politician asking for help, but have so far failed to secure much action beyond a phone hook-up with One Nation MP Len Harris who, after initially promising to help, has also withdrawn his support. They have compiled 1500 pages of documentation to support their theories and, as recently as 2004, were holding public forums which attracted both interest and scorn. Wendy also occasionally takes people interested in her theories on a personal tour of the site and, at the time of our meeting, had just escorted an American filmmaker keen on making a documentary around the issue of the faulty door. Such is her degree of suspicion, Wendy later accuses the American filmmaker of being a 'spook': another ASIO or CIA spy. She also believes her movements at the historic site are monitored.

'I have been watched, followed and threatened...we are usually under surveillance when I go to the Port Arthur site. I was under surveillance when I went there a fortnight ago with a group of 36 at that time.'

Graeme, a large, quietly spoken bloke who buys and sells wool from properties across Tasmania's midlands, is fiercely supportive of his wife's views. He has seen Wendy suffer greatly from the anguish of her unending quest, but believes she is right in her pursuit. He, too, believes Bryant was under some form of mind control and was set up as a patsy for persons unknown.

They are beliefs born of stress; compounded by what the Scurrs claim has been a blatant and ongoing disregard for what people at the site suffered that day. They feel forgotten.

Wendy acknowledges she has suffered severe post-traumatic stress disorder, which led to an attempt in 2001 to take her own life through an overdose. Graeme found her after hearing a noise in their bedroom and immediately rang an ambulance.

'I found every tablet I could in the house and I took them in three handfuls. For some reason that night I just thought I had had enough and I couldn't go on any more. I am not very proud of what I did to [Graeme] and I am not proud of what I did to my kids because I worried them. I wouldn't do it again, but sometimes you can only take so much.'

Depression remains a constant battle. Wendy spent close to three years in and out of hospitals for a range of health problems immediately after the shootings. 'Up until a year ago I was having these recurring thoughts about five minutes apart. There were just constant images from the day, running through my mind.'

Electric shock therapy was part of her initial treatment, but this, she says, caused memory loss, lapses in concentration and a lack of motivation. These days she prefers a rigid regime of vitamin and mineral supplements to 'balance me out'.

Wendy's health struggle has meant she has not worked since the massacre and has forgone any involvement in first-aid training as it is too close to the memories of the Broad Arrow.

She now lives a quiet life, punctuated by lawn bowls once a week which she took up again, after a ten-year absence, in 2003. A group of women from the nearby town of Oatlands convinced her to start playing. 'They never gave up on me, those ladies. They persisted, even when I was in the Hobart [psychiatric] Clinic for two weeks, they would bus me out for a game and take me back when we had finished. Half the time I was as high as a kite on anti-depressants and was surprised the bowls landed where they were supposed to.'

Wendy laughs as she recalls her somewhat unconventional team competing in the Southern Tasmania Mitsubishi Fours in early 2004 – and winning.

Her Melbourne psychiatrist has also convinced her to try to write a 'positive' book about her journey through trauma, rather than remain wedded to the conspiracy theories. Wendy says Andrew MacGregor and Stewart Beattie now run the bulk of the campaign on the Port Arthur cover-up – they don't use the word conspiracy – but she hopes to continue to tell her personal story in the hope of flushing out 'the truth'. 'There is the frustration; the sheer frustration of not being able to get some finality to this. I will pursue it as long as I can draw breath.'

In early 2005, Graeme Scurr was diagnosed with bowel cancer, from which he was expected to fully recover, but which prompted the Scurrs to leave Tasmania for Sydney to be closer to family. Wendy continues to work behind the scenes on pushing for a coronial inquiry into the massacre.

The video

It was footage that nobody outside of the Tasmanian police force was ever expected to see. The crime scene video was shot by police forensic teams as they moved through the bloodied rooms of the Broad Arrow Café, around the tour buses and up to the toll booth; carefully documenting each of the tagged bodies of Bryant's victims. So sensitive was the footage that it was kept in secure storage at Tasmania Police headquarters in Hobart's Liverpool Street and anybody who wanted to access the video needed the permission of no less than the Deputy Commissioner of Police, Jack Johnston, who kept a log on who had borrowed the video and when it was returned.

Yet, on a beautiful August afternoon in 2004, I was watching this very footage in the darkened, smoky lounge room of Wendy Scurr's home in Kempton. Two weeks earlier I had emailed Wendy, who agreed to be part of this book, to ask if I could visit and take her photograph. She was pleased I had made contact, she said, as 'something big' had happened and it 'changes everything'. It was too sensitive to discuss via email or telephone, she said, so she would wait until my visit to tell me the full details of this 'huge thing'. Knowing Wendy's obsessive belief that the Port Arthur massacre was a 'government-sanctioned terrorist attack', I was sceptical about what this 'huge thing' might be. It was, I thought, most likely another piece of evidence that Wendy had unearthed to support the 'terrorist' theories.

On the agreed day of our meeting, we wandered over to a nearby park to take the photographs and, as we crunched our way back along the gravel footpath, Wendy revealed the story of the video.

She had a friend, she explained, who bought used videos from Tasmanian tip shops (shops which sell salvaged goods) to use for recording. They were cheap, maybe ten or twenty cents each. As Wendy explained it, among the videos her friend had bought from a Hobart tip shop for ten cents was a police training video based around the Port Arthur massacre. It showed the gruesome aftermath of the massacre inside the Broad Arrow Café and beyond, she said.

I swallowed. If this was true, then this was a huge news story about a major security breach within Tasmania Police: there were few issues, if any, more sensitive in Tasmania than the Port Arthur massacre.

Back in her lounge, Wendy pulled out a CD-ROM copy of the video. The original, she explained, was stored with a trusted friend. She played it on her desktop computer and, much to my disbelief, it was indeed the forensic footage. I watched it through splayed fingers, trying to again imagine how it must have been for those who witnessed the massacre first-hand. The video shows tables and chairs strewn across the Broad Arrow Café, having been pushed aside as people tried to escape or to make room for treating the injured. Each of those killed in the café remained in situ, frozen in the positions in which they died. The police camera methodically moves between each tagged body, a low, male voice providing a solemn commentary on the age and sex of each victim. The same procedure was followed as the camera scanned the bodies on Jetty Road, around the buses and in the car park.

Not only did the Scurrs have a copy of this highly sensitive footage, which had been copied and circulated to some of their friends and supporters, but letters kept by the Scurrs revealed the Tasmanian Government and Tasmania Police had known about the leak for at least three months. Despite this, there were no public warnings to the families and friends of Port Arthur victims that this material had been stolen and released. The police minister, David Llewellyn, instead hoped he could convince the Scurrs to return all copies; an unlikely scenario given the Scurrs' suspicion of government authorities. Fortunately in those three months the material had not been circulated on the Internet, although some people claim to have seen it there since.

I wrote the story about the video for *The Australian* newspaper at the same time as Wendy caught the *Spirit of Tasmania* ferry to Melbourne to avoid what was expected to be a media frenzy in the days immediately after. There was. She had already suffered a relapse, she said, after watching the film and could not take any more pressure.

The media later named Wendy's friend as Launceston woman Olga Scully, who had a public profile of her own as a vocal anti-Semite and denier of the Holocaust. As Deputy Commissioner Johnston told me later, it was too much of a coincidence in his mind that such a video would accidentally fall into Mrs Scully's hands via the tip shop. Within a fortnight, the tip shop itself would be torched, causing $30,000 damage.

Mr Johnston denied the video was a police training film. Instead, he explained, a series of police videos had been spliced together to discredit the police by making it appear as if they were using sensitive Port Arthur footage in the training of recruits. It was true, however, that someone had removed the Port Arthur forensic footage from the secure area, taken an illegal copy and, it appeared, released it to further the campaign by those convinced the massacre was a government-sanctioned conspiracy.

Eight months after the footage surfaced, the Tasmanian police wound up their internal investigation without finding the person responsible for its release, although there was one disgruntled former officer who some suspect used the leak to embarrass the force. Most, but not all, of the copies were returned to police after those holding them were accused of gross insensitivity. While the public was justifiably outraged by the video's release, it appears the answer as to who wanted to reveal the footage – and why they were able to do it so easily – will remain a mystery.

Conspiracy theories

Those who believe Martin Bryant is an innocent man are nothing if not imaginative. The World Wide Web is alive with theories and counter-theories about what really happened at Port Arthur on 28 April 1996, all based on the belief that Bryant was simply too stupid and too hopeless with a gun to have unleashed such lethal force.

Instead, the conspiracy theorists argue, the massacre was a carefully managed terrorist exercise that involved, depending on the particular point of view, a complex web made up of the CIA, ASIO, the state and federal governments, police, medical professionals, the national and international media, unnamed corporate giants, crack marksmen wearing wigs, and mind controllers.

Among the key perpetrators of the conspiracy theories was a Perth-based pensioner and writer, Joe Vialls, who died in July 2005. After Martin Bryant's sentence of imprisonment for life, Vialls, who described himself as an independent investigator, self-published a book, *Deadly Deception at Port Arthur*. The book, which according to Vialls's website is in its third reprint, outlines in forensic detail what he claimed was undeniable evidence of the massacre being a government-sanctioned plot to crack down on gun ownership and turn the nation against sporting shooters.

Martin Bryant, according to Vialls, was framed using a form of mind control practised by the Tavistock Institute in Britain. This mind control began, it is alleged, when Bryant was first assessed by psychiatrists as a teenager to determine if he qualified for a disability pension on the grounds of intellectual impairment. It appears those supposedly behind the massacre were a patient lot.

Indeed, Vialls would have had us believe that the massacre was not the work of a vengeful loner, but rather what he called a meticulously planned 'psyop': an operation that psychologically manipulates a nation for political or military reasons.

One of Vialls's websites went on to explain it this way:

Because of their illegal nature, psyops are never formally ordered by governments, but are discreetly arranged through multinational corporations and others. Some psyops ordered during the last forty years are known to have been carried out by independent contractors hired from a small specialist group, staffed mostly by retired members of American and Israeli special forces.

And what was the outcome of this 'psyop' at Port Arthur? According to Vialls, an unnamed but obviously highly influential multinational corporation successfully removed 600,000 firearms from the community as part of the campaign by the anti-gun lobby to disarm Australia. These weapons, he argues, should have at least been oiled up and stored away by the federal government so that the good citizens of Australia could access them at a minute's notice if the nation needed defending.

Despite his ludicrous arguments, Vialls found a willing audience on the Internet, where chat rooms harbour numerous souls who mull over the voluminous 'facts' he compiled to support his views. Unfortunately, the detail of his work can make it appear credible and persuade even clear-thinking people that there may be 'something in it', much to the despair of most of those who lived through the experience.

By late 2004, Vialls was still lobbying for a retrial of Martin Bryant and seeking donations to cover the court action, but even Wendy Scurr, a former supporter of Vialls, was no longer backing his efforts. They had a falling out, according to Wendy, over his fundraising methods.

Having gained a degree of notoriety for his theories around Port Arthur, including his decree that 22 November – the day of Bryant's sentencing – be officially declared Martin Bryant Sorry Day, Vialls spread his investigative wings.

A quick glance at his work published on a United Kingdom website called The Truth Seeker, revealed he had undertaken no less than 83 separate investigations into the 'truth' behind everything from the September 11 attacks on the World Trade Center, through to the murders of British schoolgirls Holly Wells and Jessica Chapman. His outrageous and increasingly anti-Semitic views, however, were proving noxious. As of late 2004, Internet domain host Yahoo had shut him down and Paypal, an online banking system, refused to accept donations on his behalf. Vialls counter-attacked by moving his website offshore and finding an inde-pendent online bank that was happy to take people's cash. Vialls's supporters are continuing to promote his work.

Unlike Vialls and his prolific work online, former Victorian policeman Andrew MacGregor and retired New South Wales gun-smith Stewart Beattie rely on good old-fashioned spruiking from the stump to deliver their version of the truth behind Port Arthur.

Wendy Scurr was once a regular part of their tour circuit of small towns across the country, but has since taken a step back, she says, to focus on her own health.

This group also believes the massacre was a government-sanctioned act of terror, but, unlike Vialls, is less clear on the motive. MacGregor suggests in his CD-ROM compilation, *Deceit and Terrorism, Port Arthur*, that the mainstream political parties were, at the time, fearful of the rising political influence of the Shooters Party. The argument follows that the major parties considered a massacre the only way to turn public opinion against guns and gun owners.

MacGregor, who sounds on the telephone like an amiable Scot, also argues the federal government was keen to expand its influence over the states, including controlling laws over firearms.

An added incentive to kill 35 people and maim twenty others, according to MacGregor, may have been the police security units hoping that the skill and prowess they demonstrated in their response to the massacre would increase their chances of providing security for the 2000 Sydney Olympic Games.

The claims may be outlandish, but they also have found trac-tion among chat room enthusiasts and others. The Shooters Party, not to be confused with the Sporting Shooters' Association, which dismisses any talk of Port Arthur conspiracies, has embraced the line pushed by MacGregor, Scurr and Beattie.

In its website, it says the evidence collected by the three categorically proves that Bryant:

> was recruited by others into playing a role in the operation which involved him dropping off his car at Seascape, him staying there, him manning the phone while others fired shots from the windows, and saying silly things on the phone which would be consistent with his role. This is all he did and it is quite clear he was totally unaware he was going to be the bunny for it all.

In the 1998 Queensland state election, the pro-gun lobby was to fall in behind the ultra-conservative political party One Nation, at that time led by Pauline Hanson. Hanson was roundly criticised in February 2001 for adding fuel to the conspiracy theories when she supported questions over why there had not been a full inquiry into the massacre to determine if more than one gunman was involved. In the wake of the furore, Hanson was forced to retreat and concede that even she believed Bryant acted alone.

Despite their marginalisation by the mainstream media, the conspiracy theorists remain active. As of early 2004, Andrew MacGregor was speaking at forums around Australia, most notably those hosted by the ultra-right-wing lobby group, the Australian League of Rights. In March of that year, he shared the stage at the Australian League of Rights' annual Inverell Forum (which proudly advertises itself as 'The Politically Incorrect One!') with One Nation Senator Len Harris.

Given its racist views, it is not surprising to find the Australian League of Rights is also a strong supporter of Olga Scully, a Launceston woman who has provoked outrage for her denial of the Holocaust and anti-Semitism. The league was right behind Scully in 2000 as she was successfully pursued by the Jewish community through the Human Rights and Equal Opportunity Commission for breaching the *Racial Discrimination Act*.

Be it through the online work of Vialls, or stump speeches at meetings of extreme right lobby groups, anti-Semitism and the conspiracy surrounding Port Arthur have become unlikely – and increasingly disturbing – bedfellows.

Wendy Scurr acknowledges some people have used Port Arthur as part of an anti-Semitic agenda, which she says she finds abhorrent and of which she wants no part. Wendy cut all ties with Scully, she says, after the release of the police video became caught up in Scully's anti-Semitic views.

Yet the connection between racist groups and the Port Arthur conspiracy movement is perhaps not surprising when it is considered that Bryant himself was anti-Semitic, or at least that was the impression he gave while talking to police negotiators.

According to the transcript of the conversation between negotiator Sergeant Terry McCarthy and Bryant while he was holed up in Seascape, Bryant described the owner of Seascape, Sally Martin, as 'a troublemaker, she's part Jewish, you know'.

McCarthy: You don't like Jews?

Bryant: Uh. I detest Jews. Do you like Jews?

Bryant then explains his hatred of Jews based on a visit to Miami, Florida, where he approached a Jewish couple who, after initially chatting with him, 'more or less dumped me'.

Bryant then asks McCarthy a second time: 'Do you like the people? Do you like Jews?' before he is distracted from the conversation by a noise.

I doubt it is simply a coincidence that Bryant's views on Jewish people match those of some of his greatest defenders. Unlike the majority of Port Arthur related coincidences for which the conspiracy lobby has a full and detailed explanation, the anti-Semitic thread is carefully avoided.

BEHIND THE LENS:
LEIGH WINBURN

Leigh Winburn was heading home from a long day cutting fire-wood when he spotted the first of the rescue helicopters settling upon the grassy expanse of the Hobart Domain. His sharp eye for the unusual came from more than 25 years' experience as a photog-rapher with Tasmania's largest daily newspaper, *The Mercury*.

Leigh sensed that the helicopters signalled trouble: perhaps a major car crash. He mused about which of his colleagues might be responding to the story, before returning to the more pleasant thought of a hot shower and a cold beer after a grimy day in the bush.

Before he could enjoy either, the newsroom had tracked him down via a phone call while he was unloading the wood at his brother-in-law's house. 'A colleague was yelling at me down the phone, saying there had been a shooting at Port Arthur and six people, seven people, have been shot and it was chaos.'

Leigh arrived in the newsroom in Hobart's Macquarie Street to find it virtually deserted. Nearly all of the skeleton staff that normally worked the Sunday shift had been despatched to Port Arthur in a scramble to get on top of the breaking story. Leigh's father, Barry, also a senior photographer with the newspaper, was among them.

Leigh remembers the unrelenting ring of the office telephones and there being nobody to answer them. Calls were flooding in from an anxious public who, having heard radio news bulletins about the shootings, were desperate to know more. The phones were also running hot with calls from interstate and, by mid-afternoon, international media outlets, trying to glean details of what was beginning to sound like a huge story.

Leigh decided the only way to handle the barrage was to disperse it. He found the phone numbers for the two other daily newspapers in Tasmania, *The Advocate* and *The Examiner*, both based in the north of the state, and redirected as many of the calls as he could. That way, 'the opposition' was left to handle time-consuming questions from 'things like the *Glasgow Daily*, or whatever, and we didn't have to deal with them'.

Against the backdrop of ringing telephones, the tension in the newsroom mounted with each radio bulletin that broadcast an increasing number of dead and injured at the site. *The Mercury*, as with every other Tasmanian media outlet, had never experienced a story of such magnitude. Indeed, one reporter recalls the then editor Ian McCausland shouting across the newsroom in his thick, Scottish brogue, 'We are at the centre of the fucking universe today!'

This was the type of chaotic event that would stretch a major metropolitan newspaper, yet it was unfolding at the feet of a small daily with limited staff. 'It was all happening on a Sunday, in a particularly low-staffed office, in the middle of nowhere. It was bizarre and very hard to know exactly where to go to next.'

Despite it being a weekend, *The Mercury* managed to muster nine reporters and four photographers for the story. As they laboured towards putting out a special morning edition, chartered planes packed with interstate media crews were beginning to arrive at the Hobart airport. By mid-afternoon, at least 80 journalists were already gathered for a long, chilly night on the police forward command station that had been set up at the Taranna Tasmanian Devil Park, about 6 km from the Port Arthur site itself and 5 km from the ongoing siege at the Seascape cottage.

By Monday morning, as Bryant was finally taken into custody, more than 150 journalists representing media outlets from across Australia and around the world had descended on Hobart to cover the story on the ground. Several dozen of these were camped outside the Royal Hobart Hospital, which was providing its own regular media briefings on the condition of the victims.

The news crews, however, were desperate to get footage from the site itself now that Bryant had been arrested and the siege had come to an end. The Tasmanian police, worried that journalists would decide to take matters into their own hands and start moving into the site themselves, decided the best way to protect the crime scene and contain the growing media pack was to organise a bus tour through parts of the site once the bodies had been removed and the area cleaned.

Leigh volunteered to join the tour as the designated photographer for *The Mercury*. 'The police, to their credit, were very proactive. They addressed everybody and said that this is such an enormous crime scene and we don't want media wandering all over the site: it is impossible for the coroner to do his job. We will take you down – delegated people in the media – and show you what has happened.'

Leigh was on board the bus as it set off from Taranna after a briefing from the then Superintendent, now Tasmanian Deputy Commissioner of Police, Jack Johnston. The media pack was split between the locals and what Leigh calls 'the gung-ho, trench-coat brigade': high-profile journalists who had flown in from the mainland and would fly out again once the breaking story began to cool.

There were differing sensitivities among the group. The local reporters, having already dealt with many in the Port Arthur and wider community in the immediate aftermath, had a personal sense of the scale of the loss. The trench-coats, according to Leigh, were by contrast pumped with adrenalin as the bus set off for its grim tour. 'There was almost a black humour when the bus tour began. People were joking about it and thinking that this was almost like a tourism event.' Leigh found the convivial atmosphere difficult to take and tried to block out the repartee by immersing himself in his thoughts.

The bus wound its way past the Fox and Hounds hotel, where those injured by Bryant's pot shots from Seascape had taken refuge. It continued on to the small Port Arthur town and the petrol station where the white Corolla driven by Glenn Pears and Zoe Hall sat abandoned, its window shattered and a large, burgundy bloodstain across the top of the sheepskin car seat cover. The media group clambered out to take notes and photographs as Superintendent Johnston explained the killing that had taken place there.

By the time the bus arrived at the toll booth and down to the bloodstained roadway where Nanette and Madeline Mikac were murdered, the media pack had fallen quiet. The black humour had evaporated and instead the group sat in stony silence as Superintendent Johnston explained how six-year-old Alannah Mikac had hidden behind a tree, was pursued and executed. The full scale of what had unfolded just 24 hours earlier was beginning to be understood.

'Some of the journalists by this stage were so traumatised, especially the women, that they didn't get off the bus. They sat at the back. By the end of it, it was a very long, very sobering trip home.'

Some people would later argue it was unwise for journalists to be exposed to the crime scene so soon after the murders. Many of those assigned to cover the aftermath would later struggle to keep working in the media. Other journalists involved have been unable to return to the site since.

For Leigh, the bus trip marked the start of what would be two long weeks of functioning on auto-pilot, as the demands of the newspaper took precedence over his personal reactions. There was little time for quiet talking or tears amid the relentless pursuit of the latest news angle which shifted from the immediate shock of the massacre to the overwhelming grief of a nation and, later, anger over the state's loose gun laws and disbelief at Bryant's complete lack of remorse.

There was also the constant conflict between the public and the media. While the community expected to turn to the newspapers and news bulletins for information about the massacre, it railed against what it saw as an intrusion into the lives of those in mourning.

'The best way I can put it is that when you're an ambulance officer or a police officer, you are there in a uniform and you are seen as being part of the cycle of it all. When you're in the media, you're just another person in a jacket and a pair of trousers. When people are so emotionally highly strung, you're the last person they want to see, so you either get their total grief, or their total anger,' Leigh says.

In the days immediately after the massacre, people on the Tasman Peninsula were more accommodating of journalists, as if talking about the events helped make sense of it all. As the days wore on, however, the community began to close in on itself, to grieve privately. Leigh recalls the 'nightmare' of driving to Port Arthur day after day for what is known in the industry as a 'death-knock': interviewing the family or friends of the deceased. It is a part of the job most journalists dislike intensely.

'Every time we went and did an interview, it was the same story. It was somebody who had lost their loved ones and you just couldn't get rid of it. It was like the world's worst recurring death-knock, on and on and on.'

The mainland trench-coaters didn't help. Hobart is a small city in a small state where people's lives cross regularly and memories are long. One of the frustrations for Leigh was watching the behaviour of some interstate journalists who, having no sense of connection to the Tasmanian community, ran roughshod over shocked locals in an incessant chase for interviews and photographs.

He recalls an incident at the state memorial service held three days after the shootings when, during the minute's silence, an inter-state photographer using a wide-angle lens began to take images of those crying: the camera often just centimetres from their faces.

'Now why on earth would you want to do that? It means nothing, it is not atmospheric; it's totally confronting…the way I see it is you will still get your picture. They will still be there in 60 seconds' time, so why hurt them? Their attitude reflects on all of us.

'It pissed me off and it pissed a lot of my mates off, because this is our community. Now the community may not see us like that, because we are just from the newspaper, but it means something to us.'

Dr Kay Chung, the former head of the Tasmanian Government media unit under Premier Tony Rundle, described another incident in her 1999 book *Going Public*, where an unnamed journalist claimed to be a relative of a Port Arthur victim so he could gain access to grieving relatives as they arrived at the Hobart airport. Fortunately, such tactics were rare.

Since the massacre, Leigh admits there have been times when he has challenged the demands of editorial management to pursue a death-knock. Sometimes he and the reporter have opted for what is called, in newsroom language, a 'grass-knock', where the journalist makes it to the front lawn, but decides not to go any further.

'We've sometimes knocked on the door, seen the look on the people's faces and walked away saying, "They weren't at home". If [management] gets upset about it, then so be it. We are at the pointy end of the spear and, at the end of the day, the paper still comes out. If you are going to shatter someone's life or hurt yourself emotionally, then it is not worth it.'

If there was a defining moment for Leigh among the frenetic days that followed the massacre, it came during the state memorial service held at St David's Cathedral on the morning of 1 May. The event was being broadcast to a grieving nation and in Hobart the sorrow was palpable as thousands filed into the church and spilled out onto the surrounding streets to listen to the service.

Leigh was stationed outside the cathedral entrance and remembers being almost overcome by the emotionally charged atmosphere just before the service started at 11 a.m.

'I looked down Murray Street and the whole street – everybody – had come out of their shops to pay their respects. All of the people that you normally see in the city and are just part of your community, they had all left their businesses and were standing there. It was unbelievable and it still upsets me to think about it now.'

After the service ended, the cathedral doors swung open and Leigh positioned himself with a long lens to capture images of those leaving. He remembers thinking it odd that there didn't appear to be a mob of other photographers around him, with most choosing to remain at a side entrance. At that moment, a weeping Dr Bryan Walpole appeared – Leigh knew him from the Royal Hobart Hospital – and was embraced by Prime Minister John Howard. Leigh raised his camera and captured their embrace. It was to be an image that appeared across Australia and gave momentum to the gun control campaign.

Seconds later, a grief-stricken Walter Mikac emerged, supported on either side by his brother and a best friend as they moved through the crowd. Leigh described it as 'an incredible sight', as if the three men were moving towards him in slow motion.

'All I can remember is that I couldn't see clearly. I was fighting back tears and I was shaking. I just held the camera up and thought, well, I was kind of focused, so I took the picture. Walter walked straight past me, just like a ghost, and went into [Hadleys] hotel. I took a couple more pictures and went back to work.'

Leigh returned to the darkroom and processed his shots. The Mikac image was 'pin sharp': a distraught Walter clutching the spray of irises and Alannah's diary, with the girls' hairbands wrapped tightly around each wrist. Leigh decided the image was too personal and left it out of the selection he presented to his editor in the news conference.

'In the end, the editor wanted to see the contact sheets and I had to 'fess up [that I had deliberately left it out], so there was a bit of friction there. He asked me why he hadn't seen that one and I said, "I can't deal with this. It's almost too much." After we printed it though, there was no other photograph. Nobody else took it. Nobody else had that frame.'

Like the photograph of John Howard and Bryan Walpole, the Mikac image was reproduced in newspapers around Australia and graphically captured the senselessness of Bryant's actions; the loss of so many lives and the unbridled sadness for those left behind.

Leigh interrupts our interview in a small room of his home on

Hobart's eastern shore to retrieve something. Stepping between the ironing board and a stack of folded laundry, he returns with a cardboard box and lifts the lid to reveal a pile of A5-sized photographs; among them is the Mikac print. He holds up the image which, like for so many people, is so familiar to me. Even after all these years it still holds immense power. Many photographers might be tempted to frame it on a wall for 'bragging' rights, but for Leigh, this is the first time he has looked at the image in years. It is not something he would ever consider as a showpiece.

Not everyone agreed with the decision to publish the photograph. Leigh received a string of abusive phone calls from people who believed it was an invasion of privacy. Almost two years after the massacre, however, Leigh was to receive another phone call. The soft voice on the end of the line explained it was Walter Mikac. He was writing his book about Nanette and the children and wondered if he could use Leigh's image. Leigh made arrangements to visit Walter while he was in Tasmania and the photograph was, indeed, included in Walter's book, *To Have and to Hold*.

Unlike in the emergency services, there are still few formal debriefing structures in place for journalists and even fewer were available at the time of the Port Arthur massacre. In what is a reminder of the male-dominated culture of newsrooms, journalists are still expected to be hard-nosed and thick-skinned. To admit an emotional reaction to a story risks being considered soft, or 'too close' to the event and possibly reassigned away from covering 'hard' news. Not surprisingly, most debriefing by journalists is done over a few drinks after work, rather than through formal counselling.

Reporters also receive no formal training on how to deal with confronting or violent situations and yet they are expected to be among the first on a scene, be it a riot, a car accident, or the bloody aftermath of a murder.

As Leigh explained, the Royal Hobart Hospital had its Code Brown plan already in place to deal with a major disaster, whereas the media response to Port Arthur came down to a pot-luck draw of who happened to be rostered on that particular day. It remains the same in most newsrooms today.

'The police and the ambos, they construct situations so they can train people. We don't do any of that. I mean, at the end of the day, every single day, we just pick up the phone and respond to the facts.'

Oddly, there is a certain bravado among journalists about who is 'lucky' enough to cover a major disaster or horrific event. Leigh calls it the war-correspondent syndrome, where reporters are lauded for putting themselves in confronting situations.

'It is really bizarre, because people would say to me, "Oh to do that gig [Port Arthur], aren't you lucky?" And I say, "Mate, you don't know what it's like to do a news story as big as that". It was a worst-case scenario and there's probably no amount of training to prepare you for it, but when you have no training at all, well...'

Leigh recalls that the *Mercury*'s managing director Rex Gardner immediately made counselling available to staff who requested it, but the counsellors had to be found out of a phone book rather than through any structured, internal system. All the same, he considers himself 'stupid' for not taking up the offer of help in the immediate aftermath of the shootings.

Instead, his personal reaction to what he had seen and experienced remained suppressed. 'I didn't think it was anybody's problem. I made the big mistake like most blokes, where I thought it was my problem and I'll deal with it. I didn't think it was fair [to my family] to come home and say that I had seen roads covered in blood and bullet shells and stuff.'

Rather than discuss his thoughts with his wife, Lou, Leigh 'bottled it up' and instead threw himself into more work. He was one of a handful of News Limited photographers chosen to cover the Olympic Games in Atlanta in 1996, which provided a mental distraction, but the physical workload only added to his underlying exhaustion.

By early 1997, Lou was finding it increasingly difficult to deal with Leigh's withdrawal and moodiness and the tension between them began to mount. 'In the end I knew I was heading for a marriage breakdown. Lou couldn't deal with it. I was just moody and difficult and sick of people wanting more and more. It was basically the classic symptoms of what you would expect to happen.'

There were also the nightmares. In particular Leigh found it hard to shake the memory of one victim who, after having held a press conference, began to scream and shout and claw at her clothes in an effort to show the assembled reporters her bullet wound. 'She had gone completely crazy and it was awful, really awful.'

It was not until after the first anniversary of the massacre, however, that Leigh finally 'cracked' and realised he was teetering on the edge of a nervous breakdown.

The night before the anniversary, Leigh travelled with a senior reporter, Mike Bingham, down to the Fox and Hounds hotel, where, over drinks in the front bar, the pair again came under a volley of abuse for 'intruding'. They tried to explain they had been invited to cover the first anniversary memorial service and were 'just doing their job'.

After a sleepless night, Leigh rose at dawn to photograph the memorial wooden cross by the water's edge and, later, joined the memorial service in the Port Arthur convict church. 'I was standing maybe two metres from Walter Mikac and his family. The TV guys had a great advantage, because their cameras don't make any sound, so they could film it live and just stand there with their hands discreetly in front of them.

'Those days, every time I picked up the camera and fired one frame, it was like a rifle shot; just, bang! Each time I took a photo, each time I picked up the camera, sets of eyes would look up at me and the looks from those eyes were just unbelievable.'

After returning to work the next day, he realised he was not coping; he felt irritable and edgy. Leigh asked if he could have a day off, just to settle the system. A senior colleague responded, 'What's your problem? You volunteered. Get over it.'

It was a flippant comment, but it touched a raw nerve. Leigh felt devalued, like he was an inanimate object rather than an individual who might react to an emotionally charged situation. 'It is probably the one thing in 25 years that upset me more than anything else and it triggered, I think, a period where I was very difficult to deal with.'

It would be another three to four months before he finally made the walk downstairs from the *Mercury* editorial department to the managing director's office and asked for an appointment to speak with a counsellor. It was a decision he now believes saved his marriage.

Today Leigh is the pictorial editor for *The Mercury*, but still takes to the road as a photographer for the newspaper: he is a man who appears more comfortable in jeans and a thermal jacket than a coat and tie. His promotion in 2002 meant he is now in a position to make changes and improve work practices for his colleagues. The Port Arthur experience, he hopes, has left him more sensitive to the pressures on staff, especially juniors.

'I am very, very aware of looking after my colleagues. We still have, from time to time, management issues where they want you to do certain things that I think are risky and I don't mind saying so. I don't always win the argument, but I agree to disagree.'

Leigh believes the Australian media, buffered by a sense of living in a secure country, can easily drift back into a comfort zone and forget the lessons of an event such as Port Arthur, both in how to deal with a shocked and grieving public and how to support reporters exposed to the coalface. He was just one of dozens of journalists to cover the Port Arthur story either through words or pictures, and his emotional struggle mirrors that of many of his professional colleagues. Former ABC television reporter Celina Edmonds, who went on to be a newsreader with Channel Ten, wrote of her experience in the monthly newsletter produced by the Port Arthur Incident Recovery Centre. 'The Port Arthur tragedy has dominated my life for the past seven months. I have lived and breathed it every day,' she wrote in December 1996.

Celina also wrote of the difficulty of the extended death-knock in contacting the family and friends of victims to ask for photographs of their loved ones. She told of the ongoing stress in covering Bryant's trial and the emotion of his sentencing. Her words reflect the conflict between remaining professional and yet, as a fellow human being, sympathising with those immediately affected. Like so many others, she was both saddened and inspired by the strength of those she had come to know as the story unfolded over the ensuing months:

> After the first day of Martin Bryant's sentencing hearing, I went home and sobbed on the couch. The details that had come out that day were extraordinarily sad. But I felt different at the end of the second day, after the victim impact statements had been read out. All of those people whose lives had been so badly affected were still there…they had not been beaten.

Ten years on, there is still no mandatory training for journalists on how to cope with covering a major trauma, although seeking counselling after the event carries less of a stigma. *The Mercury*, for example, has since contracted a counsellor to support its staff.

Leigh believes failing to include grief and trauma in media training is a major flaw, especially as Australia is immersed in the global threat of terrorism. 'We see news companies looking at the small stuff through various management courses, but I have never heard anyone say that we may well have a terrorist attack in Australia in the next five years and we should get journalists and photographers together who have experience in mass fatality incidents and spend two days with the cadets, telling them what they might experience and what they can expect.'

Today, there is perhaps less likelihood of another Port Arthur style massacre in Australia, due to tighter gun control, but many believe there is an increased risk of a major terrorist incident with the potential for an enormous loss of life. It is a chilling thought and one which inspires Leigh, at the end of our interview, to take the matter further and speak to senior management about staff training.

'This raises an issue for me in that I haven't actually done anything about it. I want to do something about it, because people will be asked to cover an event like that in their normal course of duty. Unfortunately, it's very real.'

Postscript

In September 2005, News Limited launched a conflict and trauma management course for photographers and reporters, News and Conflict, which was the first of its kind for the Australian newspaper industry. According to News Limited, the course has an emphasis on managing personal safety in situations of conflict and aggression, but also offers 'ways to build resilience for handling distressing jobs where there has been loss of life'.

The first two courses, held in Melbourne and Sydney, were booked out.

—— 7 ——

A COUNTRY PRACTICE:
PAM FENERTY

Within a week of moving to the Tasman Peninsula to run the sole medical practice, Dr Pam Ireland was beginning to think she had made a mistake. It was 1992 and she and her medico husband, Steve, had relocated from Hobart to Nubeena, about 15 km west of Port Arthur. On the surface it appeared an idyllic existence, with Nubeena in the heart of a stable, intimate community that enjoyed a laid-back lifestyle built around farming, fishing and the growing convict tourism trade. The Irelands believed the decision to take over the combined medical practice and pharmacy would give them a chance to share a reasonable workload and still have time for their young son, James.

It didn't take long, however, for the demands of serving a close-knit, ageing population to come to the fore. While they loved their job, it came at a price. Between them, the Irelands were either working or on-call virtually 24 hours a day, seven days a week. They handled six to eight patients per hour, plus ran a small pharmacy service. If any of the 2000 people on the peninsula needed to see a doctor, the Irelands were *it* and they were expected to 'be there'. It was exhausting work. In an attempt to ease the burden, Pam began to lobby the state government and various medical bodies for relief doctors to serve the peninsula and, as a result, found herself appointed to the Rural Doctors Association. The association has since gone on to propel the drastic rural doctor shortage into the national spotlight, but, in the early 1990s, it was all meetings and more meetings, with few changes on the ground.

Some desperately needed help arrived in August 1994 in the shape of the Mikac family. In the previous summer, Walter and Nanette Mikac had visited Nanette's parents, Keith and Grace, at nearby White Beach. During their holiday, Grace suggested Walter, a Melbourne pharmacist, consider opening a stand-alone pharmacy in Nubeena. It would be a first for the area and Walter was seduced by the idea of running his own business. For Nanette, a registered nurse, and their two young girls, it would mean being closer to parents and grandparents.

Walter decided to discuss the idea with the Irelands the very next day. He writes of his first meeting with Pam Ireland in his book, *To Have and to Hold*:

> Meeting Pam, I felt somewhat intimidated by her presence. A solidly built lady with a pleasant face and straight, dark-brown hair, she gave the impression of not interacting with people well. Her manner, without being unpleasant, was blunt and matter of fact.

Despite being a little taken aback by Pam's no-nonsense style, Walter would take up the challenge of running the pharmacy and the two couples would go on to become close friends, linked by their professions and similar ages. Within just two short years, however, both their worlds would be ripped apart by Martin Bryant's actions: the consequences of which pushed Pam to the brink and which continue to resound through her life.

It was shortly after 12.30 p.m. on Sunday 28 April 1996, when Pam Ireland dropped by to visit Nanette Mikac. Nanette had been going through a low patch that weekend, about exactly what Pam now can't recall, but Pam thought an impromptu visit might help lighten her mood. She arrived to find the Mikac house at Nubeena empty. Walter was playing in a local golf tournament and Nanette and the girls, unbeknown to Pam, had already set off for their picnic at the Port Arthur Historic Site. Oh well, thought Pam, she would just catch up with them later. In a small, quiet community like Nubeena, there was always later. By about 1.30 p.m., Pam had settled on the couch with *The Weekend Australian*. Her memory of the next few hours is a mixture of absolute clarity and moments of complete blankness. She recalls what she was wearing that day — black pants and black jumper — yet she can't remember loading her doctor's bag into her white Nissan Patrol, or if she or Steve drove the vehicle once they left the property in response to the phone call. It was from Julie Skipper, a duty nurse at the Tasman Aged Care Facility in Nubeena, saying there had been a shooting at Port Arthur: there was a gunman, there were four dead and more injured and could she come at once?

Pam immediately drove to get Steve, who was working in one of the paddocks on their 130 ha farm, praying under her breath that she would find him close to the house, rather than having to make the half-hour climb to the 'top paddocks'. Fortunately, Steve was sitting on his tractor a mere 50 m from their house. The pair drove quickly towards the Port Arthur site, passing the tranquil Nubeena Bay where their twelve-year-old son, James, was sailing with friends. Steve turned to Pam and said, 'We'll be back in an hour to pick up James'. In fact it was to be almost midnight before they were to leave the drama that lay ahead.

They arrived at the Broad Arrow Café to find the Nubeena volunteer ambulance officers, Gary Alexander and Kaye Fox, already at the scene. Some of the injured had been removed or run from the café, while others needing medical attention had received preliminary treatment by Port Arthur staff and off-duty doctors and nurses who happened to be visiting the site that day.

'Somebody had done a pretty good job of the triage — sorting out the injuries — and they had done it mighty quick. Whoever it was, the doctors and nurses and first-aid people, they had done a bloody good job in those first fifteen or twenty minutes,' Pam recalls.

Pam cannot remember exactly how her first twenty minutes on the scene unfolded, but she knows her medical training was reduced to the most basic of responses. There was no time for taking pulses or applying blood pressure cuffs. Instead it was a matter of 'shoving in drips' where the badly injured needed them, administering morphine to those in extreme pain and sorting out a priority list for the rescue helicopter.

Among those Pam later despatched was the Broad Arrow kitchen manager, Brigid Cook. 'I remember putting Brigid in the helicopter and the driver saying that the door could fly open. He said he could take a sitting one, if she can hold the door shut. We said, well this one's just got a leg injury. You know, *just* a leg injury, I mean how she is alive, I don't know.

'Brigid probably doesn't remember me, but I remember patting her and saying, "You'll be okay Brigid…just hold onto that door". I looked her straight in the eye and said, "You just hold that door shut" and off she went.'

Six years later, after the Bali bombings in October 2002, Pam found herself watching the television reports and thinking about how the dead and injured would be triaged; how many hospital beds would have been available and the prioritising of patients. It was an instinct created by the Port Arthur experience.

Particular moments within the chaos after the shootings stand out to Pam, such as her brief conversation with a former Port Arthur Authority Board member, Michael Langley, who has since died of cancer. Pam remembers seeing him at the site, his face blank, 'as if he wasn't there'.

'I said something stupid to him like, "There'll be some meetings out of this, Michael". I mean, you say some stupid things…and he just said to me, "This is like war, Pam. The last time I saw anything like this was in Vietnam."'

What Pam considers remarkable now is that at no time while treating the wounded did she worry where the gunman might be, or if there was more than one gunman at large. The medical crews simply got on with the job. Only after the last of the injured had been moved off site did Pam's thoughts turn to a gunman being possibly on the loose.

The uncertainty made her feel particularly stressed about Steve joining a medical crew that set off to see if there were any dead and wounded at other locations. As Steve drove out of the site, Pam had an overwhelming feeling of dread that she would never see him again.

'All I remember is them taking off in two vehicles for a search, which was very brave. I wanted to go, but not out of bravery. Bugger the bravery; it's the last thing that's in your friggin' mind at times like that. That is one of my pet hates, bravery awards...they gave one to each of the site people who were there that day, but most people when they heard the gunshots did what any normal person would do: you run and hide. You don't jump in front of a gun so you can get a bravery award.'

As Pam would learn later, Steve and the medical crew did, at one point, think they had come face to face with the gunman when, on the road to the Fox and Hounds, a car came speeding towards them. They veered into a ditch and ducked for cover, before realising it was a fleeing tourist.

While Pam waited anxiously for Steve's return, which would not come until several hours later, she joined those tending to the shocked and grieving relatives. If there had been any screaming, there was none now. Most of those left behind stood in silent, mind-numbing disbelief.

'I was just reacting, or performing, or trying to help, just like everybody else. We were just reacting to what was going on. It was as if we were no longer in the world. We had been cast onto the flipside of the universe. There's a dark side and we were in that other space: that's how it felt.'

Walter Mikac was among those desperately searching for his family. He approached Pam to ask if she had seen Nanette and the girls. He had found their car by the waterfront and, as it approached dusk, his panic was rising. Pam knew they were not among the bodies in the Broad Arrow Café, but recalled Kaye Fox mentioning something about children being among the bodies near the toll booth. It gave her a bad feeling. She asked a site guide, Paul Cooper, to take Walter into the safety of 'Clougha', one of the historic homes used by the Port Arthur management, while she and Kaye Fox walked up Jetty Road towards the bodies.

'There were police there and the bodies were covered with blue tarpaulins. I asked the police if they knew who they were and they said, "Not exactly", or "No, we don't". I said who I was and that "I think I might know who they are". And they were Nanette and the girls.'

Upon seeing the bodies, Pam felt completely numb; consumed by the single thought that she had to tell Walter. It was all she could focus on. She returned to 'Clougha' where Walter sat awaiting any news of his family. Pam took him into a separate room, knelt at his feet, clasped his hands firmly in hers and stared straight into his eyes to tell him what she knew.

'He just made the most horrible sound I have ever heard. I have since made that same sound myself, so I know that sound.'

Not long after breaking the dreadful news, Pam heard more gunshots outside 'Clougha'. Those huddled inside were told to plunge the building into darkness as fears mounted that the gunman had returned. Pam remembers pulling the plug on the photocopier machine to kill its green, glowing light that appeared to illuminate the entire room. She also glanced around the room looking for a window they could smash to escape if the shots moved any closer. 'Everyone was in a state of heightened alert and we only found out much later that it was somebody shooting rabbits.'

It was an atmosphere of terror that was broken only by the arrival of police who, finally, swarmed through the building and moved the group up to the nearby Port Arthur youth hostel. Pam was stunned to find the state coroner Ian Matterson was already at the hostel, together with a team of social workers who were starting to debrief the traumatised families and Port Arthur staff.

'I remember thinking, what? This isn't even over, but we're doing debriefing. I felt really strongly about going in there and ordering them out, but it was beyond me. I kept wondering why [the coroner] didn't step in and stop what's going on in there, because it's all wrong. These people needed a cup of tea and an arm around them.'

As the hours ticked by, Steve Ireland returned safely and Keith Moulton, Nanette's father, arrived at the youth hostel from White Beach. The Irelands, Keith and Walter Mikac all sat and comforted each other, unsure of exactly what to do next.

'There was another feeling and that was nobody wanted to go home. It was very powerful that night. Nobody wanted to go home. It was sort of like we were in a new space in the world and it wasn't anything like the world you knew. You felt you were in this new world and you didn't really want to go back to the old one. I know it sounds fanciful and airy, but I didn't want to go back and now, eight years on, I know why.'

In the years since the massacre, Pam, in her own words, has watched her life 'flip upside down completely'. Every cornerstone of her existence – her son, her marriage, her career – has been destroyed and, if she stops to consider it, the dismantling can all be related back to the events of 28 April 1996.

It began in the week immediately after the shootings, when relief doctors were sent down to run the general practice while the Irelands took a much-needed break. The week of rest, however, was filled up with visits, phone calls, meetings and the peninsula recovery program that had been launched by the state government.

'They were calling it a "recovery program" within the first hour, I think before people were even buried. I dispute the word "recovery" at such an early stage, but that's what they were calling it.'

If they weren't involved in meetings, the Irelands were talking with bereaved families, while also coming to terms with their own grief, especially over the loss of Nanette Mikac and the girls.

'I had some really weird experiences in those first few months. I used to smell Nanette's perfume. James and I would go for walks and [I would] smell her perfume, I don't know what it was, but it was very distinctive. I remember, oh maybe six weeks after, we went for a walk and I got a whiff of her perfume and I would say, "Nanette, go away. Please leave us alone". We were probably mad, really mad.'

When the Irelands formally returned to work a week after the massacre, the avalanche began: dozens of traumatised people from across the peninsula came to seek help. 'Every single day in those first few months – and I don't know how many months it was, four or five – we were seeing eight to ten severely traumatised people every day.'

Pam didn't recognise it at the time, but she was suffering her own post-traumatic stress disorder as a result of the massacre and yet was receiving no personal counselling or structured support for the practice. She and Steve instead naively thought that by having experienced the event, they would be better placed to understand the feelings of others.

'I mean, how stupid is that? It is almost a conflict of interest…I was in a state of severe, utter psychological shock and then every day I would go to the surgery and hear people run through their experiences. It was like getting Chinese water torture every day.'

In an effort to ease the load, doctors were provided from around the state to assist with the Tasman Peninsula practice, but it was 'patchwork' support rather than consistent. Almost 28 doctors passed through the practice in the first few years after the shootings. They would stay a weekend, or a couple of days. There was no sense of continuity. The assembly line of doctors proved unsettling to traumatised patients who, desperate for a sense of comfort and security, would still make an appointment to see the Irelands to debrief about the doctor they had seen. As patient numbers swelled to 180 people a week, the pressure on the practice began to build to breaking point: these were not ordinary patient demands.

In desperation, Pam decided to contact doctors in the Scottish community of Dunblane, who were dealing with the fallout from a massacre of schoolchildren that happened just weeks before the Port Arthur shooting. Pam wanted to know how they had coped.

'I ended up ringing Dunblane to find out what the hell they'd done for the practice there and, you know, it was entirely different.

They had been given their own psychologist and they put in a doctor to look after the practice and they basically gave them whatever they needed. We didn't get any of that coordinated care. I am not saying for us, I am saying for the practice. I swear to the day I die that we didn't get it. It was very badly managed. I was made to feel that I should be grateful for any help received.'

In the middle of helping to manage the grief of the wider community, Pam faced her own personal trauma. Her only child, James, who was then thirteen, was badly burnt on the face and chest just four months after the massacre, after playing with petrol on a farm. Pam was to suffer a similar accident using petrol on a fire the following January. The burns were to be challenging enough, but by the October after the shootings, her personal life had also begun to seriously unravel. Steve announced that he was involved with one of the secretaries of their medical practice and wanted a separation. The next few months before Steve finally moved out were a time of tension, anger and despair, during which Pam finally hit rock bottom and attempted suicide by drug overdose.

'I remember waking up and apparently a series of people had been coming and going and sat with me as I snored it all off. The very next day I went to work at the practice…It was crazy stuff. I mean, I should have been hospitalised and getting professional treatment. I wasn't actually fit to work.'

Two days before Christmas 1996, Steve moved out and the Ireland's eighteen-year marriage had come to an end. It was impossible for Pam to continue the practice alone. She remembers 'throwing the pager against the wall' and saying: 'I can't do it. I'm not doing it anymore.'

The state and federal governments paid for locums to temporarily take over the running of the practice for six months while Pam decided what to do next. Part of that recovery time would be spent recuperating from the burns on her hands and face from the farm accident in January. She also used the time to start counselling with Hobart psychiatrist Dr Ian Sale, whom she still describes as 'a rock: my professional doctor rock'.

By mid-1997, the funding for the locums had dried up and

Pam was under pressure to decide whether she would keep the practice or give it up permanently. She still isn't sure why, other than 'madness', but she decided to return and operate the practice part-time. Within a year, the effort of running the practice, handling a marriage breakdown and raising a teenage child had taken its toll. Pam suffered a second collapse in May 1998 and, she says, 'spent six months on the couch'.

'I just had this drive that someone had to do it…I really shouldn't have gone back to medicine, looking back on it, but I had worked in some capacity ever since I was fourteen, you know. It was all I knew.'

After Pam's second breakdown, the Tasman practice was passed into government hands and Pam stopped working for eighteen months. By November 1999, she was able to tackle some part-time work on the Tasman and at various medical centres on Hobart's eastern shore, but her medical career was virtually over.

The word that Pam uses to best describe her feelings in the years immediately after Port Arthur is 'betrayal'. It is a strong choice, but Pam Fenerty – she has since returned to her maiden name – is still refreshingly blunt. She believes the practice was hung out to dry by the state and medical authorities, including her union, the Australian Medical Association. There was inadequate support to cope with the patient load, many of whom were suffering extreme emotional stress or struggling through complex workers compensation claims.

Instead, Pam and Steve were left to feel constantly guilty about not being able to cope with the demands of the community. If Pam wound back her hours, she felt she was letting the community – *her* community – down. She lived and worked among these people and was a highly visible member of a peninsula that relied heavily on its only doctor.

Pam believes she was abandoned. The mounting pressure, she says, ultimately split her marriage.

'I reckon we were doomed. We were doomed as a family unit. We were doomed as a practice. We were doomed in every sense of the word. Could someone have done something? You know what?

I think we should have been given tickets out of there.'

It may sound strange to want to leave a community she loved, but Pam believes she was thrown into an impossible position. It was an overwhelming sense of responsibility that she and Steve tried to manage, but which eventually consumed them both.

'[What] I would categorically say to anyone in a small community who is involved in a catastrophic event such as that is that you attend it, you do the best you can — which I think every single person did that day, they went to their limits and way beyond — you console the relatives who have lost people, you go and visit the injured in hospital, you go to the funerals and then you piss off. You get out of there; you leave. We should have left.'

When I first spoke to Pam about this book, she was reluctant to be involved. Like many others, she wanted to try to put Port Arthur behind her and was hesitant about the spotlight being placed on her story when there were so many stories from the day. After speaking on the phone about how I intended to tackle the book, she arrived unexpectedly on the doorstep of my office armed with two books.

She spoke rapidly, nervously even, but her stocky body effused strength and her dark eyes were warm with generosity. 'Well, if you *are* doing a book on Port Arthur, then you had better read these,' she said, passing over a copy of Mike Bingham's book, *Suddenly One Sunday* and Walter Mikac's *To Have and to Hold*.

The Bingham book had a picture of James on the cover, among a group of young boys at a memorial service for the Port Arthur victims. The latter has a personal inscription from Walter which reads: 'To My Beloved Pamela Ireland, Know that you will always have my utmost respect and love. We have a bond that very few could ever appreciate. Lots of Love, Walter Mikac.'

Pam was embarrassed when I read it. It soon became clear that Pam is embarrassed by any personal attention related to her role in the aftermath of the massacre: she was nominated for Tasmanian of the Year in 1998, but had to be convinced to attend the award ceremony and almost ran out the door the minute it was over. Yet the Irelands kept coming up time and again when I talked to people about this book.

Having dropped off her two books and 'checked out' who I was in person, Pam left the office with a promise to at least think about being involved. I liked her upfront yet immediately engaging style. That was early August 2003 and I made a note to chase her up with a phone call.

A month later, I had still not heard from Pam, but had begun the first interviews for this book, beginning with Glenn Imber on 10 September 2003. Glenn, at the time of the massacre, was a volunteer ambulance officer on the Tasman Peninsula. Our interview was interrupted by a phone call from his mother, where the talk centred on buying flowers for a bereaved family. After hanging up the phone, Glenn said that James Ireland, the son of Steve and Pam, had suicided the day before. As Glenn went on to explain, it was his former wife who had left him for Steve Ireland in 1996. Now all the families were struggling to come to terms with the suicide of James who, on the day of his death, had just returned from working in the Northern Territory. I didn't really know Pam, but I felt immediate sympathy: what more could life throw at her?

It would be another eight months before Pam and I were to sit down and talk about her story. The telling was physically exhausting for Pam and would take a series of interviews in my office overlooking Salamanca Place in Hobart where, over coffee, we would spend 45 minutes, maybe an hour a time, as she unpacked each part of her life since the massacre. There wasn't the need for many questions as Pam, her eyes often gazing to another place, just let the story spill out of her.

Having lost her only child, she had decided there was nothing more to lose in offering up her story. James, she believed, was another victim of Martin Bryant, having experienced the break-up of his parents when he was twelve and their estranged relationship since.

'It was because of the enduringly bitter relationship between James's father and myself that we didn't pick up on what was happening with James, or we didn't pick it up quickly enough. The separation between James's father and myself came about from Port Arthur.'

What was 'happening' was that James had allegedly become involved with cannabis while working on an Aboriginal station in the Northern Territory. Pam was told after James's death that some of those working at the station were smoking the drug virtually continuously throughout the day. Pam was unaware of his drug use and suspected little when he returned home from Alice Springs looking 'absolutely radiant…like a Greek god. He almost radiated a light or something. His skin was beautiful, his teeth were beautiful. The way he moved. He was just so perfect.'

It was the morning of Tuesday, 9 September 2003 and Pam remembers a feeling of absolute 'bliss'. She was at her farm on the peninsula with her new partner, Andrew Chappell, whom she had met through a personal advertisement two years earlier, and her son was home from a month away: life didn't get much better than this.

What Pam came to later believe was that James was already suffering a cannabis-induced psychosis and was in a state of euphoria.

The pair spent the morning together at the farmhouse before arranging to have a roast dinner the following night. Pam was heading up to Hobart to spend the evening at Andrew's home. James decided to stay at the farm and help clean up the aftermath of a severe storm the night before. Pam's last sight of him was leaping a post-and-rail fence with one hand, cowboy-style.

'I rang James about 7 p.m. that night, because I was feeling a little guilty that I wasn't there, and he said he was in the tavern with some mates, having a few drinks. I could hear the noise in the background. He said, "Mum, do you know I worked so hard for you today, my hands are bleeding" and I was worried that his hands were alright.'

Later that night, as Pam was drifting off to sleep, her mobile phone beeped with a text message. Pam had no idea how to retrieve it, so it was Andrew who read out the message that had arrived at precisely 11.34 p.m.:

I love you Mum. I'm sorry to do this to you, but it's the easiest way out. I'm in the shed. I love you Mum. James.

Pam remembers making 'the most horrible noise', like that she had heard from Walter Mikac on that unforgettable Sunday.

'And I said to Andrew, "He's done it".'

Pam and Andrew drove immediately back to the peninsula, but James was already dead. As his body lay under the cover of the ambulance blanket, the first thing Pam looked at was his hands. 'There wasn't any blood. I now know he was psychotic and he was psychotic in my opinion because of the drugs.' James was nineteen.

Shortly after James's death, Pam went in search of answers. She and Andrew drove more than 3000 km from Nubeena to the Northern Territory and back, just so she could see where James had worked and what he had been exposed to.

She was determined to pursue those she believed were responsible for making the cannabis available, if only to try to save another life. Pam Fenerty is not one to give up easily, but she admits today that she is tired and overwhelmed by the enormity and complexity of the drug problem. 'I don't know if I have the energy for it anymore.'

Pam's days now are divided into three parts: medically assisted sleep, a few hours of 'normal' activities, such as simply getting out of the house, and what she calls 'James time'. That is from 3 a.m. to 5 a.m. when she lies awake, tormented by what happened to her son and how she couldn't save him.

'Part of me died when James died and part of me is still here, so I feel like I am living in two places. It doesn't make a lot of sense, but I know that part of me is with him.'

Andrew remains a solid force. She doesn't believe she would have mentally survived the loss of James had Andrew not been in her life. The pair still divide their time between his home in Hobart and the peninsula, where she has since sold the farm and bought another property at Eaglehawk Neck, overlooking the ocean.

She has only minimal contact with the world of medicine, but has developed another passion: the transcription of convict records at the Port Arthur site. It is Keith Moulton's former volunteer job and one he passed to her shortly before he left the peninsula in late 2003.

Keith and Pam remained close after the massacre. He was one of the first people Pam called after James's death and Keith conducted the funeral service.

In the months after the funeral, Keith explained to Pam how transcribing the records had helped him recover from the loss of Grace, Nanette and the girls. She decided to give it a go.

'It was really hard the first few times, even walking into the building, because you feel like you are a social leper when you have a suicide: it is such a socially isolating thing. I feel very ashamed that James has suicided and that I didn't save him, so when I first went to Port Arthur, I sort of fled in there and hid in my little corner. I didn't even look at people when they walked in.'

Pam has since come to consider the work a deep privilege, in that she may be the first person to transcribe records of lives long forgotten, but so worthy of their place in history.

'It was a gift that Keith gave to me, truly a gift. I have had the conservation manager say how good it is of me to do it, and I say, no, turn that around, it is really good of you to have me. I really believe that.'

Two months after the last of my three interviews with Pam in 2004, there was a major feature in the *Sunday Tasmanian* newspaper on a protest against a development plan for Crescent Bay, east of Nubeena. The pristine bay is a sweep of squeaky, white sand that is buffeted by a turbulent ocean from which the ragged edge of the peninsula emerges like jagged teeth. Neil Noye, the son of the former Tasman mayor by the same name, was planning a $9.5 million tourist resort for the area. Most of the locals were unhappy, fearing the project would ruin the unblemished beauty of the bay, which can only be reached by the public on foot.

The newly formed lobby group, Friends of Crescent Bay, was particularly angry, with a photo of a group spokesperson capturing their mood. She stood firm, arms crossed, resolute: the face of Pam Fenerty was unmistakeable.

'Seeing what was being planned for Crescent Bay brought me out of this big, black hole. It was a catharsis that helped me on the first rung of the ladder out of this enormous grief. The beauty of the place reintroduced me to life. It was like, "There is still a world out here, pull yourself together and do something".'

Pam is still up for a fight when an irreplaceable treasure is under threat.

As this book went to press, the bay remained untouched.

Moving the cross

Before the reflective pool and memorial garden were opened at the Port Arthur site on 28 April 2000, the 35 victims of the massacre were remembered with a tall cross of Huon pine, placed at the water's edge. It was a plain yet poignant symbol of loss that, unlike the official memorial, was not a compromise reached after lengthy and often highly charged debates. The cross was made by a local craftsman, Mick McMillan, and erected in the days after the shooting with little fuss. It simply stayed there – until a few days before the fifth anniversary of the massacre, in 2001.

Without explanation, the cross was suddenly relocated to the back left-hand corner of the memorial garden. Nobody seemed to know how it got there and those who did ask questions via angry letters to the newspaper, including Ron Neander, failed to prompt any answers.

Pam Fenerty is one of the few keepers of the secret behind the mystery.

Pam was elected chair of the memorial committee set up to decide how the massacre would be officially remembered. In an indication of the sensitivity around the issue, it took four years for the group to settle on the memorial garden and reflective pool, designed by Tasmanian Torquil Canning, and incorporating the shell of the Broad Arrow Café. There were 165 separate suggestions for the memorial that were lodged from around Australia, after a call for ideas.

As Pam explains, the committee – and those caught up in the massacre – were deeply divided over whether the Broad Arrow Café should have been preserved or bulldozed. 'The fighting that went on in the committee! I mean at various times, we could have easily had people rolling around on the floor, wrestling and tearing each other apart, and a lot of it was over whether the Broad Arrow should stay or go.'

Ironically, a similar argument had raged more than a century earlier when the Port Arthur convict prison was closed in 1877. At

that time, Tasmanians were at odds over whether the convict buildings should be razed or left as ruins. According to an information
board posted at the historic site today:

> People had strong opinions. Many Tasmanians called for total
> obliteration because they felt the convict past reflected badly
> on themselves and the British Empire as a whole.

It was decided, however, that the ruins stood as testament to a past
which, as unpalatable as it was, could not be ignored:

> Ruins are evidence that something, usually bad, has ended.
> The idea of keeping ruins managed to satisfy people with
> opposing opinions. It was partial obliteration that kept
> something intriguing for tourists.

The memorial committee for the 1996 massacre was less concerned
with keeping 'something intriguing for tourists', but still grappled
with the same issues on how to acknowledge the most recent
chapter in the site's dark history.

The committee decided to consult grief counselling specialists
on the merits of keeping the café, which resulted in the café being
kept as a roofless shell. It was important, the counsellors advised, to
retain a physical reminder of what had happened that day so those
who chose to could come and grieve. The café shell would also
provide a 'living' reminder of those who died there, just as the remnants of the convict buildings evoke a feeling unlike any to be
gleaned from reading a plaque or looking at a photograph. To stand
there, among the ruins, is to feel the past.

When the memorial garden, tranquil pool and café shell were
officially opened by former Governor-General Sir William Deane in
2000, the Huon pine cross remained by the waterside, but seemed
disconnected from the commemorative area. To Pam and others, the
area felt disjointed, as if the memorial was now split in two.

'When you have a memorial site, you don't have bits of it
draped around everywhere, do you? You have a site. A few of us

always felt very strongly that it should be all contained within the one site and make a clean fist of it.'

The location of the cross was never officially part of the memorial committee discussions and, when it was raised, it only served to heighten tensions. Pam knew there was no chance of reaching a resolution on the cross without more months of meetings and public consultation.

A group of six, including Pam and several members of the memorial committee, made an executive decision to move it themselves. It was agreed the group, which included four senior citizens, would meet in the early hours of Easter Monday on 16 April 2001, before the usual Port Arthur ground staff began to arrive for work. The clandestine group picked out the new location for the cross in the memorial garden and set about organising spades, gravel and a private contractor who could supply a forklift.

The scene was set, but then things began to go awry. The day the cross was to be moved, Pam was ill in hospital. The remaining five committee members decided to press ahead and agreed to meet at the site at 4.30 a.m. One arrived with a ute-load of gravel, three more arrived with shovels, while the fifth slept in and missed the whole event. The contractor who was to operate the forklift also overslept and had to be woken from his bed by a phone call to his mother. A mild panic was starting to set in as the first rays of light began to filter through the clouds and the cross was still nowhere close to being moved. After finally regrouping at the site, the four quickly set about digging a deep hole around the cross, which had been set into a brick pallet that was then buried. After some frantic shovelling, the contractor moved in, slid the pallet onto the forklift and carried the fully upright sculpture to its new resting place.

'They picked it up, scratched around on the ground where it was to go, put it down, poured the ute-load of gravel onto it and got the hell out of there before anybody got to work,' Pam explains.

The ongoing sensitivity about the site for the cross deters Pam, even now, from revealing the names of those involved in its relocation. The site management, however, believes the new location is better for everyone. It has protected staff – many of whom lost colleagues in the shooting – from having to constantly explain 'what happened' when they walked tour groups past the solitary cross at the waterfront. People can stand under the cross beams, sit by the reflective pool, or wander through the shell of the Broad Arrow and get an overpowering sense of it themselves.

8

THE MAYOR OF TASMANIA: NEIL NOYE

The address on the condolence card from Wickenham, United Kingdom, is optimistic in its brevity: The Mayor, Tasmania, Australia. The population of Tasmania has grown considerably since the British established a settlement in 1803, but the letter still found its way, eventually, to its intended recipient in Neil Noye, the then mayor of the Tasman Council. As news of the Port Arthur massacre began to filter out, Neil found himself elevated from the mayor of a community of 2000, to the civic face of an entire state. 'I remember taking calls from the BBC in London wanting to talk to "the Mayor of Tasmania",' he tells me with a smile.

Soon after the airwaves broadcast Neil's gentle voice telling of the many lives lost at Port Arthur that day, calls and cards began to pour into the council offices from around the world.

Perhaps the Wickenham writer was among those listening.

The Noyes have farmed the Tasman Peninsula for six generations; long enough to have a road or two named in their honour. By the time of the massacre, Neil, who had celebrated his sixty-fourth birthday a month earlier, had served on the Tasman Council for 28 years. He was to be mayor for fifteen years. The Tasman Peninsula was an area that thrived on stability. It was this deep familiarity with the peninsula that was to prove both a blessing and a curse for Neil as he found himself catapulted from worrying about 'rates, roads and rubbish', to helping rebuild a community that had had its heart ripped out.

Neil was repairing fencing in one of his paddocks with his son when the first ambulance shot past his Nubeena property, followed shortly by another. Like others, he thought there had been a nasty car accident in the area, which was not uncommon on the sharp bends of the peninsula. Neil ambled down to his old farmhouse to call the local nursing home which, he thought, might have news of the accident.

They told him there was a gunman running amok at Port Arthur, but had few other details. A call to a friend closer to the historic site confirmed the unthinkable: yes, there was a gunman and he was still on the loose.

Even after being told the news, Neil found it hard to believe such violence was unfolding on the peninsula. This was a district of rolling hills and plump, sleepy-eyed cattle, where the only gunshots to be heard were those of the occasional spotlighter chasing possum or rabbit. Neil's first response was to call the council general manager, Greg Burgess, to discuss what they should do in the face of such an unbelievable event. The pair decided to open the council chambers in Nubeena so that they could make the phone and fax lines available if needed. It was not long before the police were on the line, asking for building plans of the Seascape cottage so they could map the layout of the property where, by this stage, Martin Bryant was continuing his rampage.

There were no such plans in the council chambers, but Neil knew the house well; Sally and David Martin were long-time friends. He had visited them at Seascape just two nights earlier. 'I knew that house inside and out, so I could give them all the information they needed over the phone.'

Neil wasn't to know it then, but his two friends were Bryant's first victims and among seven people who died that day whom Neil knew personally. He would later spend hours crying with the families of the Martins, the Mikacs, and the parents of Elizabeth Howard and Nicole Burgess; supporting them in their grief, but also sharing in it. It was a pattern he was to continue for the next two years as he opened his home to anyone needing a quiet chat or a cry. They did come and they talked – often for hours – and the tears were many.

By late on the Sunday night of the shootings, news about the massacre had spread widely and Neil was being inundated with requests for media interviews. He gave his first in the council chambers at about 12.30 a.m., after a Melbourne television crew bluffed their way through the roadblocks by falsely claiming that 'they had an appointment with Neil Noye'. He finally made it home to bed by about 1.30 a.m., but his respite was brief. An hour later, the phone was ringing again, this time from the police in search of a bulldozer. The phone line to Seascape had been lost after the batteries on the cordless phone being used by Bryant had gone dead. In desperation, the police considered using the protection of a bulldozer blade to carry in another telephone line. Again, Neil didn't actually have a bulldozer, but he knew a list of locals who did. Within the hour, a huge bulldozer was propped outside Seascape, but the telephone plan, which at the very least was ambitious, was abandoned after the police decided Bryant would shoot at anyone trying to drive a vehicle onto the property.

By 8 a.m. the following morning, Neil was back at the council chambers to meet with stunned colleagues to try to plan how they could cope with the aftermath of such a large-scale tragedy. The Tasman Council had a permanent staff of just five and faced a daunting task. There was the pall of grief – which for some would later turn to vocal bitterness and anger – which hung over the community. There was also the very real threat of economic ruin for the peninsula, which depended heavily on the Port Arthur site – overnight, it had gone from the state's leading tourist attraction to a place nobody wanted to visit. Added to the mix were the growing demands from the media which, for the first ten days after the shooting, Neil and the rest of the council handled unassisted. Only later was a media officer provided to the council on loan from the state government.

Support staff would eventually be allocated to help ease the burden, but Neil would spend most of the next two years immersed in the fallout from Port Arthur.

At one point, he was simultaneously on the Port Arthur Historic Site management board, a member of the committee set up to determine how the massacre would be memorialised at the site, a member of the council's community recovery taskforce and one of three volunteers appointed to determine who would receive compensation from the $3.6 million fund donated from across Australia. He also remained a friend, confidant and mayor to a shell-shocked community.

It was a time of 5 a.m. starts and midnight finishes, with little room for much in between. A 30-minute bath each morning became a ritual, where Neil could let his mind go to a place other than the frantic world which awaited him. If he needed a break during the day, he would drive his tractor up a paddock and just sit there, his worker's hands resting on the steering wheel, as he surveyed the peaceful scene below.

'I had people asking me if I wanted counselling, but I felt I didn't need it, because I was talking to people all the time. I was sort of in semi-counselling – on the Tuesday after, I was going around to all the relations of the victims and just stopping with them and crying with them. I spent hours with Walter Mikac and Keith Moulton; crying with them. It was all part of it for me.'

Trying to determine who should receive what amount of compensation after an event such as the Port Arthur massacre is an unenviable task. How can you ever put a figure on either a physical injury, grief or trauma, or perhaps the three combined? For Neil Noye, it was made even more difficult by the fact he lived and worked among some of those who were to apply for compensation from the $3.6 million public fund.

Neil, together with a retired Queen's Counsel, Henry

Cosgrove, and Bob Grierson, from the Tasmanian Department of Premier and Cabinet, made up the volunteer committee which met solidly for three months to wade through the applications for help and decide who would receive what, if anything at all. There were at least 200 individual claims, some of them several centimetres thick, as they outlined in detail their suffering; either from being injured themselves, or through losing a loved one. The committee had the job of deciding who would receive funds and who wouldn't, based not only on need, but on what other forms of compensation also may have been available to victims.

While the fund paid for the funerals of all victims, except one by the family's choice, it was inevitable some people would miss out on further compensation, or feel they had been treated poorly compared to others. Even though the decisions were not his to make alone, much of the flak came back onto Neil's shoulders, largely because, as a local, he was such an accessible target.

'It was bad, yes, because I had people come up to me and say "Oh, you gave such and such so much money. What did you do that for?" and I had to wear that. I would try and explain that sometimes I had different ideas, but the decision had to be the majority of the committee and that was that.'

Neil similarly wore a significant dose of the community angst around what should happen to the Broad Arrow Café, with people adamant it should either stay, be bulldozed or be 'pulled apart brick by brick, buried and then rebuilt later when everything had settled down'.

In the first twelve months after the massacre, it seemed no matter what the Port Arthur Authority Board did, it was wrong. Neil, who was a member of the board at the time, believes it was being hit with not only the raw reactions of shattered people, but every past grievance between the site and its staff, and the site and the wider community. The chairman, Michael Mazengarb, was particularly targeted.

'He was doing a marvellous job, but people were against him and they didn't want this and they didn't want that. We were eventually dismissed off the board after twelve months to try and alleviate the friction. There was an enormous amount of tension and you became a whipping boy.'

Neil would often be confronted face-to-face by angry site staff and locals who would vent their frustration over the seeming lack of support for their situation, or to disagree loudly with the recovery plan for the site. He recalls one man turning up to his property on a Sunday afternoon and berating him for three hours solid over all the things which 'should and should not' have happened to help the community after the massacre. 'I was copping a lot at the time and it hurt, but people were also hurting and they didn't really know what they were doing. It was just seen as "everybody's fault".'

Yet Neil knew perhaps better than most what the wider community was suffering. He had lost friends and he had also taken a financial hit of his own. The two years of work on rebuilding the community meant he had to neglect his own cattle and chicken business and lose up to $40,000 in income, but he is reluctant to talk about his own financial loss.

Instead, he believes it gave him an insight into the strain that was imposed on local traders, some of whom were forced to relocate in order to survive. 'The peninsula was hurting bad. The shops were suffering, the accommodation places were suffering, the vegetable and fruit growers who supplied these industries were suffering, because nobody was moving here, nobody was staying here. There were people in Hobart, even friends of mine, who wouldn't come down here for a long, long time. People were really terrified, yet Port Arthur wasn't the problem, it was one man.'

Indeed in the week after the shootings, hotels and airlines began to record blanket cancellations for Tasmania, as the once idyllic island shifted in people's minds to a place of exceptional violence.

Given that tourists were no longer coming to Tasmania – let alone Port Arthur – Tasmania decided to go to them.

In May 1996, Neil, the then Liberal Premier Tony Rundle and the Port Arthur board chairman Michael Mazengarb, began a punishing six-day tour up the east coast of Australia and across to Adelaide in an effort to convince people not to abandon the state because of Martin Bryant's madness.

The trio worked from the early hours in the morning to late at night, appearing on top-rating television and radio shows, visiting schools and hospitals, wandering through shopping malls: whatever it took to show that Tasmania was still open for business and that it needed that business more than ever.

In between the hectic media commitments, the three men met privately with the families of some of the victims, including a quiet dinner with the children of Mervyn and Mary Howard in country Victoria, and took time out to personally thank many of the Victorian police who had helped contain Bryant during the Seascape siege.

Neil was surprised at his own energy and resilience. 'It showed me that I never got upset; that I could handle things more than I thought I could. I thought I would really go to pieces on stress, but...you really do seem to find an inner strength and...you know you have to keep going whether you like it or not. There were times when you wanted to say, "I give it away", but there was no way you could do that.'

The whirlwind tour was noble in its intent, but tourists would not return to Tasmania in any significant numbers for another four years. For many of the local businesses, it was far too late. Many Tasmanians remember the years immediately after the massacre as being like living under a steel-grey cloud that showed no signs of lifting. There was no joy, no vibrancy and no sense of a real future. House prices had stagnated, more people were leaving the island than moving to it and the economy, which was already staggering under crippling debt, had taken a king hit.

'I thought we would come out of it a lot quicker than we did,' says Neil. 'I thought within two years we would be out of the main part, but it took four years and, of course, for those who lost loved ones, you never expect to really come out of it.'

The year after the massacre, Neil was made a Member of the Order of Australia in recognition of his community effort and was to be a runner-up for Tasmanian of the Year behind the national president of Canteen, Fiona Taylor. These are accolades you still need to drag out of him, as he remains a man who prefers to talk about the good work of others, rather than his own. He and his wife, Kath, also a former member of the Tasman Council, decided to finally retire from civic life in early 2002 when Neil was 70. Neil admits his health these days is 'perhaps not as good as it was'. Probe a little deeper and he reveals he had heart bypass surgery in 1998 that uncovered nine blockages in his arteries.

Yet he continues to live in the original Noye farmhouse and to work the land on behalf of his only son, also named Neil, who lives in Hobart, but who will eventually continue the Noye tradition. When we meet, Neil makes tea and invites me into his cosy yet formal lounge, where he has spread out bags of 'Port Arthur material' on a long dining table that, judging by the deep lustre of its dark, aged wood, has hosted innumerable family gatherings. His classic country home exudes a warmth that comes from years of absorbing a little of each life that has passed through its walls. Those same walls are, today, lined with family portraits of the Noyes. As Kath offers slices of warm sponge cake, Neil speaks of his connection to this place.

'I would never leave the peninsula. There would not have been a month go by since this house was built in 1891 that a Noye wasn't living here. [In that time, there have been] nine children born in this house and twins are buried in the yard out here,' he says, finishing his sentence by pointing through the large windows that overlook a garden crowded with trees and flowering plants.

It is this profound sense of history, of belonging, which cannot be easily erased, least of all by a weak character such as Martin Bryant.

Not surprisingly, the massacre gave Neil an even stronger appreciation of the importance of family and he is extremely close to his five children and a growing line of grandchildren.

The fallout from Bryant's actions also taught him a lot about people. 'I grew up and learnt a lot more in those three or four years about people and life than I did for a long time before that. How people react: the goodness that can come out and the bad and how people react to the system. Some carry it and travel really well, some fall over much later, and some will always stay bitter.'

Neil says that before our meeting in May 2004 he had begun to put the immediate pain of Port Arthur behind him. It was only in preparing for our interview that he dug out some of the many boxes of condolence cards and letters that arrived in the weeks and months after the shootings. He is, again, visibly moved by 'the extreme kindness' shown to his remote community. Among the letters are those penned by an entire class at the Streaky Bay area school on the remote Eyre Peninsula of South Australia.

There are the poems and drawings from other schoolchildren who, in bright crayons and capital letters, say how sad they feel inside and how they wished they 'could make everyone feel better'. And there are the piles of Christmas cards from complete strangers, writing to let the Tasman Peninsula know it is in their prayers. Every letter that arrived, the council attempted to answer.

Reading them again eight years later, Neil, his spectacles slipping to the end of his nose, falls quiet. The words, he says with a deep sigh, remind him of what the human spirit is all about.

'I look upon life now as every day being a bonus. Money is not a priority anymore. I just live life every day and enjoy it, because a lot of those at Port Arthur that day, they never had a chance.'

The eighth anniversary of the massacre, in 2004, was the first time Neil missed the memorial service at the Port Arthur site. Many of those who once attended each year have since chosen to remember the day privately. Neil is among them. He spent the day cutting wood 'up on the hill'. There, he stopped for a moment of reflection, feeling the same sense of sorrow and yet gratitude for the richness of his own life, that he felt when he would retreat to his tractor in the years immediately after the shootings.

'These days when it comes up, I just get away on my own a bit.'

Neil will probably spend a quiet moment on his land again this year, and the next as, with each passing year, the ragged tear that was left in his community after 28 April slowly begins to heal. The peninsula remains his home; the farm, his piece of paradise. In a speech penned shortly after the shootings, Neil asked others to remember how much the peninsula was loved by the local people who had lost their lives and implored others not to abandon it in its time of greatest need: 'I am sure if Dave, Sally, Nanette, Elizabeth or Nicole could speak, they would say, "I loved the peninsula. It was my home. Don't let it go backwards. Get up and get on with it." To honour those we have lost, we must go forward.'

Neil Noye will never leave.

9

THE FRONTLINE:
THE DELLS

Colin and Robyn Dell were once part of that special group known as the 'vollies': ordinary people who, at a minute's notice, are prepared to put themselves into often extraordinary situations as volunteer firefighters, ambulance drivers or rescue workers.

Tasmania, for simple reasons of geography, has more than its fair share of these selfless souls. In a state of less than 500,000 people, nearly 60 per cent live outside its capital city of Hobart and are sprinkled sparingly across its mountainous terrain. The state's emergency services depend heavily on people prepared to interrupt their lunches and cancel their dinner dates to attend a car accident on an isolated road or help search for a missing bushwalker. Indeed, of the 8500 emergency service workers in Tasmania, almost two-thirds are volunteers.

In 1996, the Dells, a middle-aged couple who loved community work, were among eighteen volunteer ambulance drivers who looked after the Tasman Peninsula region by way of two ambulances that were rotated between the homes of those on call. On the day of the Port Arthur massacre, one of the ambulances was stationed at Nubeena, where Kaye Fox and Gary Alexander were on duty, and the other in the driveway of the Dell home; a rustic brick house surrounded by bushland, tucked off the main road at Taranna. Colin, at that time a home maintenance worker, and Robyn, a senior nurse, were out collecting their winter wood supply from a bush block on their property when the pager sounded just after 1.30 p.m. Mobile phones at that time were virtually useless in the area, which still suffers communication blackspots, so Colin silenced his chainsaw and went inside to phone the Hobart headquarters. While only Colin was rostered on that weekend, Robyn followed him indoors to hear the reason for the emergency.

'They said to me, "There is a mass shooting at Port Arthur",' Colin recalls. His immediate response was to ask when the 'training exercise' was expected to finish. His throat tightened when the communications office replied that it was far from a training exercise and he had to get to the site as quickly as possible.

Given the potential number of injured, Robyn joined him.

Colin remembers the apprehension that filled him as he floored the ambulance towards the site. It was one thing to be called out to car wrecks and farm accidents, where years of training helped him to slip into automatic pilot, but an entirely different set of emotions was involved when you were heading into the unknown. 'I felt absolute fear. I was terrified from the minute I left here, absolutely terrified. I didn't feel concerned about my own person, it was a fear of the unknown.'

Robyn, although an experienced nurse, admits she also felt worried for her own safety, knowing the gunman was still at large.

As they approached the historic site, tourist Anne Wardle flagged them down and warned them not to go the most direct route past the Seascape cottage, as Bryant was still firing at passing cars and at the two policemen bunkered in the leech-infested ditch. The pair turned the vehicle around and took the back roads towards the site, their speedometer nudging 140 km/h, but 'feeling more like 50,' as Colin would describe it. They would later learn that paramedic Jim Giffard, who had a farm at nearby Dunalley and had just finished a night shift only hours before the massacre, gunned his ambulance straight past Seascape. Giffard and his two volunteer colleagues, Jodie Branch and Roger Garth, unknowingly exposed themselves to Bryant's line of fire when they spotted the two policemen in the ditch and slowed to see if they were hurt, only to be waved on frantically.

Just before reaching the Port Arthur site, the Dells were again redirected, this time by ambulance headquarters, asking them to stop at the Fox and Hounds hotel to help those injured by Bryant's random shots at cars.

Colin still remembers being astounded by the level of medical care the wounded had already received, well before any medical help had arrived. 'We had four patients there, but the first aid that was already done before we got there was absolutely magnificent. The patients had already had their dressings applied and were in appropriate positions for their injuries. I still don't know who did it, but they did a fantastic job.'

The Dells helped work on the four most badly wounded, including Linda White, who had a shattered forearm and Susan Williams, with a severely injured hand, as the 'pop, pop' of Bryant's shots could be heard in the distance. The Dunalley crew soon arrived to take some of the injured to Hobart, while others would be taken to the site to be airlifted out. After the first of the patients was loaded into the ambulance, Robyn began to feel her composure unravel. As the adrenalin needed to care for the injured subsided, the enormity of the situation began to seep in and the tears came easily.

Jim Giffard took her by the shoulders and shook her, saying, 'Come on, pull yourself together. We've got work to do.'

'If he had allowed me to weep then, that would have been it for me. I would not have been able to do any more,' Robyn says.

There was still much more to do, as the pair drove to the site itself. Like Ian McElwee was to later do with his bus, Robyn guided the ambulance through the covered bodies that lined the top of Jetty Road, prompting Colin – who was in the back of the ambulance attending to Susan Williams – to ask her why she was swerving so badly. 'I said, "Can't you drive straight Delly?", before she explained what was going on,' Colin says.

Despite the confronting scene on Jetty Road, as soon as the ambulance pulled into the site, Colin felt his fears slip away. He could see the other volunteer ambulance crews at work, the GPs Pam and Steve Ireland prioritising the patients and the helicopters flying in and out to ferry the injured to Hobart. The Dells were no longer working alone, but were part of a much bigger, coordinated emergency operation: this felt familiar and safe. Unlike hundreds of people still on site, including the other medical teams, they also had the mental advantage of knowing that Bryant was not at large, roaming around the area. 'Nobody at the site knew where he was, but I didn't know this at the time. I wasn't aware until a long time later that they didn't know where he was,' Colin says.

A paper prepared by the Tasmanian Ambulance Service in the wake of the massacre would describe how medical crews worked for two hours at the site before the first on-duty police arrived and, even then, the officers were unable to confirm whether Bryant was contained at Seascape. So real was the threat, fuelled further by rumours that Bryant was indeed on the move, that several ambulance crews turned their reflective jackets inside out to make themselves less of a target. They did not, however, stop working.

After arriving at the site, the Dells parked their ambulance in front of the Broad Arrow Café and passed Susan Williams into the care of the Irelands. Colin also checked on the injured Brigid Cook who was propped on the verandah, nursing her leg. 'I asked her if she was being attended to, and she said she was. She had a smile on her face; she was a lucky girl.'

Jim Giffard was by this time inside the café and, stepping from the doorway, he beckoned to Colin to come and see the aftermath himself. As Colin explained, going inside was the right decision.

'Jim tapped me on the shoulder and said, "I think you had better come and have a look in here. There'll be a lot of lies told about what's in there and you had better see it so you know what the [truth] is." So I clenched my teeth and I went in with Jim and looked around and saw things that I never expected to see in my lifetime: I knew this was something that I was going to have to share with Robyn.'

Colin called to Robyn and the pair spent a couple of minutes absorbing the surreal scene that, at once, was overwhelmingly appalling, but also reminiscent of mannequins prepared for a film set. One gentleman, his head slumped forward, still clutched a cup of tea in his hand; another held a fork as if he was about to take a mouthful of food.

'As everybody in there was deceased, it had a calmness. It had a calmness, but it affected me deeply,' Colin says quietly.

Fortunately many of those who had suffered disfiguring wounds had been covered by tea towels, so the Dells were spared the shock of seeing the very worst of the injuries. They were also unaware that among the dead was Elizabeth Howard, or Lizzie Campbell as they knew her, who had grown up with their own children. 'I don't think I would have survived the day if I had seen Lizzie. I must have seen her, but I didn't have time to register who it was because their heads were covered,' Colin says.

Colin believes that by going into the café and seeing the devastation first-hand, he and Robyn were able to remove themselves from the swirl of myth-making that followed the massacre. They have their own truth, he says, seen by their own eyes.

'That recommendation by Jim Giffard was the best thing; absolutely the best thing. We have had people absolutely and blatantly try to lie to us about what was in the Broad Arrow because they say, "Oh I this and I that" and they know eff all.'

Although they both walked through the café, or perhaps because of it, the Dells have never talked at length about it to each other. Instead, they share an unspoken connection for having faced the gruesome reality together: there is no, as Keith Moulton would say, 'imagination' at work.

'We still haven't talked about it much. We'd sometimes just stand and cuddle each other and cry,' Colin says.

'And we would know what it's about without talking,' Robyn adds.

After leaving the café, the Dells escorted Ian McElwee's busload of walking wounded as far as Taranna, before they sped past the bus towards the Royal Hobart Hospital with the injured Susan Williams, who had been unable to secure an airlift by helicopter.

Today their tears come from their pride at being part of a medical response in which not a single life was lost during the rescue operation. Despite the horrific injuries and blood loss suffered by so many, every patient brought out of Port Arthur survived.

'Everybody who was recovered, lived: I am proud to have been a part of that,' Colin tells me through tears.

Robyn also recalls the many people who, having heard about the massacre on their car radios, pulled over to the side of the road as the ambulances raced, lights ablaze and sirens screaming, towards Hobart. She will never forget driving through Midway Point, a strip of water-locked land between the Tasman Peninsula and Hobart, linked by two thin causeways. A long line of people had stopped on the causeway to Hobart and stood outside their vehicles as the ambulances flew past. As the Dells drove by, each of the local folk raised their hand in what was a simple gesture of support. Robyn still cries when she thinks of the people who, their faces blank with disbelief about what was happening just a few kilometres away, stood for a moment to let the 'vollies' know they were not alone.

The next day, both Robyn and Colin attempted to go back to work, but soon realised they were numb and operating on auto-pilot. Colin, thinking he was still on call for the volunteer ambulance that week, even responded to a call-out before the Hobart base radioed through and told him to go home: they would handle it.

Whether people should be formally debriefed immediately after a catastrophic event is still a subject of divided opinion, but the Dells believe the debriefing offered to them in the hours after the Port Arthur shootings helped them to move on. The Critical Incident Stress Management (CISM) program is a peer-based program that had been operating for Tasmania's emergency services since 1988, but it was put to the ultimate test in the aftermath of Bryant's rampage.

The Dells were among the ambulance workers and volunteers taken to the Hobart ambulance headquarters the night of the massacre for a CISM session.

Robyn and Colin were part of a small group of about twelve, including Jim Giffard, who together openly shared their stories, their tears and, without embarrassment or shame, their moments of doubt and fear. 'We were able to get it off our chests; tell everything you were feeling,' Robyn says.

Colin found the session much more rewarding than that which followed several days later at the Nubeena tavern, where government-paid counsellors encouraged those gathered to share their thoughts. The Dells were like many of the locals who saw the counsellors as 'suits from town' who, although well meaning, were perceived as being physically and emotionally detached from the very people they were trying to help.

'I came away thinking it was a waste of time and we never went to another one. We didn't have any more counselling at all. We just looked at each other after that and said, "We have to get on with it".'

The Dells joined the 1 May memorial service at St David's Cathedral and then left for a holiday to Alice Springs, planned before the massacre, during which they sat in their hotel room and watched the unveiling of the Port Arthur memorial cross on television. It was a poignant yet strange moment, made all the more surreal by the housekeeper who, having arrived to clean the room, left her laundry trolley to one side and asked if she could watch the service with them. All three sat on the bed and cried as the ceremony unfolded.

Colin and Robyn believe the two memorial services gave a sense of closure that they would not have achieved from ongoing counselling. 'The counselling seemed...an open-ended thing and I wasn't prepared for it to go on and on,' Robyn says.

Colin describes it as 'getting on the train' and that, in his view, some of those involved in the massacre remain stuck in a cycle of ongoing counselling and medication and are unable to get off. 'I still feel very saddened that I see some of our volunteers who are still suffering, who are still on the train, as I say. They got on the train with counselling and medication and I see one or two of our residents still suffering greatly, psychologically, as a result.'

Colin Dell blames the emotional impact of Port Arthur for changing the personalities of some of his former ambulance colleagues. It was for this reason that in 2000 he and Robyn decided, after almost twenty years of service, not to continue their volunteer role. Where personalities once gelled, they now clashed, or disintegrated into petty rivalries. Colin still feels distressed by having had to make such a decision, but doesn't blame anyone for what he considers was yet another consequence of one man's crazed actions.

A big man with Popeye-strength forearms, Colin admits he cries far more freely than he did before the massacre. Yet he believes the experience has made him tougher, in that nothing he could expect to face in life from here could compare to the trauma of the shootings.

'I am different in that I have had that experience. Most people in their lifetime wouldn't have that experience. I don't know what a war experience is like, but I imagine it's something like...that...,' Colin says.

It is at the end of our interview, when the tape recorder has been turned off and we turn our attention to a plate of warm savoury scones, that Colin lets his emotions flow unchecked.

Leaning his elbows on the table, his large body shakes and tears tumble down his face as he tells of one of his most challenging moments shortly after the shootings: the day he decided to forgive Martin Bryant. Robyn rubs his shoulder, swallowing her own tears, as Colin tells the story.

It was about six weeks after the massacre and Colin was standing in his peaceful native garden, struggling with the incongruity of his beautiful surrounds and the intense anger and hatred he felt towards Bryant. On one hand he understood why he felt that way; on the other he knew his hatred was debilitating: a poisonous grip that was gradually tightening around his heart.

'I knew then I had to forgive him. Not for him, but for me. If I was to move on, I had to forgive him. I am not a religious man, but I knew that if Jesus Christ could forgive, then I had to forgive too. So I forgive him, I forgive him.'

Now both retired, the Dells spend their days either enjoying their rural block or being part of the growing tribe of 'grey nomads' who strike out to see Australia in a motor home. Colin modified a car-caravan for their travels and, judging by the string of coloured pins which snake across the map of Australia on their lounge room wall, it has served them well. Call the Dell household these days and you are just as likely to find them 'gone for six months' as they explore another state; slowly.

Yet while they travel, the Port Arthur experience sits within them. It has become a quiet yet permanent reminder to cherish every moment on the road – and they do.

Talking it out

Tasmanian psychologist Ian Sale, who went on to individually counsel some of those involved with Port Arthur, told an ABC radio program in 2004 that, in his view, some of the debriefing in the wake of the massacre became completely over the top.

'There were people saying that it's like controlling an infection: you go into this place, you do your debriefing to help the people there and then you get debriefed yourself before you leave.

'It was quite extraordinary and, looking back on it, a slightly bizarre set of ideas and operations that was happening,' Dr Sale told the Radio National program *Background Briefing*.

Dr Sale also took issue with the debriefing process being forced upon people who may have been better left in the comfort of their families, such as one of the police officers who had been trapped in the ditch outside Seascape. After being rescued and taken home sometime after midnight, he was called out for a counselling session.

'I believe he was actually in bed…and he'd had a couple of cups of tea and a warm shower…but it was felt important that he also have a psychological debriefing. So he was summoned back and that's what I saw that night in that rather exhausted figure just leaning by a corner of the Command Centre.'

One person who closely examined the debriefing of emergency service workers involved with the Port Arthur massacre was Hobart psychologist Dr Julian Watchorn.

Watchorn based part of his 2001 doctorate through the University of Tasmania around a detailed study of how professional emergency service workers coped with the massacre and the effectiveness of the Critical Incident Stress Management (CISM) program for those involved. Watchorn's study involved an assessment of 96 professional emergency service workers over a two-year period, firstly eight months after the shootings and then again at twenty months. The 96 were among 685 emergency service workers involved in the Port Arthur response, including 526 police, 62 ambulance officers and 49 firefighters. Some were involved for a single day; others saw their working lives inextricably linked to the massacre every day for more than four months. There were those who worked at the crime scene and others who had the grim task of identifying bodies in the Hobart mortuary. Some worked on piecing together the criminal case against Bryant, while others were kept fully occupied with compiling the 1055 witness statements.

The extent of the debriefings after the massacre is captured by Watchorn's study, which reveals 113 debriefs and 51 defuses were held in the first thirteen days after the massacre alone. A defuse is held within twelve hours of the traumatic event and usually lasts between 30 to 45 minutes, during which those people involved are encouraged to talk about what they saw and experienced. A debrief is either held individually or in a group, in the first 24 to 72 hours after the event and is a more in-depth exploration of feelings and reactions to the incident and a discussion of how to cope with these reactions.

Of the 685 emergency service workers involved in the immediate response to the massacre, 269 eventually were to be 'defused' and 495 were debriefed.

When Watchorn asked his 96 participants what aspects of the event they found most distressing, the most common response was, not surprisingly, the shooting of the Mikac children. The sight of the children's bodies left even seasoned emergency workers shaken by the brutality of Bryant's actions.

The crews also found it hard to cope with thoughts of the utter defencelessness of Bryant's victims and identifying with how terrifying it must have been for them. Others talked of the fear of being under threat themselves and not knowing, for hours, exactly where the gunman was. There was also the stress of dealing with the grieving relatives of those killed and the overwhelming magnitude of the crime.

The emergency service workers interviewed by Watchorn were, like Wendy Scurr, also unnerved by the bodies piled near the broken rear door of the souvenir shop.

As Watchorn reported, the professional training which normally helped emergency service workers detach from a tragic event was not nearly enough for the Port Arthur situation. 'As they described, this was due to the enormity of the incident, the number of bodies, the level of personal threat and/or the surrealness of the scene in the café,' he writes.

Like the Dells, those who were part of the initial response to the shootings said they experienced immense stress through 'fear of an unknown danger' as they drove into a potential death trap. It was akin to driving into a battle for which there was little or no preparation and, for the medical crews at least, no way of defending themselves.

Judging by Watchorn's findings, the Dells were far from alone in their reactions. Even the professional crews who were mentally and physically trained to deal with disaster on a daily basis struggled to cope. Watchorn tells of one police officer, for example, who remained terrified of the dark for months after the event. It took a fortnight before he felt safe enough to walk around even his own home and it was another month before he could venture outside in the night.

Another policeman told of seeing the face of one of the young victims every time he closed his eyes for the next two months after the shootings. Some emergency service officers would be unable to work in the job again.

If there was one positive for the emergency service workers, it was the community response to their efforts. Many told Watchorn that they felt 'proud to wear their uniform' and 'more valued by the general community': an attitude which many said helped their recovery.

So did the formal debriefing offered by the state's emergency service CISM team help? For those prepared to talk freely and openly at the sessions, Watchorn found that it did.

Indeed, Watchorn goes so far as to say that talking it out in the debriefing may have been critical towards avoiding ongoing mental and physical problems. The debriefing was especially valuable for those who had experienced a sense of disconnectedness and were prepared to talk openly about it. Watchorn found that of the 96 people interviewed, 55 experienced 'dissociative' symptoms at the time of the massacre, such as blanking out details, running on auto-pilot, feeling disconnected from their body, or a pervasive sense of unreality.

Watchorn says those who spoke freely at the debriefing sessions about these seemingly strange reactions suffered fewer ongoing problems. He stresses, however, that more investigation is needed into the impact of various parts of a debriefing session, such as the timing, who runs it, where it is held, how it is structured and its purpose. Those who feel uncomfortable about opening up before a group of colleagues should also be given the chance talk freely in another setting.

In Australia, the Port Arthur massacre remains – thankfully – one of the few occasions when debriefing approaches could be tested on a large scale and, hopefully, improved so that there are more stories like the Dells' and fewer like Wendy Scurr's.

10

A MAN OF MANY HATS:
IAN SALE

The last mundane part of Sunday, 28 April 1996 for Dr Ian Sale was listening to the Brisbane Bears bag a ton of goals against Fitzroy. Ian, a respected Tasmanian psychiatrist of almost twenty years' experience at the time, was motoring down the Midland Highway – a well-travelled strip connecting Launceston to Hobart – having just finished a seminar on the *Workers Compensation Act*. He remembers the forum was interesting; the one-sided football game being broadcast from Brisbane wasn't.

'Suddenly there was a newsbreak and they mentioned the name Luppo Prins. That made my ears prick up, because it is such a unique name. There must be only one Luppo Prins who has ever lived in the history of the planet, so that drew my attention and then it became pretty clear that something extraordinary was happening.'

Tasmania Police Assistant Commissioner Luppo Prins was in charge of the major incident room in response to the Port Arthur massacre, the first details of which were now trickling out through the media.

Ian tightened his grip on the steering wheel and turned his ear to the radio as the newsreader told how an unknown gunman had been on a shooting spree at Port Arthur and was now at the centre of a siege at the Seascape cottage. As soon as Ian heard it had developed into a siege situation, he knew he could expect a phone call from the police hostage negotiation team.

Assisting in siege negotiations was a role he had performed before. As a forensic psychiatrist, Ian specialised in psychiatry linked to criminal and legal cases. He had developed a close friendship with Superintendent Jack Johnston when they both worked in Launceston, where the CIB occasionally used his skills to help crack a particular case. The friendship continued after Superintendent Johnston took over the hostage negotiation unit in Hobart, where he arranged for Ian to have specific training to back up the team if required. The majority of sieges were handled by the police internally, but in extreme cases, where the individual involved could be deeply psychiatrically disturbed, Ian would be called in to help guide the negotiators. Port Arthur was an extreme case. Superintendent Johnston was on the phone as soon as Ian arrived home.

Within minutes, Ian had joined the negotiation team at Tasmania Police headquarters in Liverpool Street, where Sergeant Terry McCarthy and police psychologist Mike Ryan were trying to unravel just who they were dealing with at Seascape and whether his hostages, the Martins and Glenn Pears, were still alive. Bryant was using the name 'Jamie' and even once his real identity was revealed after he told police to recover his passport from the glove box of his Volvo, little was known about the man.

'There was nothing the police could pick up in their first sweep through the data. There was just no information whatsoever about [Martin Bryant]. He didn't even seem to have a driver's licence, so he was a complete unknown.'

According to Ian, the police were, however, able to link Bryant's name to a relative who worked in the corrections industry. The relative was interviewed, but inadvertently put the negotiation team on the wrong track by repeating a family misconception that Bryant was schizophrenic.

Ian was sceptical of the schizophrenia diagnosis, as Bryant's phone calls with Sergeant McCarthy did not appear to match the behaviour that could be expected from someone suffering a psychotic episode.

'The conversations were more sort of childlike, with an almost playful quality to them: nothing remotely suggesting a psychosis. There was no real dialogue and he made no sense at all. We couldn't get any idea of what his goals were. It was not like any scenario they had been trained for, or that I had come across.'

While Sergeant McCarthy managed to make contact with Bryant six times during the afternoon and evening, the negotiation efforts came to an abrupt halt when the cordless phone Bryant was using at Seascape lost power shortly after 9 p.m.

The negotiation team had no choice but to relocate from police headquarters in Hobart to the site of the siege itself, but Ian first joined two detectives in a desperate search for more clues to Bryant's unusual character by visiting his home.

The trio walked up the heavily overgrown front garden of 30 Clare Street, New Town, where the weeds brushed shoulder height, and into the darkened rooms of the rambling mansion. It might have been eerie, but it was not an obvious lair of a lunatic. 'It was a very strange place, very unusual, but later you realised that what you were seeing in that house was not so much Bryant – there was some influence of him there – but the old lady [Helen Harvey].'

Bryant was living virtually as a squatter in the house, which had been owned by an eccentric middle-aged woman, Helen Harvey, who crammed it with piles of hoarded clutter. There were piles of books, some bound together by string, others just jammed into boxes. There were several hundred videos – 'enough to stock a video store' – showing an eclectic taste ranging from Jackie Chan and Arnold Schwarzenegger, through to *The Sound of Music*. Some of the videos remained sealed in their wrappers, and there were multiple copies of others. Ian remembers a documentary about the history of Port Arthur being among the collection, although, with the site being a high-profile part of Tasmania, he did not consider this in itself unusual.

The group wandered into the spacious lounge room, which was largely empty but for a strange wooden cage, stretching two metres into the air, which Ian later discovered was used to house Bryant's African Gray parrot. Carleen Bryant had taken the bird after Bryant failed to care for it, but when Ian later spoke to Carleen and 'met' the parrot, he was taken aback to hear its voice: it mimicked Bryant's perfectly.

In another room, Ian found a life-size doll of cartoon character Bart Simpson, while in Bryant's bedroom there were piles of brand new, highly fashionable clothes, on which Bryant splurged regularly. It was an eccentric home, but other than a couple of military magazines, the first search through the house produced nothing of substance. It was only later that police would return for a more thorough search and find a firearm hidden in the piano.

By about 10 p.m. that night, Ian joined the negotiation team for the 85 km trip to the police forward command post at Taranna, but there was to be no further communication with Bryant. Instead, Ian recalls the fruitless attempts to secure a phone hook-up with the Seascape cottage that occasionally bordered on the farcical.

One idea was to use a small robotic device called an Echidna, which was normally used to detonate bombs, to deliver a phone to Bryant as he remained holed up in the house. The device, however, operated from a power cord and this cord was too short to cover the 300-metre safety perimeter set around the cottage by police. It was then suggested a bulldozer be used to deliver the phone, until it was realised that someone would still need to drive the machine and expose themselves to Bryant's firepower. The cumbersome machine sat idle on the roadway, having been rustled up by Tasman mayor Neil Noye in the middle of the night.

Ian raises a wry smile when he recalls the arrival of the state-of-the-art negotiator van that had been purpose-built to deal with siege situations. The van, which had arrived in Tasmania only months earlier, was in Launceston on the day of the massacre and had to be brought down to the command station at Taranna. The van lumbered into Taranna about the same time as Ian and the rest of the negotiation team arrived from Hobart, but shortly after they climbed into the unit they realised they were locked in.

'Here was this amazing van with all the bells and whistles and super-duper electronics and yet it had a faulty lock. Fortunately we had this snip of a man from Telstra in there with us and he was able to climb out through this little hatch and, even more fortunately, he was able to do it without the press noticing.'

The woeful communications situation on the Tasman Peninsula also proved to be a major headache for police as they worked to contain Bryant. Superintendent Barry Bennett, who was in charge of the forward command at Taranna, would later tell the Police Association of Tasmania's periodical, *Association News*, how the area's undulating terrain created a virtual mobile phone blackspot. The ironstone in the surrounding hills played havoc with radio signals and it was the media who eventually found the only 'live' mobile spot, in the middle of a roadway. Even the police radio network was 'very scratchy and very poor' and was reduced to only one reliable channel.

Indeed, the radio network reception was so poor that the police had to dial the major incident room back in Hobart on one of the three landlines available at the Tasmanian Devil Park at Taranna and leave the phone off the hook as a permanent link. A police car was parked as close as possible to a window in the park office, so that details received from those outside Seascape via the police car radio could be relayed back to Hobart via the landline.

The fact the police negotiation team was originally speaking to Bryant from Hobart also created problems, with police at the Taranna command station unable to listen directly to what was unfolding between the negotiators and 'Jamie'. Instead they had to rely on information passed down the telephone line from Hobart which, in turn, had to be passed on to the Special Operations Group (SOG) officers stationed outside Seascape, a further 5 km on from Taranna.

As Superintendent Bennett was to explain, the terrain also rendered useless the secure radio network he would normally use to communicate with the SOG officers. For most of the long night, a police officer had to drive between Taranna and Seascape to pass messages between the forward command post and the SOG.

It was the biggest police operation ever mounted in Tasmania and yet those involved were forced to rely on a form of bush telegraph. As a result, critical information from the negotiating team in Hobart was passed through several people before it reached the SOG officers who had their rifles trained on Seascape.

Superintendent Bennett later expressed his frustration to Police Association reporter Jenny Fleming:

> Our SOG would normally monitor negotiations for obvious reasons, to see if they could make some tactical decisions on what was going on inside the stronghold. They had no contact with negotiators throughout the night, so they were getting it through me third or fourth hand, which really caused me some heartburn and slowed things down tremendously.

Earlier in the day, there had been even less communication between Taranna and the devastating crime scene at the Port Arthur Historic Site. There, a handful of police officers had been doing their best to calm frightened and severely traumatised staff and visitors, without confirmation, until much later that night, that Bryant was actually contained. For hours, they also remained uncertain if Bryant had acted alone or had an accomplice.

It was only towards daybreak that a reliable communication link was finally established between the Taranna command post and the SOG group outside the Seascape cottage, although it still involved the SOG officers having to move repeatedly to keep their reception. No line of communication, however, was to be re-established with Bryant directly.

Ian remembers those seemingly endless hours of no contact, during which the entire police response was desperately trying to determine if any of the hostages inside the cottage were still alive.

As daylight came, smoke began to billow from the cottage and the need for a decision on whether to storm the building became critical. Ian was by now convinced that the hostages were dead, given there had been no firm evidence to the contrary, but then an officer spotted a curtain flapping and thought it might have been someone waving.

Superintendent Bob Fielding, who had by this time replaced Superintendent Bennett on the command post, had to decide whether to risk the lives of his officers by ordering them to move in, or continue to sit tight and possibly let a hostage or hostages burn to death.

'It put Bob in a real crunch situation,' Ian says. 'Here was possible information that a hostage was alive, although we had formed a view that there probably wasn't, but here was this highly dangerous and unstable situation. Bob, to his credit, held back. We had to see how it unfolded. We couldn't send people in there.'

Superintendent Fielding would later tell the Tasmania Police *Association News* that he felt justified in his decision not to potentially sacrifice the lives of up to ten officers, who would have been easy targets for Bryant, on the slim chance that a hostage may have been alive. It was only minutes after this crucial decision that Bryant burst from the house and stripped himself naked from his burning clothes.

As Superintendent Fielding told the *Association News*, all that Bryant was armed with by that stage was 'his mutton gun and that's not going to penetrate any ballistic shield'. The comment, passed on to a SOG officer as they prepared to move in and arrest Bryant, was, Fielding says, one of the few lighter moments of a very long and anxious night.

Ten years on, Ian still has his practice tucked above Hobart's Salamanca Place. A security buzzer and electronically locked reception door offer a reminder of the risks of his profession, but his modest office is welcoming. A wooden yacht, complete with hand-sewn canvas sails and a mast stretching well over a metre tall, provides an instant talking point and Ian delights in revealing its history. A man with a small frame and ruffled pewter-coloured hair, Ian speaks with the voice of a counsellor, his tone soft and soothing.

Wearing his trademark grey suit, Ian leans back in his office chair, cups the side of his face and tells of the many hats he wore in the weeks, months and years after the massacre.

As a forensic psychiatrist, he provided tactical advice to the police during their initial interrogation of Bryant in the days after his arrest, although their efforts at digging any confession out of him came to naught. Instead, Bryant rambled about surfing at Roaring Beach, before later admitting only to stealing the BMW and taking a hostage.

In an effort to learn more about Bryant, Ian later interviewed Martin's mother, Carleen Bryant, and his younger sister, Lindy, during which he learned of the family's struggle with an intellectually impaired child, the impact of the loss of his father and details of Martin's extraordinary life with Helen Harvey.

Ian also interviewed Bryant twice on behalf of the Director of Public Prosecutions, although the conditions of the interviews at Hobart's Risdon Prison were far from conducive to building any trust with the man. 'There was no sense of rapport and that wasn't just because he was defensive. I had to make allowances for the fact that I wasn't allowed to interview him without [Bryant having] shackles on, which is crazy. That was an absurd situation. He was kept in his own individual wing in the prison hospital and was shackled to the table with some big lads right outside the door. It wasn't a very suitable way of trying to interview him.'

Again, Bryant made no admissions about the massacre to Ian, although he did reveal a few details about his personal background.

Ian recalls how Bryant displayed odd body language, making extravagant gestures that appeared out of sync with what he was saying. And as police negotiators had already found, his voice was more like that of a teenage boy than an almost 30-year-old man, yet he was articulate and gave the impression of being far more intelligent than suggested by his IQ of just 66.

Ian eventually concluded that Bryant suffered a form of Asperger's syndrome, similar to an autistic disorder, which manifested itself through extreme emotional detachment and obsessive behaviour.

Dealing with Bryant face-to-face was not the most difficult aspect for Ian, despite the enormity of the crimes of which Bryant was accused. It was, as for Dr Pam Fenerty, handling the incessant flow of grief and trauma from those who were victims of Bryant's actions, either directly or indirectly. As Ian explained, it this way: before the massacre, one of his jobs was to help assess public service workers compensation claims on behalf of the state government's insurer, MMI. The Port Arthur Historic Site, as a government business enterprise, came under the MMI banner. 'I got to see the bulk of the workforce over the next few months. Just about everyone [was assessed for personal injury] whether they were there on the day or not. There was a lot of secondary damage; the people who were there obviously had a lot to cope with.'

Even those who were not directly involved were still exposed to the trauma of working in a highly stressful environment, particularly those kitchen staff who were asked to collect supplies from the Broad Arrow Café for the mobile kitchen that was set up to replace it. The café had been cleaned, but still bore the bloodstains and bullet holes from the massacre. 'Some of these people became damaged because of the strange environment they were working in, in the aftermath. There were a lot of problems among the workforce.'

Ian spent more than a year listening to the harrowing stories of staff and emergency service workers, while also dealing with the aggression and agitation of those employees who did not want to talk. He also provided a private practice service once a month at Nubeena to help ease the load on the local GPs, Pam and Steve Ireland.

Being almost permanently immersed in a sad pool of Port Arthur stories began to take its own toll, even on a man who had spent close to two decades in forensic psychiatry. 'What happened to me was that although I had not been to the Broad Arrow and chosen not to go there, I had actually built up almost like a virtual reality of what had occurred there and what it looked like afterwards.

'It was beginning to feel as if I'd almost been there and it was beginning to really trouble me.'

By mid–1997, the strain was starting to show in his behaviour. Ian would unknowingly repeat the same story about Port Arthur, over and over, with close friends becoming increasingly concerned that he was losing the professional detachment so necessary for his field.

'One of my good mates said to me, "You've got to back off, you've got to take it easy, because you can't stop talking about it. It's becoming a central feature of your life." And he was right.'

Another 'warning sign', as he calls it, was his emotional fragility. At one stage he 'barely held it together' while watching the movie, *Face/Off*, on a flight to Perth: it contained a sentimental scene involving a child, which before the massacre, he would have absorbed easily. Ian also found it increasingly difficult to sleep and would wake at the slightest sound.

Troubled by these symptoms of stress, Ian contacted MMI and said he needed to back off from his workers compensation role. A Melbourne psychiatrist was sent to help fill the gap. Ian believes the decision kept him from perhaps walking away from his profession altogether, although he still finds it difficult to remain completely detached from another person's suffering.

'I'm more troubled by people who have had a genuinely hard time; it's not quite as easy to be disinterested and that's a very important state of mind to do my work. You just have to be disinterested in outcomes. You have to just do your job, call it as you see it and not really be bothered if side A or side B gets up. That's not as easy as it once might have been.'

Ian rarely visits the Tasman Peninsula now, despite having once thoroughly enjoyed its rugged walks and wild beauty. Now when he drives past the Fox and Hounds hotel, past the Seascape cottage, through the Port Arthur village and into the site itself, he feels ill at ease from the memories of what happened there.

He remains similarly affected by news of major disasters around the world and cannot tolerate the emotive, drawn-out media coverage that follows an event such as the 2002 Bali bombings.

'I guess anytime there is a disaster, I have a greater sense, a greater empathy for what is the true effect. You hear of a bombing in Istanbul, for example, where 25 might be killed and you think, that is about the same as for Port Arthur and who knows how wide the ripple effect is going to be from that 25.'

As of late 2004, Ian was still seeing – in some cases for the first time – clients who were traumatised by what had happened at Port Arthur almost ten years earlier. It is the sadness of this ongoing individual pain, which lingers long after the headlines have subsided, that stands out for Ian as he reflects on the day.

'There is still so much distress and so many people with dislocated and ruined lives. I don't know how many there are – some are the children of others – but their lives have come to an end in many ways.'

11

THE TRAUMA BAY:
BRYAN WALPOLE

Police had already cordoned off the Royal Hobart Hospital by the time Dr Bryan Walpole pulled into the car park on the afternoon of the massacre.

Bryan, a former head of emergency services at the hospital who had since become the director of patient services, had spent the weekend hosting a severe-trauma management course in Hobart for trauma doctors from around Australia.

By 1 p.m. on the Sunday, Bryan had signed off the last of the pass/fail assessments and, apart from a few wind-down drinks in Salamanca Place with some of the interstate doctors, he was looking forward to a quiet afternoon with his family. He had barely pulled the key from the front door of his Sandy Bay home when his wife said the hospital had phoned. They needed him – immediately. He called work: there had been a shooting at Port Arthur.

Bryan quickly drove the handful of kilometres back to the Royal Hobart Hospital in downtown Argyle Street. As he looked east, over the River Derwent and towards the soft mounds of the Tasman Peninsula, he could see black specks in the sky: rescue helicopters were powering towards the site.

Bryan arrived in the emergency department, where he was

employed as a specialist, to find his director, Dr David Smart, had already set up a series of trauma bays. They were anticipating perhaps seven injured people. Then the calls began to come through from the ambulance headquarters that the number was more likely close to twenty. The hospital eventually mustered 70 emergency medical staff in preparation for a crisis of a scale never before seen in the state. While most of the interstate doctors involved in the severe-trauma management course had already caught flights home, several of the local doctors suddenly found themselves shifting from theory to practice in the space of a few hours. Initially, all the assembled medical crew could do was sit and wait and absorb the tension of wondering just what was heading their way.

'There was a period that I call the "phoney war", where we were all set up, we were sitting around and we had limited information,' Bryan recalls. 'There was a fairly high level of anxiety about what to expect, because in civilian life you don't see many firearm injuries and you usually only see them one patient at a time; attempted homicide, failed suicide and misadventures. The thought of a multiple homicide, or a multiple of people shot; that really taxed our minds.'

As it happened, the hospital had spent the previous twelve months revising its disaster plan and the final draft had been tested in a mock plane accident the very weekend before the massacre. What was known as a Code Brown operation, tailored to manage a large number of critical patients at once, was activated immediately.

By 3.18 p.m., the first of the helicopters had landed at the Hobart Domain and the victims began to move through the hospital in waves. Pam and Steve Ireland, the two GPs on the ground at Port Arthur, had prioritised the injured to make sure the very worst arrived at the hospital first. This group of five was quickly assessed, resuscitated, and moved on to intensive care for immediate surgery. As the surgical team went to work, the next wave of wounded arrived. There were people shot in the back, thigh, arm, shoulder or hand; each needing a complex set of medical treatments.

Bryan was part of the team that looked after this group of injured. 'Some required resuscitation, they required x-rays, blood tests and, in a number of cases, scans. It was quite a complex logistical problem, because we were working with half a dozen surgical groups – plastic surgeons, neurosurgeons, orthopaedic surgeons, vascular surgeons, anaesthetists and general surgeons – and we had to work out who would be first, second, third and fourth priority to go to theatre and make sure they had adequate analgesia and were properly resuscitated.'

It was a scene of frenzied yet skilfully coordinated activity which continued for the next five hours as the injured were taken through various levels of care. By late Sunday afternoon, a ward holding people due for elective surgery on Monday morning had been cleared and turned over to the Port Arthur victims. Having the wounded grouped together helped with management, communication and security.

By 9 p.m., as the patients settled and the immediate chaos gave way to quiet, Bryan Walpole was able to go home. The only major hospital in Australia's smallest state capital had been forced to cope with the horrific injuries resulting from a mass shooting and not a single life of those brought into the hospital had been lost.

There was one patient, however, who was yet to arrive. He would be admitted for burns treatment – under police guard.

Bryan Walpole recalls the mind-flip that was needed to try to return to 'business as usual' – attending to sprains, aches and pains – on the Monday morning after the massacre.

'We arrived back at work the next day and we were all feeling pretty shell-shocked after [the Sunday], but we had to get back into it again and deal with the ordinary humdrum stuff of everyday life.

'Then we heard somewhere around 10.30 that Bryant had been captured, he had been burnt and he was coming to the hospital.'

News of Bryant's impending arrival sparked a frenzy among the media, which was hungry for any developments on the story. National and international news crews – CNN was among the first on the scene – had been camped outside the hospital most of the night and were desperate to photograph Bryant as he arrived by ambulance. Bryan well remembers the chaos.

'One of the most dramatic scenes I have ever seen in civilian life was the police forming a wall, an arm-to-arm barrier, right across the emergency entrance, about 50 officers forming a visual barrier. When the ambulance arrived with Bryant in it, the ambulance actually backed through this line of police which then reformed around it.'

Senior photographer for *The Mercury*, Fred Kohl, was among those who managed to capture a single frame of Bryant as he was stretchered inside, his body and face hidden by a tangle of blankets. All that could be seen was the top of his head with its distinctive blond, wavy hair.

Medical staff were given the option of not treating Bryant, because of what he was accused of having done, but, as far as Bryan could recall, nobody flatly refused. The hospital remained under duress, however, as people vented their frustration against Bryant being cared for in the same place as his victims. There were also those who questioned why he should be treated at all, when he had callously taken the lives of so many others.

Peter Stride, one of two paramedics who escorted Bryant by ambulance to the hospital, summed up the mood when he later told reporters: 'I must be one of the most hated people in Australia at the moment [having delivered Bryant alive].'

Graffiti was daubed on the hospital walls and several anonymous callers made bomb threats, leading to evacuations of hospital wards. In another instance, a man attempted to break into the Burns Unit where Bryant was being treated for twenty per cent burns to his back and buttocks, but was discovered by security guards in the stairwell before he could cause any damage.

Bryant's presence was an added strain on an already pressured workplace and Bryan Walpole was among those glad to see him go after six days, when he was bustled out of the hospital under tight security and immense secrecy to the forensic hospital at Risdon Prison.

In the ten days after the shootings, the Royal Hobart Hospital was
to completely regear itself so that the ongoing treatment and care
of the Port Arthur victims remained a priority. Other, non-urgent
surgery was cancelled and wards cleared as needed. The cumulative
damage caused by bullet wounds makes them particularly difficult
to treat and some victims required successive surgery: one patient
was taken to theatre five times in one week for reconstructive work.
It would be another two months before the last of the Port Arthur
patients was discharged.

Apart from caring for the living, hospital staff also had to
manage the dead. Bryan recalls the overwhelming procession of
bodies that was trucked into the hospital late Monday afternoon;
the first opportunity emergency workers had to remove them from
the Port Arthur site. Forensic services are part of the Royal Hobart
Hospital and bodies are normally assessed by a doctor – to certify
they are dead – in an emergency bay before being transferred to the
morgue in another part of the building. This time, the extraordinary
number of bodies meant Bryan and a team of two nurses had to
direct the mortuary truck straight to the morgue, where they would
begin the identification process.

'Bear in mind at this stage that most of the people had not been
identified and, as many of them were tourists, they had no identification at all. Some of those who had been in the café had left their
ID on the bus, so what we had to do was say we had a 35-year-old
female wearing jewellery, with a scar on the left chest etc, so that
when the relatives turned up, we would be able to select a body for
them to identify and avoid misidentification.'

Under the often disconcerting gaze of at least a dozen super-
vising police officers, Bryan and the nursing staff worked until the
early hours of the morning, weighing and carefully documenting
the bodies. A radiographer later joined them to check each body for
bullets that might have to be retrieved and used as evidence. It was
a physically and mentally exhausting process.

Bryan recalls being stunned when, having finished the last of
the 32 bodies (another three bodies recovered from the Seascape
cottage would arrive the next day), the team headed to the doctors'

mess to unwind over a few beers. He asked the police crew to join them. Unfortunately, they explained, they couldn't: they had to attend a compulsory debriefing session – immediately. It was 2 a.m.

'My jaw nearly dropped off. I said, "What, at this hour?" I think the whole business of critical incident stress debriefing after Port Arthur got completely out of hand.'

By the Tuesday morning, relatives of those killed began to arrive at the hospital from across Australia to identify their loved ones. Again, it was the nursing team who faced the grim task of jotting down the description provided by the relatives and matching it to those meticulously compiled in the morgue the night before. Once a match had been made, the body would then be retrieved for the family to identify. A ward was emptied for the identification process, since the morgue was so small and depressing. The cancellation of non-urgent surgery in the wake of the massacre meant that it was not hard to find the space.

As Bryan remembers it, they only got one identification 'match' wrong and retrieved the wrong body. 'Every other one we brought up was the correct body for them to identify. Then there was a tremendous amount of grief counselling and support to deal with around that.'

A large part of what kept the medical team going in the face of such intense emotional strain was the many gestures of overwhelming generosity. From early Monday, local restaurants and bakeries were supplying trays of free food to the hospital staff. By Tuesday, almost an entire shift of nurses and doctors arrived by bus from the Launceston General Hospital, 200 km north of Hobart, to relieve the exhausted Hobart crew. By the middle of the week, a team of senior doctors and nurses had also arrived from Melbourne, with Qantas providing free airfares, a local hotel organising free accommodation and the Tasmanian medical board waiving the normal registration requirements so they could set to work.

'It was excellent, because it actually meant we could stop and have a cup of coffee and a bit of a talk about it. We could go home to our families for a while. It was one of the most practical, heartwarming things that happened,' Bryan recalls.

The exemplary performance of the Royal Hobart Hospital staff after being put to the ultimate test most likely saved the hospital from being sold off. Before the massacre, the hospital had been under attack for being over-budget and there were rumblings it might be privatised. The government had already taken the step of restructuring the hospital into saleable 'business units' as part of an 'efficiency' drive. Bryan believes its ability to have six theatres, 25 surgeons, fifteen anaesthetists and twelve intensive care beds all up and running within minutes showed the immense public value of the institution.

'It had a really profound effect on the hospital because, you know, we'd faced something that really nobody in peacetime had ever faced in Australia before. It absolutely tested every single aspect of the hospital and yes, it came up trumps.' Today, suffering the funding squeeze of most public hospitals, the outside of the Royal Hobart Hospital looks rundown and parts of its interior are badly dated and in desperate need of a fresh coat of paint, but the reputation of its staff for medical excellence remains.

During the immediate response to the shootings, Bryan retained the professional detachment that allowed him to attend to the dead and wounded without the fog of his own emotions. It was to be the sight of a weeping Walter Mikac as he left Hobart's St David's Cathedral which finally broke his composure.

As the head of emergency medicine at the Royal Hobart Hospital until 1995, Bryan had developed a tough hide. He had to. Years of exposure to human injury and illness has left him with the slightly gruff, even blunt, manner common among emergency service workers, but to dismiss Bryan as standoffish belies his warm sense of humour and concern for others. The emergency bays at the Royal Hobart Hospital may not be the place for fragile hearts, but Bryan rediscovered his in a moment that was to help change a nation.

Dressed in his white medical coat, with a balding head and a closely cropped grey beard, Bryan resembled both a Lutheran pastor and a family doctor as he emerged from the Port Arthur memorial service on the Wednesday after the massacre.

As he moved down the sandstone steps, his eyes fell on a sobbing Walter Mikac who, with his head bowed, looked as if he might crumple to the ground were it not for one arm being supported by his brother and the other by a best friend. The scene was too much for Bryan who, having been absorbed in the aftermath of the shootings himself, was briefly overcome with empathy for the bereft young father.

As grief tightened his chest and he fought back the welling tears, Bryan saw a familiar figure walking towards him. Prime Minister John Howard, who was just two months into his first term in office, grasped Bryan's shoulder firmly, leaned towards him and whispered brief words of comfort.

Bryan's composure unravelled and, as the tears finally came, the cameras of the media waiting outside the cathedral captured the moment on film. The image of Prime Minister Howard comforting a distraught medico – a potent symbol of those who had worked the frontline – was published in newspapers around the country.

Bryan hadn't planned to wear professional clothing to the memorial service that day. He would have preferred to just blend into the crowd, but his medical director suggested he wear a white coat and a stethoscope so that he visibly represented the hospital's medical team. It was a uniform which instantly drew the sympathetic eye of the nation's most powerful political figure and, in one split, serendipitous second, Bryan would be given a significant tool with which to pursue his long-held belief that Australia needed tighter gun controls.

'John Howard was walking the line and he fixed me with his eye. I had never met him before in my life...but he just came up and sort of put his arm around me as if to say, "There, there old fellow, everything will be alright" and suddenly I was blinded by about 50 flashes going off.

'I said, "Oh, thanks very much" and shook his hand and he wandered on down the line and I completely recovered. It was one of those defining moments when the sadness of the whole thing overcame me, but if he hadn't transfixed me with his eye, it might not have happened. It was just one of those things.'

Bryan didn't know it then, but the image of this embrace was to raise his personal profile well beyond Tasmania, which in turn focused further attention on a series of gun control rallies that he was invited to address in the weeks after the shootings.

Lobbying for stricter gun control was not new to Bryan. He had spent the previous 25 years trying to change Australia's inconsistent and in some cases frighteningly lax gun ownership laws.

Before Martin Bryant cut loose in the most dramatic and lethal manner, calls for tighter gun laws had fallen on deaf ears. No political party, it seemed, was willing to take on the pro-gun and sporting shooters' lobbies, which could wield significant power in critical rural seats.

Yet medical professionals like Bryan had spent decades dealing with the tragic consequences of these laws, be they fatal hunting accidents, suicides or attempted murder. Bryan recounts a story from the 1980s when he was working at the Footscray District Hospital in Victoria and a 22-year-old woman was brought in by ambulance after being shot through the groin. She had been simply walking with her baby daughter near a vacant block in suburban Sunshine when a bullet ripped through the fence, kept going and plunged into her upper thigh. The wound severed an artery and she bled to death. The unsuspecting killer was a middle-aged man who had been collecting high-powered firearms for some time and who occasionally used the vacant block for shooting practice.

'I remember thinking at the time, what on earth was this man doing with a range of high-powered weapons in a shed when he's a suburban factory worker? I mean he wasn't even a sporting shooter or something.'

Bryan at that time wrote a discussion paper on the gun control issue for the Victorian branch of the Australian Medical Association and was part of a subcommittee which drew up a national firearms policy for the AMA. It was 1982, a full fourteen years before the Port Arthur shootings, and there was little movement towards national uniform gun laws.

When Bryan relocated to Tasmania in 1984, he found a state that, despite a population of less than half a million, had the highest number of firearm suicides in the nation. At that time, about 80 Tasmanians a year were choosing to die by a gun: double the national average. Bryan studied the statistics closely. 'When we looked at those, they were nearly all impulsive; they were nearly all sporting weapons that had been left sitting around the house and they were nearly all young people [who were suiciding].'

The shameful figures prompted Bryan, together with Hobart lawyer Roland Browne and a group of like-minded supporters, to form the Tasmanian Coalition for Gun Control, which campaigned widely and loudly across Tasmania in the late 1980s and early 1990s.

The coalition campaign was instrumental in making sure gun control was at least part of the political discussion in Tasmania and, by the early 1990s, the Tasmanian Greens, in particular, were pushing hard for legislative change.

It took the previously unthinkable scenario that unfolded on 28 April, however, before the state – and the nation – was shaken from its complacency about firearms in the community.

After the image of John Howard embracing Bryan was published around Australia, Bryan found himself something of a celebrity. He was invited to speak before crowds of several thousand people in gun control rallies in Sydney, Melbourne and Hobart and also gave inter-state lectures on the medical response to the crisis. Particularly grat-ifying was his involvement in a round-table conference at the federal Parliament House in Canberra, where he was able to speak directly to then Attorney-General, Daryl Williams, about the government's proposed legislation for tighter gun control in the wake of the massacre. A separate meeting in Canberra of all the state police ministers, held shortly after the massacre, also gave Bryan and other members of what was by then the National Coalition for Gun Control an opportunity to speak directly with some of the heavyweight journalists sent to cover what had become a highly topical event. 'Even [the high-profile, conservative News Limited columnist] Piers

Akerman was amazed and wrote positive articles,' Bryan says with a laugh. It was a dramatic change from the years of trying to be heard, but getting nowhere.

'We realised we had this amazing opportunity. We could educate [the journalists] about the data, about how long we had been going and what policies we had and why you need the cooling-off period, and what was the problem of high-powered rifles and semi-automatic rifles, the issue of youth suicide…and so the next few days we got amazingly good coverage because we were actually able to get the message out.'

The subsequent gun laws and gun buyback amnesty – in which 600,000 firearms were handed in from across Australia – has, in Bryan's opinion, made a significant difference towards reducing mass shootings.

'If you look back before Port Arthur, there was something like 25 massacres where at least three people, including the perpetrator, were killed at once. In the ten years since, there has not been one,' Bryan says. 'What this did was put the focus squarely on firearms as a public health problem, and a public health solution – removing the agent – fixed the problem.'

The world of medicine remains important to Bryan Walpole, even though he was momentarily lured into the world of politics. A disgruntled former supporter of the Tasmanian Greens, Bryan was persuaded to run for the Australian Democrats at the 2002 Tasmanian state election. He agreed on one condition: that he had no chance of winning. The hook for the Democrats was the promise of almost guaranteed media coverage for his campaign, not because of Bryan's links to Port Arthur, but the fact that in 2002 he was in the middle of a twelve-month contract with the Australian Antarctic Division on remote Macquarie Island, a speck in the ocean south of Tasmania. His distant posting made for quirky stories during an otherwise lacklustre election campaign, with Labor dominating the opinion polls, and gave the Australian Democrats coverage in a state in which they are virtually invisible.

'It was great fun because it was mid-winter and a fairly cold, bleak and dark time down [on Macquarie Island] and it really livened things up,' Bryan says. As part of his 'campaign', Bryan threw an election party in which his small band of colleagues were encouraged to dress as their favourite politician. Four came as Bryan, with shaved heads, outsized glasses and fake beards. He eventually polled 685 votes – 'a number that I could go around and thank them, *all*, individually' – and was delighted with the result. 'I was the only person in the state on election night who was thrilled not to be elected.'

When we speak, he is back at the Royal Hobart Hospital training overseas doctors for practice in Tasmania. The state remains at least 100 doctors short in Bryan's view. When he is not involved in retraining overseas doctors, he is helping teach the new brigade of medicos coming up through the ranks of the University of Tasmania. He also performs a day or two of clinical work each week at the Hobart Private Hospital which sits next door to the Royal Hobart Hospital. This is Bryan, at 60, slowing down.

The gun control issue for now, however, is off his agenda. Bryan occasionally sees his former Tasmanian Coalition for Gun Control lobby colleague Roland Browne around Hobart, but has no active involvement in any campaigns.

He also, he says, rarely thinks or speaks about his experiences in the aftermath of Port Arthur: the professional detachment has returned.

'I see two or three of my colleagues [at the hospital] every now and then, but we've never really mentioned it because I think, you know, for most of us it was just a day in your life – an extraordinary one – but a day.'

12

THE PERFECT STORM: MARTIN BRYANT

Martin Bryant may have intended to die in a hail of bullets at Port Arthur, or when he later set fire to the Seascape cottage, but he is among rare company in gunning down scores of people without then taking his own life. Many massacres come to an end through the perpetrator killing themselves – many wish Bryant had.

Despite having been imprisoned in Hobart's Risdon Prison for ten years, Bryant, who will turn 39 in May 2006, remains an enigma. He has never made any public confession as to why he carried out the massacre, or shown any significant remorse.

It is impossible to ask Bryant about regret or motive directly, as the Tasmanian Government does not allow media interviews with high-security Risdon inmates. The scale of Bryant's crime places him particularly off-limits.

'I just wish the fucking cunt would die,' said one state government media adviser when I asked about the possibility of interviewing Bryant. I took that as a 'no'.

In the absence of Bryant's own explanation, medical professionals have tried to piece together what sort of human being could be capable of such a heinous act. Some questioned whether Bryant could be considered human at all. Others just wanted Bryant to disappear and, by not mentioning him again, perhaps they could convince themselves he had.

In late 1999, a coffee-table magazine, *Australian Style*, published a collection of photographic portraits under the title 'Stars of the 20th Century' which featured famous and infamous figures. The diverse collection ranged from larger-than-life personalities such as Kylie Minogue and Mel Gibson, through to the corrupt former New South Wales detective, Roger Rogerson.

Opposite a beer-swigging portrait of former Prime Minister Bob Hawke, there is a page devoted to Martin Bryant under the title 'The Reaper'. The blurb reads, in part:

> Bryant's act was so dreadful, so hard for even the professionals to fathom, that the authorities don't want to believe it anymore. So they're erasing it. They exile journalists, shut down websites. They're packing up history and wishing it away. It won't work.

The piece goes on: 'We shouldn't forget Bryant. Let's talk of the prick, violently. Until every village idiot gets the message.'

Above the words there is no photograph, just a blank, white space with a date in black numerals: 28.4.96.

The public has not seen a photograph of Martin Bryant since his imprisonment, other than a grainy video image screened live from Risdon Prison during part of his trial. His face today, like the man himself, is a mystery.

One of the few people who got to know Bryant after the massacre was his Hobart lawyer, John Avery. Avery, a bearded, ruddy-cheeked man with a beguiling sense of humour, gives the impression he is keen to share his insights, but he is prevented from doing so by lawyer–client confidentiality for as long as Bryant lives – and perhaps beyond. Avery at first agreed, and then later declined to be interviewed for this book. He has intimated he may eventually write his own book on the Bryant case, which catapulted him from a small-town lawyer into the national spotlight. He remains a high-profile criminal lawyer in Hobart, where he still takes on some of the state's most controversial cases.

In the immediate aftermath of the massacre, thousands of words were written about Martin Bryant, as reporters scoured the streets of Hobart and the farms along the Tasman Peninsula for anyone who might have, if only briefly, known the 'monster' responsible. Within days, contradictory pictures of Bryant had emerged as the media tried to piece together clues about his past. He was, according to some reports, obsessed with guns, cruel to animals and a sociopath who feasted on a diet of pornographic videos, military magazines and violent films. To others, Bryant was a slightly weird, but seemingly harmless and lonely soul, who spent his days wandering the neighbourhoods of inner suburban Hobart in search of someone to talk to.

In light of the carnage caused by Bryant, the media was compelled to try to find answers for a nation grappling to make sense of it all. Soon there were reports of Bryant being schizophrenic, which, without anyone actually saying so, brought almost a collective sigh of relief: the enormity of his crimes could all be put down to a neat, identifiable mental illness, rather than an act for which there was no explanation.

Others spoke of the massacre being linked to Bryant's apparent obsession with violent films, while one newspaper made much of his penchant for sleeping with pigs. There were also suggestions he had murdered before, with rumour and suspicion surrounding the suicide of his father and the death by car accident of his closest friend, Helen Harvey.

All these chunks of information helped to build an acceptable picture of what sort of depraved man could commit such atrocities. In the eyes of the public, Bryant had to be a non-human, a monster, someone with a deviant mind and a deprived background who was destined to kill.

It was a shock, then, when the first photograph of Martin Bryant was splashed across the front page of every News Limited newspaper on the Tuesday after the massacre. The image was not that of a crazed lunatic – a clichéd, Unabomber-type character with unkempt hair and dirty clothes – but a blond-haired, blue-eyed Aussie surfer with a gentle face and relaxed stance. In that image and those published since, Bryant looked anything but a killer. In his faded sloppy joe and tracksuit pants he was just like 'the lad next door' and that made him all the more terrifying. From appearance alone, there was not a single clue as to what was going on inside his mind.

Publishing the first photo of Bryant was a journalistic coup for the Hobart daily newspaper, *The Mercury*, but how it came to be secured caused a major ruction between the Tasmanian police force and the newspaper. As is normal practice for such a big story, two journalists – Stuart Potter and Sue Bailey – and a photographer, Fred Kohl, were immediately despatched to Bryant's New Town home once his name had leaked out to the newspaper. It was around 2 a.m. Sunday night and Bryant was still staging his stand-off with police at the Seascape Cottage.

By the time the reporters arrived at the Clare Street home, it was under police guard. The reporters, however, were under pressure to find out any details, however minor, of the man believed to be responsible for what was the biggest Australian crime story in years. The police patrolling the property allowed the trio into the front room of the house, where Bailey and Potter quickly surmised by the cluttered state of the place that Bryant's living conditions were, at the very least, unusual. While Bailey chatted amiably to the officers in the front room, Potter slipped quietly into the kitchen where, as luck would have it for him, there were numerous photographs laid out on a table. Dr Sale had noticed the same pile of photographs during his visit earlier in the night.

Taking photographs and being photographed in return had become one of Bryant's obsessions, so there were literally dozens of images spread out for the picking. Potter grabbed one of the many photographs of the thin, blond-haired man that stared up at him and discreetly made his exit; the police guard being none the wiser. Armed with the picture, Potter had to wait until the next morning to doorknock neighbours to confirm if the photo was in fact that of Martin Bryant. They confirmed it was. From a journalistic perspective, Potter had hit paydirt. From a police perspective, the newspaper had breached the rules of ethical behaviour.

On the Tuesday morning of 30 April, the tabloid-sized newspaper ran the photo poster-like across its entire front and back pages under a large headline: 'This is the man'. The accompanying story began each paragraph with 'This is the man...', printed in bold type, outlining in gritty terms what were still, at that stage, allegations. The Tasmanian Director of Public Prosecutions, Damian Bugg, QC, was furious and threatened *The Mercury* and *The Australian*, another News Limited publication which reproduced the same image, with contempt of court proceedings. While Mr Bugg expressed outrage at the actions of the newspapers, which he feared might have compromised any chance of a fair trial, the fact the papers printed the image just hours *before* Martin Bryant was charged at his hospital bedside with the first of the murders may have given the media a legal escape hatch. As it was, the matter was eventually dropped by the Director of Public Prosecutions after Bryant pleaded guilty.

The Australian also attracted its own, separate, criticism, since its reproduction of the photo enhanced the whites and dilated the pupils of Bryant's eyes, changing his facial expression from docile to wide-eyed and staring. The paper ran an apology for the distorted image, putting it down to a production error that arose from trying to remove a shadow from Bryant's face. There are those, however, who remain convinced it was a deliberate, if clumsy, attempt to make the suspect killer look more like the crazed man everyone believed he must be.

Bryant's story, however, is more complex than him simply being 'crazy' and does not provide any neat answers as to why he was capable of indiscriminate slaughter. Instead, it was a unique combination of factors that led to his unleashing of such a violent force on 28 April 1996.

Martin John Bryant was born on 7 May 1967 and was still a toddler when his parents, Carleen and Maurice, began to notice there was something not quite right with their first child. His speech was slow to develop and he was showing signs of hyperactivity. What was tiring behaviour at home became unacceptable behaviour at school and, shortly after enrolling at the respected Hobart Quaker school, Friends, he was in trouble for being disruptive, aggressive and antisocial.

A change of school to New Town Primary brought little relief for the Bryants, as Martin continued to misbehave in class, bully his classmates and demand attention from all those around him. His irritating antics earned him the schoolyard nickname 'Silly Martin'.

So worried were his parents, who by this stage were also caring for a second child, Lindy, that they sought professional advice on how to deal with their son. Medication and a special diet for hyperactive children were tried, but had little effect. Bryant was barely eleven years old when he was first suspended from New Town Primary School for his delinquent behaviour.

Shortly after Bryant was banned from school, Carleen and Maurice again sought help with their son, who by now was also making life extremely difficult for his little sister with his bullying and, at times, inappropriate sexual behaviour. Assessments by the Hobart Diagnostic Centre, which were later included in a report for Bryant's defence lawyer by Melbourne forensic psychiatrist Paul Mullen, revealed Bryant's continued slow speech development and, more disturbingly, a tendency to torture and harass animals.

Bryant was barely coping academically and, after moving into New Town High School, was placed in a special education unit where at least his behaviour could be better managed.

When asked later by Professor Mullen what his memories were of school, Bryant would not recall the usual playground experiences of games with friends, only years of loneliness and misery from which he tried to escape. At times he would refuse to go to school, or pretend to his mother he was ill, because, he said, he was 'terrified' of being bullied. His own behaviour was not mentioned. 'I was hazed and knocked around all the time. Nobody wanted to be my friend,' he told Professor Mullen.

Bryant would remember having only one schoolfriend, Greg Lahey, and even that friendship was fraught with difficulties around Bryant's often inappropriate antics. His odd behaviour included pretending to stab Greg with a fishing spear during dive trips and, on several occasions, aiming an unloaded air rifle at him and pulling the trigger. Bryant's aggressive behaviour soon brought an end to the friendship. Bryant spent most of his school years alone, as other children found his bullying and hyperactivity increasingly irritating.

A UK relative of Bryant's British-born father would later tell the media that Bryant was 'a nice boy', but 'there was something lacking': 'He would just do as he wanted and sometimes he didn't know right from wrong.'

Bryant's poor academic performance and lack of social skills made it obvious to his parents that he would not be able to continue at school beyond the compulsory attendance age of fifteen and that he was even less likely to be able to hold down a permanent job.

With this in mind, the Bryants had their son assessed for a disability pension while he was still a teenager. It was a misunderstanding of this diagnosis, prepared by clinical psychiatrist Dr Eric Cunningham-Dax, that was to lead to a perception within the Bryant family that Martin was schizophrenic. It was a false impression that was to stay with the extended family right up to and beyond the events at Port Arthur. Even as police negotiators and psychiatrists sat talking with Bryant on the phone hook-up to Seascape, they believed they were dealing with a schizophrenic man, based on what they had been told by a relative of Bryant's at the time. The misconception, while genuinely believed by the family, proved confusing for the negotiators, who saw no evidence of schizophrenia in their conversations with Bryant.

The report by Dr Cunningham-Dax in fact found that Bryant was suffering some form of personality disorder, that he was intellectually handicapped and that he was *at risk* of perhaps developing a schizophrenic illness later in life. Carleen Bryant read the report as confirming that her son was indeed a schizophrenic. She was to later pass her assessment on to two other general practitioners who treated Bryant some years later, with the result that Bryant's medical files referred to his suffering schizophrenia when this had not, and has never, been diagnosed.

After the massacre, Dr Ian Sale was asked to prepare a psychological assessment of Bryant for the Director of Public Prosecutions, for which he sought the advice of clinical psychiatrist Noele Page.

Bryant refused to be interviewed by Dr Page, but by viewing his past medical and educational history, she concluded that Bryant displayed evidence of some form of frontal lobe dysfunction. This section of his brain was simply not working normally, which would explain, at least in part, his slow learning and impulsive behaviour as a child.

In his report, Dr Sale explained that people with such frontal lobe dysfunction often had bland and superficial personalities and showed a distinct lack of guilt, conscience or remorse.

A separate assessment of Bryant after the massacre, by Victorian forensic psychiatrist Ian Joblin, would find that he had an IQ of 66 – the equivalent of that of an eleven-year-old child. Another test, comparing his ability in a specific task to that of most eleven year olds, again showed Bryant to be at the bottom end of the intellectual scale. His performance on that test showed that 90 per cent of eleven year olds would have scored higher than him.

All of this was unknown to Carleen and Maurice Bryant at the time they were dealing with their demanding teenage son. As Martin grew older, physically stronger and more of a handful, it was Maurice who felt himself best placed to cope with Martin's erratic and increasingly embarrassing behaviour. He would try to keep his son occupied by taking him crayfishing, diving and horseriding down on the Tasman Peninsula, where the family had a holiday property at Carnarvon Bay, just south of Port Arthur. It was during this time that Maurice was forced to confiscate his son's air rifle after Martin saw nothing wrong with taking shots at passing tourists.

The Bryants' family doctor would later comment that it was Maurice who kept Martin Bryant's violent tendencies in check. As part of an assessment in 1991 to see if Martin could still be considered eligible for his disability pension, the GP made the comment that Martin's 'father protects him from any occasion which would upset him, as he continually threatens violence'.

The GP then added prophetically, 'Martin tells me he likes to go around shooting people'.

Maurice, a Hobart wharfie, eventually took early retirement to help his son keep busy through a small business of gardening and selling vegetables and fresh rabbits to locals around their New Town neighbourhood. One of their best customers was an eccentric, wealthy woman who lived with her elderly mother in a sprawling house in Clare Street, which was within walking distance from the Bryant family home in Augusta Road. Helen Mary Harvey was to become – and remain – Bryant's only close friend. Her wealth, however, was to inadvertently play its own part in Bryant eventually acting out his violent 'shooting people' fantasy with devastating consequences.

Bryant's friendship with Helen Harvey was well documented after the massacre, in court transcripts, media coverage and in Tasmanian journalist Mike Bingham's 1996 book, *Suddenly One Sunday*.

When Bryant and his father met Helen in the mid-1980s, she was barely coping with the demands of caring for her immobile mother, Hilza, and the two-storey mansion in which the pair lived at 30 Clare Street, New Town. The grounds surrounding 'Wibruna' were overgrown, the house itself was squalid, teeming with cats and dogs and the Harvey women had retreated to just two rooms, filling the remainder with a voluminous array of clutter.

It was the sort of forbidding, unkempt house that would attract the finger-pointing and stares of local schoolchildren, and the complaints of neighbours for its foul odours and overgrown garden.

Helen herself, by then a stout, 40-something woman, was known around New Town as a kind-hearted, if slightly bossy, eccentric who was never short of money. As an heiress to George Adams's Tattersalls lottery fortune, she received monthly payments totalling more than $150,000 a year and she wasn't afraid to spend it. With a bottomless income and nobody to shower it on, money had little meaning. Rather than buy a few videos, for example, Helen would buy dozens, including many of the same film and some that would remain unopened in their shrink-wrap. She would also think nothing of spending wads of cash on a new car then, if she was between cheques from the George Adams Trust, selling it to make ends meet before buying another one. In one incident, after she met Bryant, she reversed a brand-new $28,000 car into a tree. The pair patched up the damage with house paint and sold the car shortly after for $7000. Registration records would show Helen owned more than 50 cars in her life.

Maurice and Martin became closely entwined with Helen's bizarre world after she and her mother were no longer able to cope in the rundown home and were admitted to hospital in mid-1990. In their absence, the two men agreed to help clean the house to comply with an official order from the Hobart City Council. It was a filthy, time-consuming job, but the Bryants managed to make the place at least habitable. Hilza Harvey was to die in hospital only a month after being admitted, but Helen returned home and, unable to cope with the huge property on her own, agreed to have Martin move in.

They made the perfect odd couple. He was the childlike 23 year old who needed constant attention, and she the 47-year-old lonely eccentric with both time and money to share. Bryant would later describe their relationship as involving 'kisses and cuddles', but it was primarily a non-sexual friendship in which two social misfits, isolated from the mainstream world, could create their own. It was a place of chaos and indulgence; a world where Helen and Bryant could surround themselves with a malodorous menagerie of feral cats and dogs, yet dine in a top restaurant to celebrate a birthday. Helen would boss Bryant about as he trailed behind her during their outings, but Bryant, feeling for the first time in his life like he had an independent identity beyond that of his family, was content.

It was October 1991 when the pair decided to move from Clare Street to Helen's country property at Copping, a farming hamlet made up of little more than a smattering of houses, a convict museum and a service station, halfway between Hobart and Port Arthur. Here they expanded their 'family' to include a variety of birds, dogs, cats, miniature horses and pigs which roamed freely around their property. Even in rural Tasmania, which has more than a healthy share of eccentric characters, Helen and her young companion stood out, not least for their drives accompanied by a miniature pony or two in the back seat of their car. Bryant, in contrast to his childhood behaviour of tormenting animals, appeared to relish farm life.

It was from this time that the story about his sleeping with a pig emerged. As Crown Prosecutor Damian Bugg was to later tell the Supreme Court, Bryant did cuddle a pet piglet at night to keep it warm and continued to do so until the pig grew too large to manage. 'I suppose since seeing [the children's film about a pet pig] *Babe*, not too many people would take a critical view of that,' Mr Bugg said.

The media, however, did take a different view, hinting at bestiality as further evidence of what they saw as Bryant's depravity.

It wasn't this odd, but ultimately harmless, behaviour on the farm that provided an insight into what was still stirring within Bryant, despite the sense of belonging that Helen added to his life. The clues came from neighbours who remembered Bryant's aggressive outbursts. In one case, a mother and daughter living on a nearby farm accepted an invitation from Helen to join her for a cup of tea, only to have Bryant order them off the property and threaten to shoot them if they returned. It is testament to Bryant's erratic character, however, that other Copping locals would remember him as 'slow', but cheerful. If anything, he mostly came across to others as being deeply lonely. While he felt a sense of security with Helen, Bryant, who was 24, still yearned to be like the young men he saw around him: enjoying a carefree life full of cars, beer, mates and girlfriends. Bryant stood on the other side of the looking glass. He didn't have a licence, his best friend was an offbeat, middle-aged woman with whom he drank tea and, despite being in his twenties, he was yet to have a serious girlfriend. Bryant's sexual encounters were restricted to monthly, anonymous visits to escort agencies. Despite his access to Helen's money and companionship, Bryant was still an outsider.

The stability that Helen's slightly dictatorial manner gave to Bryant's life came to an unexpected end just a year after they moved to Copping. Helen and Bryant were returning from a shopping trip in nearby Sorell, when, about 6 km from their home, Helen's Mazda 121 veered onto the wrong side of the road and collided head-on with another vehicle. Helen died instantly, while Bryant was seriously injured and admitted to hospital with head and spinal injuries.

The local talk quickly turned to accusations that Bryant had caused the accident by lunging at the steering wheel while Helen was driving. Helen had complained of this before, telling Tasman Mayor Neil Noye that Bryant was prone to such 'silly' pranks and that she was at a loss as to how to control his errant behaviour. Bryant would later explain that the accident happened while he was trying to separate two of their dogs that were fighting on the back seat. Helen's driving ability was also questioned after an accident six months previously in which she was rear-ended after braking for a kangaroo, but some locals were convinced that Bryant was responsible for the fatal crash.

Despite the accusations, Bryant appeared extremely distressed by Helen's death and was prescribed medication by his family doctor after complaining of recurring nightmares and anxiety attacks after the crash. There are some who still firmly believe that Helen was Bryant's first victim. Such a theory doesn't explain, however, why Bryant would want to kill the one person whom he would later recall as his only true friend in life.

Helen's death on 20 October 1992 led to significant changes in Bryant's life. First, his father, having separated from Carleen, moved into the Copping property to take care of things. Bryant lost the sense of independence he had had with Helen and was, like a child, back under the care and control of his father. At the same time, Bryant became extremely wealthy as the sole beneficiary of Helen's estate. When her will was executed in June 1993, Bryant inherited hundreds of thousands of dollars worth of property and savings, although he never quite grasped the extent of his wealth. In his bizarre lifestyle with Helen, money was never important: it was always there.

Despite Martin's newfound wealth, he continued to live simply with Maurice, enjoying the rural lifestyle he remembered sharing with his father as a child. Then, on 14 August 1993, just ten months after Helen was killed, Maurice Bryant went missing. He was found two days later, weighed down in a 2-metre-deep dam on the Copping farm.

Again the local gossip put Bryant in the frame for murder, particularly after his reaction to Maurice's death appeared in gross contrast to that of a grieving son. As the police were searching the property for his father, Bryant busied himself by trimming long grass along the fence lines. Later, having been asked to identify the body hauled from the dam, Bryant was seen laughing as he returned from his grim task. It was the same, completely inappropriate, emotional reaction that he was to express three years later as 35 charges of murder were read to him in the Hobart Supreme Court.

The rumour mill had also generated a widespread belief that Maurice Bryant had been found with a gunshot wound to his body, but this was false. It was one of numerous rumours that swept Tasmania after Bryant's arrest for the massacre and in the context of a statewide media blackout. The seven-month media blackout meant Tasmanians received only the most cursory details of the case leading up to the November trial. Not surprisingly, without access to the information being reported interstate, Tasmanians passed on their own snippets of gossip and untested theories, some of which, as rumours tend to do, became 'fact' through repetition.

It later emerged that Maurice Bryant had battled depression for many years and, despite receiving psychiatric care, his mental health had continued to decline. He had turned to his family doctor for help with anxiety and depression but, by mid-1993, had decided he no longer wished to live. In an almost clinical preparation for his death, Maurice Bryant began to put his affairs in order: he made arrangements for the Public Trustee to monitor his son's financial affairs under the *Mental Health Act* and he transferred his bank account and utilities into his wife Carleen's name.

Although Maurice was separated from Carleen, he telephoned her twice from the Copping property on the day of his death. He seemed confused and distressed and Carleen was worried about his intentions. Sometime after speaking to Carleen, Maurice wrote a note which he pinned to the front door of the farm house. It said simply: 'call the police'.

Despite suggestions that Martin Bryant didn't get along with his father, he would, in an interview with psychiatrist Paul Mullen after the massacre, describe him as 'a nice, quiet, friendly man' with whom he had a good relationship. Being under suspicion of killing both his father and Helen added to Bryant's sense of isolation from a world in which he had always struggled to fit in. Worse, the two critical anchors to an otherwise directionless life had slipped away. There was nobody to stabilise Bryant's unpredictable behaviour. The storm clouds of an increasingly disturbed mind were beginning to gather.

After his father's death, Bryant left the Copping farm and moved back to the Clare Street property which he now owned. Carleen attempted to move in and care for him, but Bryant was having none of it. He didn't share the same close relationship with his mother as that he'd had with his father and saw her attempts to help him as smothering.

Clare Street was home, but Bryant began to feel uncomfortable there. He would later tell Professor Mullen that the big, empty house had strange vibes; that he would hear noises in the night and that he believed it was haunted. In the six months leading up to the massacre, he occasionally heard women's voices as he lay in bed alone at night. They would say only brief phrases, such as 'Come on' or 'Here', but it was enough to frighten him and compound his sense of loneliness.

The one means Bryant could use to try to escape his isolation was money. In a delusory attempt to make friends, he would buy tickets to destinations around the world: not to experience the delights of foreign countries, but to connect with fellow passengers as they sat trapped in their seats on long-haul flights from Australia.

What became an excessive amount of travel began in December 1993, less than six months after Maurice's death. Bryant's first trip was a test run: a three-day holiday in Singapore. The following April, feeling more confident, he flew from Melbourne to Bangkok and on to London, then, after only a few days in the United Kingdom, travelled to Sweden. From Sweden, he flew back to the United Kingdom and then on to the United States. It was a frenetic pattern that was to be repeated over and over again as Bryant crisscrossed the globe in a desperate yet misguided search for companionship.

When not travelling overseas, Bryant would fly around Australia. Between 1993 and late 1995, he took dozens of short, interstate trips, sometimes barely staying a day in one place before flying to another. Such was his patronage of the airlines, they would despatch complimentary taxis to his Clare Street home to escort him to the Hobart airport: Bryant was an excellent customer.

In search of friendship, Bryant could not have chosen a more isolating experience than travelling alone at length to foreign countries. There is a particular loneliness to standing in a foreign country as anonymous crowds rush by, keen to get on with their own business and suspicious of strangers wanting to make small talk. Without the social skills to engage people beyond a simple conversation, Bryant became increasingly bitter about people's apparent unwillingness to connect with him, no matter where in the world he might be. 'I wanted to meet up with normal people. It didn't work,' he would say to Professor Mullen of his travels.

Even this one clumsy outlet for Bryant's frustrations, however, was to be curtailed after the Public Trustee committee overseeing his finances expressed concern at the amount of money being spent on seemingly frivolous travel. It was early 1996 when Bryant was told his overseas travel would be limited to one or two trips a year.

One of his last international trips was a six-day visit to London in January 1996, just three months before the massacre. On the 24-hour flight home to Melbourne, he sat next to a Hobart woman, Rachel Lee, whom he declared he was going to marry. Ms Lee would recall him telling her how shaken he was by his father's death and how he had 'not been able to work since'. He was, she later told reporters, 'very sweet and gentle, but really intense'. His marriage proposal was, again, a telling sign that Bryant was becoming unhinged as he faced continual rejections which he couldn't understand. He was well-dressed, he was rich and he was, in his mind, friendly: why didn't people like him?

In the twelve months leading up to the massacre on 28 April, Bryant's life had been sliding into a downward spiral. His overseas travels were unfulfilling and, although he was 28 years old, he still struggled to maintain an intimate relationship with anybody. Bryant didn't know how to behave towards women and would often make inappropriate comments that didn't so much frighten women as make them think he was a pathetic loser.

Bryant began to drink more heavily, shifting from drinking only occasionally to, in the six months before the shootings, drinking every day. Often he would take his first alcoholic drink in the morning and then continue throughout the day, with a preference for sweet, strong drinks such as Bailey's Irish Cream or the aniseed-flavoured Sambuca. He drank, he would later explain, to relieve his loneliness and pass the empty hours. The alcohol, however, only heightened his depression.

In the winter of 1995, despite a growing feeling of resentment towards the world and the wrongs he saw within it, Bryant did meet a girl who was prepared to try some form of relationship. Jenetta Hoani was a seventeen-year-old Hobart TAFE student when she and Bryant met through the friendship of their mothers. The pair dated casually for eight months, but Jenetta, a striking girl with long, dark, curly hair, had tired of Bryant's immature and often bizarre ways long before the relationship ended. She stuck with him until January 1996, she later said, because of the sort of things that matter in a boyfriend when you are seventeen: his body and his money.

During their time together, Jenetta would later tell the media, Bryant would make strange sexual suggestions as he began to explore his sexuality beyond the realm of escorts. He would talk about bestiality and, at other times, express interest in the young men cavorting by a hotel swimming pool. He flirted with the idea of threesomes and golden showers and at one stage shaved his chest to make himself more feminine. It was as if Bryant was a curious, prepubescent boy – the budding eleven year old of his IQ – discovering the gamut of sexual possibilities and wanting to try them all, if only in boast.

It was Jenetta who would also reveal Bryant's love of violent movies, particularly *Child's Play 2* featuring an evil, murderous doll, Chucky. It was a different picture to the one Bryant later painted of himself in interviews with Professor Mullen. He nominated as his favourite music anything by Cliff Richard, and the soundtrack to the children's movie, *The Lion King*. His favourite movie, he said, was *Babe*, followed by Steven Seagal action films and the thriller, *The Protector*. Despite the desire to trawl through films and songs to find clues to Bryant's sudden violent behaviour, the answer as to why he would murder dozens of people was not made clear by his video and music collection.

Nor was it obvious from the magazines and jottings found in his house after the massacre. Aside from a couple of military-style magazines sold at news stands, police could find no evidence of a person capable of committing mass murder. When Dr Sale uncovered a diary in the house, he was prepared for it to be full of paranoid ravings but, he said, there 'was not a sausage'. It contained, instead, details of Bryant's rigorous exercise routine.

By the time Bryant met Petra Wilmott, a seventeen-year-old horticulture student who lived a sheltered life in Tasmania's Huon Valley, he was already preparing to kill. Petra, who has since avoided all public attention, casually dated Bryant for about eight weeks and spent the night before the massacre with him.

Bryant was Petra's first boyfriend and, judging by photographs taken of her by Bryant just days before the massacre, they appeared happy together. Bryant, however, had decided at least twelve months earlier that life was no longer worth living. Although he had met Jenetta, he remained despondent, angry and resentful that people, in his mind, didn't appreciate his worth. The ending of his brief relationship with Jenetta only cemented this belief and Petra's attentions came all too late.

As Professor Mullen would later explain, Bryant was extremely self-absorbed, with a highly egocentric view of the world. Rather than feeling worthless, he felt he was not being appreciated for what he saw as his open, kind and generous ways. Instead, he believed people were against him and that, regardless of how he tried to reach out, he would be spurned.

Isolated and bored, Bryant had plenty of time to sit in the cluttered surrounds of 30 Clare Street, drinking and mulling over the many wrongs he felt he had suffered in life. Past humiliations became virtual obsessions as Bryant withdrew further into his own distorted view of the world as a cruel and lonely place.

'He said, "All I wanted was for people to like me". Their failure to respond to his overtures led him to feel "that I'd had a gutful",' Professor Mullen wrote in his report.

Among his obsessive thoughts were those around Seascape, the picturesque waterside property owned by David and Sally Martin on the Arthur Highway, 3 km from the Port Arthur site.

Bryant knew the Martins and their two sons well, having spent time at the Martins' second property, a farm on Palmers Lookout Road, which was not far from the Bryants' holiday home at Carnarvon Bay. Carleen Bryant would later tell Dr Ian Sale that, several years earlier, her husband had expressed an interest in buying Seascape after news filtered out that the elderly owner was keen to sell. Before Maurice was in a position to take any action on the sale, however, David Martin had already negotiated a deal to buy the property.

Years later, a cashed-up and cocky Bryant would make approaches to the Martins to buy their farm on Palmers Lookout Road, but the Martins had no reason to sell.

Being unable to buy a particular property would not, to a clear-thinking person, represent much more than a disappointment, but to Martin Bryant it became the nucleus of a growing and irrational hatred towards the world. The Martins, in his mind, were standing between him and 'happiness' in buying the farm, just as they had, in his view, stripped his father of his chance to buy Seascape. From the viewpoint of an eleven-year-old mind, this disappointment was an explanation as to why Maurice, Bryant's only real companion at the time, would drown himself in a dam.

As Carleen later explained to Dr Sale, Bryant held deep, unrelenting grudges. Professor Paul Mullen would go further, saying

Bryant had the type of rigid personality that, once having decided on a course of revenge, would stick with it, despite the impact his actions would have on himself or others.

From the second floor of 30 Clare Street, Martin Bryant had a clear view across the tiled rooftops of the 1940s red-brick homes that line the inner streets of New Town, into the front window of Terry Hill's firearms shop, Guns and Ammo. It once traded at 93B New Town Road, in a square-fronted building later used by a pet-grooming business.

At the time Hill operated his gun shop, Tasmania was awash with firearms and had the weakest gun laws in the country. If you were an adult without any major criminal convictions in the last eight years, you could apply for a gun licence that lasted for life, requiring only an updated photograph every ten years. Owning a gun was part of Tasmania's rural culture, where children – including Bryant – were exposed early to the possum, rabbit, deer or duck hunting trips that still make up a large part of life in many of the state's remote communities.

As an adult, Bryant didn't have a gun licence – he felt he lacked the intellect to apply for one – but he had the money.

In his statement to police after the massacre, Terry Hill said he had had 'spasmodic' dealings with Bryant, whom he said he knew as Martin Ryan. They first met, he said, when Bryant was a teenager and interested in air rifles. By early 1996, Bryant's interest in firearms had graduated to far more serious weapons. According to Hill's statement, Bryant walked into his shop in March 1996, just a month before the massacre, with an Armalite AR10 military rifle covered by a towel. The gun, Bryant complained, had something wrong with it. Hill took the rifle from Bryant and was shocked to find it loaded.

Hill said he then asked Bryant if he had a licence for the weapon and Bryant produced a Tasmanian photographic gun licence with the name Martin Ryan on it. Bryant, according to Hill, produced this same licence the last time he saw him, on

Wednesday, 24 April – just four days before the massacre. On that day, Hill said, Bryant purchased three boxes of Winchester shells.

Hill maintained he never sold Bryant any guns and that he handed over the faulty AR10, left behind by Bryant for repair, to police on 30 April after he recognised Bryant's face on the front page of *The Mercury*.

Bryant, however, gave a different version of events to Detective Inspectors Ross Paine and John Warren when they interviewed him at Risdon Prison on 4 July.

According to Bryant, he bought two guns from Hill in the two months leading up to the massacre. The first was the Colt AR15 with a scope, which he went on to use at Port Arthur. The second was a Daewoo 12-gauge shotgun which he took with him to the historic site, but never used because it had previously 'frightened' him. The Daewoo cost $3000 and the Colt AR15 was $5000, including a scope, a shoulder strap and some extra ammunition thrown in. Bryant paid for both guns in cash.

During his interview with the detectives, Bryant expressed concern that Hill might have gone out of business as a result of his dealings with him.

'Why did you ask that, Martin, if Terry is still in business?' Inspector Paine asked.

''Cos I didn't have a licence. I had no gun licence,' Bryant replied.

'Did you make out you had a gun licence when you purchased them?'

'No, I never discussed it. I never. I just said I had the cash on me and he said that's alright.'

According to Bryant, Hill also sold him the correct ammunition for the Armalite AR10 after he complained of having problems firing the gun. Hill sold him 3000 rounds of the 'military, hard-top bullets' for another cash sale of $930.

As Bryant was to tell the two detectives, not having a gun licence proved no impediment to his desire to own high-powered weapons. 'When you got the money it helps. People pass things over if you've got the cash.'

Hill, who could not be contacted for this book, has since told friends that the fallout from the Port Arthur massacre ruined his life.

Bryant's ability to pay for expensive, military-style weapons gave him access to powerful guns that would normally have been beyond his reach. Many people of Bryant's intellectual capacity would be financially constrained by a disability pension or at least the budget of their carer. Not only did Helen Harvey's bequest leave Bryant with limitless cash, but Tasmania's weak gun laws made it easy for him to buy the weapons. At the time Bryant began accumulating his arsenal, he had lost the two restraining forces in his life – his father and Helen – and he held an irrational, all-consuming grudge against the Martins who, as Dr Sale describes it, happened to live near 'a vulnerable site in the middle of nowhere'. The Port Arthur Historic Site, as a popular tourist spot, was also likely to be full of the type of happy, everyday people who Bryant had grown to resent bitterly for what he saw as their cruel rejection over so many years. The means and motive for Bryant's deadly act were in place.

David and Sally Martin were always going to be Bryant's first victims: revenge was his priority. The deaths that followed at Port Arthur – all anonymous faces to Bryant – were not about settling scores, but an indiscriminate assault on the wider world from which he felt so isolated.

Dr Ian Sale, who has more than 25 years experience in psychiatry, believes it helps to better understand Bryant's actions if he is viewed as a freak of nature, rather than try to link his rampage to human malice. Malice alone could not explain why a despicable act of vengeance against two individuals ballooned into unrestrained violence against dozens of people who happened to be at the Port Arthur Historic Site.

'If you could reorient people into seeing [Bryant] as something that is one of mother nature's errors, rather than human malice, it might be a good thing,' Dr Sale reflects. 'With Bryant, that makes sense, because he really is sick; he's strange. It seemed to be a coming together of all sorts of issues that allowed this to happen.

The fact that there were ways for Bryant to get a weapon is pretty important [and] there were no restraints on him. Dad had gone. Helen had gone. Mother had pretty well been defeated. He had the money, he had the [means] and he had the distress of his father's death.'

I asked Dr Sale: 'So all of these things came together, much like a tidal wave?'

'It was the perfect storm, yes.'

Having interviewed Bryant twice at Risdon Prison, spoken to his mother Carleen at length and reviewed all of his past medical and educational files, Dr Sale considers Bryant's history and personality type to most closely match Asperger's syndrome although, as with most things in Bryant's life, he was not a perfect fit.

Bryant's childlike voice, his inability to empathise with or to read the emotions of others, and his obsessive behaviour all, in Dr Sale's view, pointed towards an Asperger's-type personality. Professor Paul Mullen, however, disagreed with this diagnosis. In his report on Bryant, Professor Mullen similarly struggled with the lack of any neat explanation for Bryant's paradoxical behaviour. Bryant was intellectually impaired, but not mentally ill. Since childhood, he had shown a limited capacity to cope with social and personal relationships, yet he constantly craved attention. He often suffered feelings of fear and inadequacy, which he compensated for through his fascination with powerful weapons, but also had an extremely self-centred view of his place in the world. He was, as Professor Mullen illustrated in his summary, a paradox who was 'constantly despondent, but only intermittently unhappy.'

Like Dr Sale, Professor Mullen believes the best way to make sense of Bryant's actions is to see them as a consequence not of one thing, but a complex web of events and circumstances. It is not as easy to understand, and certainly makes it harder to see the next 'Bryant' coming, but the Martin Bryant who committed the massacre was a unique mix of his own mental deficiencies and personality defects, combined with a series of chance events that led to his being able to carry out his violent fantasy unhindered.

As Dr Sale later wrote in his report for the Director of Public Prosecutions, 'perhaps, fortunately, he may be unique'.

As Bryant himself told one police interviewer: 'It was set in my mind; it was just set that Sunday. I wasn't worried about losing my property or never seeing my girlfriend again. It was just in my mind to go down and kill the Martins and kill a lot of people.'

The shell-pink colour of the sandstone walls of Hobart's Risdon Prison, about 20 km from the city centre, has seen it dubbed the 'pink palace' by locals, but it is far from being any comfortable castle. Like Port Arthur a century before, Risdon Prison was considered a model jail when it first opened in the 1950s, but its antiquated and overcrowded conditions have since seen it the subject of numerous inquiries and reports, including a scathing State Ombudsman's investigation into several deaths in custody in the 1990s. It is in the middle of a $50 million upgrade to improve conditions, including those within the prison hospital, a separate wing used to house the criminally insane, suicidal, infectious and drug-addicted. Its inmates have included the former CSIRO scientist Rory 'Jack' Thompson who murdered his wife, dismembered her and attempted to flush her down the drains, but Martin Bryant is its most infamous resident.

Bryant spent the first eight months of his life sentence in total isolation within the hospital wing. His specially designed cell contained a stainless steel bed, a seatless toilet and a television, which he smashed soon after he arrived. According to the prison psychiatrist at the time, Dr Wilf Lopez, Bryant believed the television programs were talking about him, just as he believed car horns tooting in the night were a sign that people were coming to attack him. Such thoughts suggested the beginning of a psychosis which prison authorities monitored closely, but which, according to Dr Lopez, was tempered by his later mixing with other hospital inmates.

Ten years into his sentence, Bryant is yet to mix freely with the general prison population, largely because his notoriety makes him a prized scalp for other prisoners. Even within the relative seclusion of the hospital wing, he has suffered several assaults, the most recent of which was in 2003 when an inmate threw cleaning fluid into his eyes and caused him to be hospitalised briefly. Bryant also, in his early days of imprisonment, made several clumsy attempts to take his own life, including one by trying to swallow a rolled up tube of toothpaste and another by trying to strangle himself with bandages. In the last recorded attempt, in December 2000, he lacerated his groin and arms with a razor blade, but caused only minor wounds.

Was this a sign of a man beginning to feel remorse, or just a desire to end his interminable incarceration? Given the lack of access to Bryant, it is impossible to know. He has also deliberately isolated himself from visitors, reportedly asking his mother, Carleen, more than four years ago to stop visiting him. Attempts by Dr Sale to meet with him have also been rebuffed by Bryant.

One of the few outsiders to have seen Bryant in jail is former ABC radio journalist Ginny Stein, who inadvertently bumped into him while preparing a documentary on his imprisonment for the Radio National program *Background Briefing* in 1997. Stein's report revealed a man who, at that time, was still self-centred and proud of his notoriety, with seemingly no comprehension of the devastation he had brought to so many lives.

Stein was interviewing Risdon's chief of security, Rod Quarry, when Bryant wandered into the corridor, approached the pair and interrupted their conversation. In his typical, egocentric style, Bryant's first question to Stein was about himself: 'You're busy talking away there: about me?'

As Quarry explained to Stein, Bryant would use his trips in the prison van between Risdon Prison and the Hobart Supreme Court to bombard the guards with details of the massacre, its impact and how important he was for having committed it. It took all of the guards' strength not to tell him to shut up, or worse.

'He still sees himself as somebody very special,' Quarry told Stein in 1997.

At one point, Bryant reportedly offered to be a sperm donor. At another, he asked one of the prison nurses how old her children were and whether she would bring them in to see him, after which he made his hand into the L-shape of a gun and muttered 'click, click' as if he were firing.

As Dr Lopez told Stein, 'Every day Bryant reminds his jailers of who he is and what he has done'.

Dr Lopez added that while such actions appeared grossly insensitive, they were all part of an impaired personality that saw Bryant disconnected from the range of normal human emotions. Bryant, he said, lived permanently in a state familiar to many of us, where we may react inappropriately to extreme stress or high emotion, such as laughing hysterically after hearing of a tragedy. While for the majority of people this is a rare or fleeting response, it is Bryant's permanent way of being. His intellect is that of an eleven year old, but his emotional reactions are those of a giggly two-year-old child.

John Avery has kept a drawing by Bryant of what unfolded at the massacre. Not surprisingly, the picture details the carnage in childish, inanimate stick figures. As Brigid Cook believed, Bryant saw his victims as two-dimensional targets, not as real people. To the frustration of those seeking an insight into Bryant's mind, this drawing and reams of taped interviews between Bryant and Avery must remain confidential, at least while Bryant is alive. An attempt by Avery to take a photograph of Bryant in prison was also thwarted after prison authorities, according to Avery, reneged on the arrangement — agreed to by Bryant — and ordered the film to be destroyed in front of them.

The trickle of information that is known about Bryant in prison today has been gleaned from those who either work at Risdon, or have had contact with him during their own incarceration; people such as 'Rob', whom I interviewed in March 2003 for *The Weekend Australian*. Rob agreed to talk about his brief encounter with Bryant, but was still nervous. He had told his estranged wife about our planned interview and she had warned him against it, saying that to talk about Bryant was 'asking for trouble' in a state where the mere mention of his name still provoked disgust and anger.

Rob, whose real name I will keep private in accordance with the conditions of our initial interview, spent time in prison in 2002 for alcohol-related offences. We met in the cluttered kitchen of his peeling, weatherboard home in Goodwood, a troubled northern suburb of Hobart that was bypassed in the city's real estate boom.

At the time of our interview, Rob was preparing to leave for Perth in search of a fresh start.

Rob met Bryant during a six-week stint in the prison hospital where Rob was sent, he says, after he faked a suicide attempt in the hope of being housed in slightly more comfortable conditions than those of the main prison.

He described Bryant as being significantly overweight, with close-cropped, gingery hair; the stubbled remnants of what had been long, blond locks. The young man who once adhered to an exercise routine is now virtually inactive and gorges on ice cream: he asks anyone with spare ice cream from a meal to give it to him. It is the same sweet tooth which saw Bryant ask his lawyer for cans of Coca-Cola before finally confessing to the massacre.

Rob, initially unaware of the identity of the obese, pasty-faced man, found Bryant to be one of the few people he could talk to in the hospital wing. 'He was obviously not the smartest boy, but he wasn't like most of the others either. He didn't smoke, he didn't have tattoos, he didn't act all tough and aggressive and brag, and he wasn't taking the "jailey" medicine [daily medication],' Rob said.

In contrast to most of the other prisoners, Rob said, Bryant was polite, quiet and talked only when spoken to. Any boasting about his crime failed to impress his fellow inmates, most of whom treated him with the same disdain as his schoolyard companions had years before.

'He is an easy victim. To a large extent he is left alone, but at the same time they are cruel to him. He doesn't get bashed up, but he gets picked on, like flicking a book at him as they walk past, that sort of thing,' Rob said. 'I was one of the few people who talked to him like he was a human being.'

Rob had spoken to Bryant several times about 'general prison stuff', but didn't recognise him until the day he saw his name written in marker pen on his prison-issue tracksuit.

'I said, "What are you doing wearing Martin Bryant's tracksuit?" and he says to me, "I am Martin Bryant".' Rob was stunned by Bryant's changed physical appearance having, like most Tasmanians, come to see him as a youthful, surfer-looking man.

Rob then asked the question that still burns for so many: 'What in bloody hell's name did you do that [the shootings] for?'

Bryant didn't talk about the Martins, or an obsessive desire for revenge, or his deep sense of loneliness in the world, but instead explained that he believed he was doing 'a favour' by attempting to kill Japanese tourists: Bryant was still painting himself as the hero.

'He told me that he [knew] that he was cracking up, that things weren't going right, that he was heavily medicated, and the way he explained it to me, not to defend himself – not in defence, but just talking to someone who was prepared to talk to him – was that he thought he was doing Australia a favour by shooting Japanese tourists.'

For all the gravity of Bryant's crimes, Rob struggled to dislike him as a person; an assessment which sat uncomfortably with his knowledge of what he had done.

'I personally do not believe he went out there knowing that he was shooting innocent people. Maybe he was crazy at the time, maybe he was off his head at the time, or maybe he thought he was on a mission for Australia, I don't know, but he doesn't seem like an evil bloke.'

When asked to describe Bryant's character, Rob leans forward on his chair and rhythmically strokes his beard before choosing the word 'pathetic'. 'I can understand all the horrible pain and anguish that he has caused from that terrible incident. In his mind at the time, he couldn't see that he had done anything wrong.

'There are a lot of very vicious people out there who will rob your house, bash you up, rape your wife, steal off your grand-mother, they would do anything: I just can't put Martin Bryant in that category.'

Bryant's days are now made up of mind-numbing routines and utter boredom, while the long nights are broken only by the dis-tressing moans and shouts of other hospital inmates, many of whom have a mental illness or have been declared criminally insane.

The hospital wing has about 30 individual cells, each meas-uring about 3.5 m x 2.5 m and sparsely furnished with a stainless steel bed and small mattress, a seatless toilet and a small basin. There are no light switches – lights are centrally controlled – and the sealed, opaque windows offer little or no view. There is a medical unit, a mess hall and a small exercise yard surrounded by high wire fences and paved with concrete; to walk on grass has become a privilege. A small library, TV lounge and a communal shower block complete the facilities.

Here Bryant's day would begin at 8.45 a.m. when the cells are unlocked for breakfast served either in the cell or the mess hall. Bryant is happy to eat with others, perhaps in the hope of striking up a conversation, although most choose to ignore him. The morning is then spent cleaning his cell and putting out any dirty laundry for collection. Lunch is served for 30 minutes from midday and the cells are then locked down for most of the afternoon. Dinner is served for an hour from 5 p.m., after which the cells are locked down for the night.

'Most of the day, [Bryant] doesn't do much, maybe go to the library, pick up a book. Everybody is bored stiff in there. Most of the time he just spends in isolation,' Rob said.

If, for whatever reason, the entire hospital wing is in lockdown, inmates only leave their cells for communal showers. During Rob's sentence, the hospital unit was locked down for ten days in succession. He, as he explains it, began 'crawling the walls' with boredom.

In the six weeks Rob spent in the hospital ward, he did not see Bryant receive a single visitor. His mother, having been told by Bryant to stay away, is still based in Tasmania, but apparently spends most of her time travelling Australia in a campervan. The last address I could find for Carleen was care of a caravan park in suburban Hobart, but my letter was returned unopened. Carleen, a religious woman, has rarely spoken publicly since the massacre, having openly expressed her sorrow in a written statement issued through John Avery on the first anniversary of the event.

'Of all people I weep with you,' it said in part. 'With your bitter tears, with our suffering tears and with unique, unshareable tears of my own. With you, I am worn out with grief.' Carleen then drew upon her faith in asking for compassion and forgiveness:

To overcome our tragedy, our best chance is to look forward with hope and overcome evil with the goodness which comes from God. Seeking healing with you, with all my compassion and love, Carleen Bryant.

Carleen's travels sometimes take her across to Western Australia, where Bryant's younger sister, Lindy, has been living. Lindy, who shares Bryant's blond-haired and fair-skinned features, is reportedly forced to relocate her home each time the media uncovers her address. She has scrupulously avoided all public attention.

Bryant, meanwhile, continues to live in his own world, although Rob believes he is 'extremely sorry for what he has done' and would rather be dead than alive.

'For this horrible, ghastly situation [he] is in, he is making the best of it he can. I think if any of us had to go into that situation, we would rather be dead.

'I think he deserves compassion – "hate the sin, love the sinner" if you will – but I think if you laid down a pill right there for Martin today, he would take it.'

—— 13 ——

BITING THE BULLET:
GUN LAW REFORMS

For $750, one could pick up a used Ruger No.1, .22 rifle through the classified ads which appeared in Hobart's *Mercury* newspaper on Saturday, 20 April 1996. There was also a second-hand 12-gauge shotgun and an Anschutz .22 magnum, with scope, selling for the special price of only $400 for the pair. Just eight days before 56 people were to be either shot dead or wounded at Port Arthur, there were five listings offering guns for sale in Tasmania's largest daily newspaper. Of the five advertisements, one attracted attention with its capital letters and bold type: 'Rifles, Shotguns and Ammo, large quantities available at special prices'. The address given is 93B Main Road, New Town, the then business address of gun dealer Terry Hill. (Main Road is the colloquial name for New Town Road.)

On the eve of the massacre, *The Mercury* carried another, equally portentous item. The paper's Saturday feature pages on 27 April 1996 were dominated by an in-depth interview with the then Tasmanian Police Commissioner John Johnson – not to be confused with the current Tasmanian Deputy Commissioner of Police Jack Johnston – who had just announced his retirement. Senior reporter Michael Lester asked Johnson what part of the job had changed most during his almost 40 years in the force.

'There is much more violence than when I joined the police force in the 1950s. Violence has always been a part of police existence, but it hasn't been as bad in the past as it has been in the last ten or fifteen years,' he replied.

Johnson added that by comparison to some countries, however, Australia was still very safe and Tasmania, in particular, a sanctuary. 'When you compare Australia with the rest of the world, this is paradise, particularly Tasmania. In a lot of countries I have visited…violence and crime is really at a level none of us dreams about or has any appreciation of until we visit them.'

It is chilling to read Johnson's words in hindsight, knowing that within 24 hours Tasmania was to experience an act of violence unprecedented for modern Australia. The Port Arthur murders became the nadir of what was a decade of mass killings by gunmen in Australia. Some of the massacres still come to mind easily: Julian Knight at Hoddle Street, Melbourne, in August 1987, followed that same year by Frank Vitkovic in Queen Street, Melbourne, and the 1991 Strathfield shopping centre shootings in Sydney by Wade Frankum. Yet these names are only three among more than a dozen men who, between them, shot and killed 77 people in a string of massacres throughout the late 1980s and early 1990s. Australians were becoming unnerved by what appeared to be a seeping of the violent American gun culture into their way of life, but political leaders remained reluctant to act. The conservative gun lobby, represented politically by the Shooters Party, was seen as a formidable force; one capable of turning an election result through its influence in rural seats, and a group that few political leaders were prepared to take on. University of Sydney Professor Simon Chapman in his 1998 book *Over Our Dead Bodies*, which details gun law reform after the Port Arthur massacre, notes that a 1987 national gun summit held by then Prime Minister Bob Hawke failed to gain a consensus on national gun laws, despite coming on the heels of the Queen Street and Hoddle Street massacres. Gun control had also been raised at twenty out of 29 national conferences for police ministers held between 1987 and 1996, and still the states could not agree on a uniform approach to owning the potentially lethal weapons.

Instead, the states muddled along with their own reforms, which resulted in a patchwork of rules and regulations that varied significantly depending on where a gun owner happened to live. When Martin Bryant bought his high-powered weaponry, the guns were perfectly legal to own in Tasmania, but had been banned everywhere else in Australia except Queensland.

The Tasmanian police minister had also, since 1991, had the power to ban semi-automatic weapons, but it was only in the days after the Port Arthur massacre that the minister felt compelled to finally enact this power. More than six months before the massacre, the then Tasmanian Greens leader, Christine Milne, had been ridiculed by her parliamentary opponents when she suggested that the power to ban a certain class of firearm be removed from political influence and delegated to the Tasmanian Police Commissioner.

Commissioner Johnson, who in his retirement interview lamented the increase in violent crime, advised the state government that he did not believe Ms Milne's suggestion would work. After all, he was reported as saying, what police commissioner would go against state government policy and, besides, he could not think of any recent incident in Tasmania grave enough to justify the ban of any particular class of weapon.

Others, however, held a sense of foreboding that it was just a matter of time until Tasmania's lax gun laws caught up with it in the worst possible way. At the time of the Port Arthur massacre, Tasmania held the dubious honour of being the easiest place in Australia in which to buy multiple firearms. As Dr Bryan Walpole was to discover after moving there, Tasmanians, per head of population, were fatally shooting themselves at a greater rate than anywhere else in the nation.

Despite such a grim statistic, the licensing of gun owners and dealers was not mandatory in Tasmania until 1993. A gun licence, which was effectively for life, allowed its holder to buy as many guns as he or she liked, including semi-automatic rifles, with no formal government record of the weapons. This made it a breeze for a firearm to be on-sold to anyone else, licensed or not, with no way of tracking where a weapon might end up. Martin Bryant, who didn't bother to apply for a licence, was able to buy two high-calibre weapons over the counter and another through the *Mercury* classifieds: no questions asked.

It was the potential Martin Bryants who most worried Roland Browne, a curly-haired, square-jawed young lawyer who had been campaigning for gun law reform since 1987 as part of the Tasmanian Coalition for Gun Control.

Browne, who on the day we speak appears the type of man far more comfortable in blue jeans than a suit, could not reconcile the Tasmanian Government's reluctance to move on firearms when it had seen fit to ban the sale of firecrackers. But then, as Browne points out with a hint of cynicsm, children don't vote.

'We licence and control the availability of most dangerous things in our community and it was always supremely ironic to me that fireworks were taken off the shelves in Tasmania in the 1980s, because a couple of kids suffered injuries one cracker night, yet Martin Bryant could pick up guns through the newspaper,' he says.

In an effort to further expose the weaknesses within Tasmania's gun laws, Browne appeared in late 1995 on the populist television show, *A Current Affair*, around the same time as Christine Milne was lobbying for the police commissioner to be given the power to ban certain weapons. The *Current Affair* crew had flown to Hobart, picked up a copy of *The Mercury* and, by that afternoon, had bought two military-style semi-automatic weapons plus ammunition. The crew promptly deposited the lot at the office of the then police minister, Frank Madill: the cameras capturing the entire process for a national audience numbering in the hundreds of thousands.

A severely embarrassed Dr Madill launched an immediate investigation into how the television crew was able to buy the guns so easily, but again failed to make any change to the availability of weapons that, as the gun control lobby was at pains to point out, were originally intended for war. 'Like a lot of public health issues, nothing changes until there is an obvious and very apparent public health impact which occurred, in, of course, April of 1996,' Browne says.

Eight days after Thomas Hamilton walked into a primary school in
Dunblane, Scotland, on 13 March 1996, and shot dead sixteen children and their teacher with a semi-automatic pistol, an exasperated
Roland Browne penned an angry letter to *The Mercury*. In it, he
warned that while Tasmanians joined the world in expressing their
shock and sadness at Hamilton's crimes, they were at risk of experiencing a similar massacre, because semi-automatic weapons were
so freely available. He wrote:

> If we want to avoid Scotland's grief, then I suggest Tasmanian
> politicians note first that people in this state can presently get
> access to high-powered and semi-automatic weapons, and
> secondly that Thomas Hamilton would, prior to the
> [Dunblane] massacre, undoubtedly have been granted a gun
> licence in Tasmania.
>
> In the absence of prior convictions or mental health
> problems, a gun licence would not be refused. We should
> tighten up our gun laws now and not wait for the
> inevitable judicial inquiry if a Dunblane type-massacre
> occurs here. Prevention is better than cure.

The letter was published on 21 March 1996, just five weeks before
Bryant struck. In fact as news of the Port Arthur massacre began to
filter through the media that Sunday afternoon, Browne and fellow
members of the Tasmanian Coalition for Gun Control were gathered around a table, nutting out their strategy for a meeting scheduled the following Wednesday with the new police minister, John
Beswick. They hoped, once again, to convince Beswick to intro-
duce tougher laws around gun ownership, especially for semi-automatic weapons.

Gun control lobby groups, namely the National Coalition for
Gun Control and the Melbourne-based Gun Control Australia, had
been lobbying almost ten years for uniform gun laws and a national
register for firearms. Various public opinion polls in the early 1990s
would also show that the majority of Australians were sick of the
increasing gun violence and favoured tighter laws. Yet all of this fell

on deaf ears, or was drowned out by the often-histrionic rantings of the pro-gun lobby who considered gun ownership a birthright, not a privilege.

Ironically, it was neither the pro-gun lobby nor the gun control groups which proved to have the most political influence, but the actions of a social misfit with a vengeful heart and a childish mind. When the change to gun laws came, however, it was momentous.

In October 2004, Prime Minister John Howard won the Liberal–National Party Coalition a fourth term in office that will take his tenure in Australia's top political position to twelve years. At the time of the Port Arthur massacre, however, Howard had been in office just 57 days. The massacre presented the fledgling Prime Minister with a major challenge to demonstrate his leadership and decisiveness on gun laws, in the full knowledge that any attack on shooters' rights would risk undermining his conservative support base. Howard, however, had talked boldly in the lead-up to the federal election about tackling gun law reform: the massacre provided an unexpected and ultimate test of his word.

In a move which would come to illustrate the decisive style of his prime ministership, Howard acted swiftly and firmly, dismissing any threats of retribution from those who vehemently disagreed with him. Just 24 hours after the shootings, Howard announced that an emergency meeting of all state and territory police ministers would be held on 10 May. The meeting, he explained to reporters, would be asked to agree to the most significant changes to Australia's gun laws ever put forward by a federal government. This time there was to be no shilly-shallying. The ten-point reform, drafted by then Attorney-General Daryl Williams, stunned even gun control lobby groups with its breadth.

Roland Browne remembers being phoned by a journalist asking if it was correct that the Prime Minister was banning *all* semi-automatic weapons, even the low-powered .22 semi-automatic rifle that the gun control lobby had come to accept would most likely remain available as a compromise.

'I couldn't understand that. Even the Tasmanian Government hadn't moved to ban that [low-powered weapons] in the days immediately afterwards. I rang the Prime Minister's office and his press secretary said, "Yeah, that's what we're doing". It turned out the Prime Minister had moved the debate a mile past gun control groups, which was an extraordinary thing. He didn't need to do that. The states weren't after it, we weren't after it, but he just moved it along.'

The reform package included a ban on all self-loading (semi-automatic) rifles and shotguns; a national registration of all firearms based on an integrated licensing scheme; strict, uniform gun storage laws; tougher criteria to become a licensed shooter, including a valid reason for owning a gun; and a ban on all private and mail-order sales of firearms so that guns could only be sold through licensed dealers. In a major concession, firearm owners would receive the market value for any weapons handed in during a twelve-month amnesty, funded by taxpayers through an increase to the Medicare health care levy.

Even those who disliked John Howard's political style and leanings were hard-pressed to criticise his resolve on the gun issue.

As Simon Chapman described it in *Over Our Dead Bodies*, the 10 May agreement among the states and territories was 'the single biggest advance in gun control in Australian history – and possibly anywhere in the world'.

With the police ministers having signed off on the plan, it remained up to the state and territory parliaments to enact it within their own jurisdictions. In the weeks that followed the 10 May agreement, both sides of the gun control debate mobilised their forces to try to persuade nervous politicians over to their side. Thousands of people joined passionate rallies that were held in major cities and country towns across Australia, lobbying loudly either for or against the radical reforms. Walter Mikac and Dr Bryan Walpole became memorable faces of the gun control campaign, while Ted Drane from the Sporting Shooters' Association of Australia and John Tingle from the Shooters Party protested vigor-ously – and often aggressively in the case of Drane – for the reforms to be scrapped.

The fight for political supremacy in the gun control debate was to provide another defining moment in the legacy of Port Arthur.

On 15 June, less than two months after the massacre, Prime Minister Howard stood before several thousand highly charged pro-gun protesters in the Victorian country town of Sale. In what was believed to be a first for any Australian prime minister, Howard chose to wear a bullet-proof vest, the stiff outline of which was clearly visible under his white shirt. The decision to appear at the rally proved a double victory for Howard. Not only did his personal popularity rating soar in the wake of such a seemingly courageous act, but it gave Australians an indication of what sort of country they might expect to live in – one tainted with the constant threat of violence – if firearms remained freely available.

Much to the anger and despair of the pro-gun lobby, the new gun laws were progressively passed by parliaments across Australia and the buyback began. It was an unqualified success. By late 1997, more than 640,000 guns had been deposited, crushed and sent to smelters for recycling at a cost of $304 million. Of all the states and territories, Tasmania produced the greatest amount of guns per head of population, with 32,000 firearms handed in to police stations around the island.

It is testimony to the success of the buyback that, at the time of writing, there has not been another massacre by rifle or shotgun in Australia, compared to the slaughter of the decade before.

Australian Institute of Criminology data reveals that Australia's homicide rate has fallen from 1.94 deaths per 100,000 people in the period 1989–1996 to 1.65 per 100,000 in 2000–01. The number of firearm-related deaths also fell by 47 per cent between 1991 (629 deaths) and 2001 (333 deaths), particularly in the category of suicides.

After announcing his retirement from politics in 2004, former Attorney-General Daryl Williams pinpointed the gun law reforms and buyback as one of the most satisfying achievements during his time in office.

In recognising this success, however, Williams also lamented that the buyback of semi-automatic rifles had exposed another gun control issue: the increased use of handguns for violent crime. A small-arms survey by the Graduate Institute of International Studies in 2003 found that 67 per cent of armed robberies in Australia in 2001 involved a handgun.

Roland Browne today admits that handguns became lost in the post-Port Arthur debate, as the gun control campaign zeroed in on the military-style semi-automatic rifles used by Bryant. Thomas Hamilton, however, had used semi-automatic *handguns* in the Dunblane slayings.

'It was only a year [after Port Arthur] that the penny dropped and we thought, shit, we've completely overlooked handguns and they're all still legal. We've potentially stopped a Port-Arthur style shooting, but we haven't done anything to stop a Dunblane-style shooting.'

In the months after the 1997 buyback, the National Coalition for Gun Control began a fresh campaign aimed at closing the loop-hole that allowed the ownership of semi-automatic handguns which, Browne argues, are potentially just as lethal as semi-automatic rifles. The political momentum which followed the Port Arthur massacre, however, had begun to fade. It was not until July 2002 that the police ministers moved to stem the rise in the illegal ownership and trafficking of handguns, although the weapons remained available to licensed users. Gun control groups argued that, as long as the weapons were available legally, they had the potential for misuse or to fall into the wrong hands.

Browne again feared it would take another dramatic shooting to push the problem to the top of the political agenda and he was right. 'You know, we were saying, "There'll have to be a massacre before this changes" and of course there was Monash and things did change, but only a little bit.'

Huan Yun Xiang provided a stark reminder that gun laws are only as strong as their weakest link when he opened fire with one of five handguns he carried to an economics tutorial at Monash University in Melbourne on 21 October 2002. He murdered two students and injured five others before being subdued by a teacher.

While not technically defined as a massacre, because it involved less than three deaths, the public shooting was a scene that had been absent from Australia's news bulletins for more than five years.

As John Crook from Gun Control Australia was to later tell ABC radio, 36-year-old Xiang was able to legally purchase seven handguns because he was a member of two pistol clubs.

'Some of those guns were not necessary for pistol club competition and, also, he wasn't required to attend a minimum number of shoots. So it was clear in the aftermath of that tragedy there were a number of major weaknesses in pistol club regulations and…new laws are absolutely necessary,' Crook said.

Prime Minister Howard returned to familiar territory when he launched a second gun buyback scheme that began in June 2003 and planned to snare 65,000 handguns at a cost of $120 million. The states and territories also agreed to ban about 500 separate models of handguns, although not all semi-automatics. Browne believes it remains an opportunity missed.

'They have banned handguns of .38 and over and those with magazines of greater than ten rounds, so what is left are normal barrelled .38 or .35 handguns with a ten-round magazine. I consider them to be very dangerous. It's just as lethal as a fifteen-round magazine. Our policy is that handguns should be the same as rifles: you can't have a semi-automatic, full stop.'

Browne doesn't relish the role of doomsayer, but expects it will take another shooting, beyond the scale of that at Monash University, to provoke sufficient community outrage about handguns.

At a time when Australia is tuned into the threat of global terrorism, where deaths are counted in the dozens – and, in the case of September 11, the thousands – gun violence may appear less ominous.

However, the Australian Institute of Criminology's National Firearms Monitoring Program, set up to measure the impact of the 1996 gun law reforms, contains a salient warning. While the number of deaths by firearms is in decline, those choosing to kill with a *handgun* is on the increase. In 1996, 28 people were identified as having been killed by a handgun, 107 by a shotgun, 231 by a hunting rifle and 38 by a military-style weapon, including the 35 at Port Arthur. By 2001, the number of handgun fatalities had climbed to 49, while those in every other category had fallen dramatically: 54 by shotgun, 76 by hunting rifle and none by a military-style weapon.

No amount of rules and regulations will ever completely end gun violence, but, as Browne argues, it is about minimising the risk. Just as we treat motor accidents, cigarettes and alcohol as public health issues, so too should gun control be considered a health issue for the wider population, not just for those who wish to own firearms. The right to indulge in the sport of hunting or to shoot targets at a gun club must be weighed against the right to feel safe in a community and not at risk of being mowed down in a shopping centre, a classroom or at a tourist attraction.

'There's always going to be people misusing guns,' says Browne. 'There's always going to be shootings – accidental and intentional. It will happen, but at a much reduced rate. The fact is, like any public health measure, there's no such thing as 100 per cent compliance and that is not the standard [for success]. If it was, you would do nothing.'

14

A VIOLENT PLACE: PORT ARTHUR

You don't so much drive into Port Arthur as descend. The 100 km journey from the Tasmanian capital of Hobart is initially dominated by the flat, open plains that surround the farming hamlets of Forcett, Copping and Dunalley, punctuated by breathtaking views back across Frederick Henry Bay. Dunalley, which straddles a thin strip of land known as East Bay Neck, marks the beginning of a different place. The metal swing bridge at Dunalley is the only road link between 'mainland' Tasmania and the Forestier Peninsula, where the open plains start to give way to thick stands of towering eucalypts surrounded at their base by dense scrub. The straight finger of road narrows as it begins to twist and turn, curling its way through the dark bush in a series of hairpin bends as it corkscrews down to the Tasman Peninsula. Even on a bright day, the sun struggles to penetrate the bush that lines this section of the Arthur Highway, creating a cloistered feeling that verges on claustrophobic.

Yet, just as the bush becomes its most dense and appears to close in on both sides, the road suddenly bursts out above Eaglehawk Neck, offering a sweeping view of its curved expanse of white sand and sparkling ocean. It is almost impossible not to gasp. One final, foot-off-the-accelerator plunge and the road flattens out onto the Eaglehawk Neck isthmus, less than 500 m wide and the only land connection between the Tasman Peninsula and the Forestier Peninsula.

Nature provided the perfect geographic location for Australia's largest and most infamous convict prison in what was then Van Diemen's Land. The Port Arthur penal colony lay 20 km from the Eaglehawk Neck isthmus, at the end of the heavily wooded, windswept and rocky Tasman Peninsula that had only one access point by land to a second peninsula which, in turn, had only a single access point to the rest of Tasmania. These two natural 'choke' points could be easily guarded and even if prisoners did escape, they faced battling a treacherous environment which, even today, claims lives. Tasmania itself is another 250 km south of mainland Australia, separated by the notorious waters of Bass Strait. For the wretched souls banished to Van Diemen's Land under the *British Transportation Act* of 1718, it must have been akin to sailing to oblivion.

Eaglehawk Neck provides the first taste of what life must have been like for the thousands of men and boys who were imprisoned at Port Arthur between 1830 and 1877. At the isthmus, there is the squat figure of a snarling dog frozen in bronze, his wet fangs bared and his thick neck straining at a chain tethered to a barrel that formed a rustic kennel. He represents the eighteen, square-chested, motley dogs that were once strung out across the isthmus, including several tethered to platforms in the water, to prevent convicts escaping. The vicious dogs were spaced far enough apart to touch, but not to fight; they were half-crazed from being chained for months at a time. The memorial plaque includes an extract from the diaries of a Harden S. Melville, who described the beasts this way:

> There were the black, the white, the brindle, the grey and the grisly, the rough and the smooth, the crop-eared and lop-eared, the gaunt and the grim. Every four-footed black-fanged individual among them would have taken first prize in his own class for ugliness and ferocity at any show... constantly being kept separate, [they] are most ferocious.

This was the four-legged welcoming committee for any convict who might consider taking a chance at fleeing the peninsula. Today, the single, rabid dog in bronze serves as a reminder of what once lay at the foot of this striking landscape, where the names of the coastal formations now reflect the terrain: the Tessellated Pavement, the Devils Kitchen, the Blowhole.

Volumes have been written on the history of Port Arthur and any Australian student has spent at least part of his or her school life learning of its dark past, the remnants of which now draw tens of thousands of tourists each year. The penal settlement began in 1830 – 26 years after the founding of Hobart Town – as an alternative to the troubled penitentiaries on Sarah Island in Macquarie Harbour and on Maria Island. While only the husks of many of the original buildings remain, Port Arthur was once a major industrial site built on the back of slave labour. Convicts were put to work building ships and boats from the tall timber hand-felled across the peninsula. They made sails, furniture, clothing and leather boots. They grew vegetables and hand-cast tens of thousands of bricks that have since become highly sought after for their distinctive broad-arrow symbol or the convict mark of a simple thumbprint.

While it is tempting to view this era as a time of bustling productivity, the cruelty and suffering that underpinned this efficiency remains inescapable. Each prisoner who arrived at Port Arthur spent his first six months in hard labour, usually felling and carrying the massive eucalypts that surrounded the site for use as building materials. Shackled at the ankles by heavy metal cuffs, prisoners would work from dawn until sunset before returning to their dank cells. Those who behaved were rewarded after six months with lighter and more varied duties, while recalcitrants were punished accordingly.

As Tasmanian historian Ian Brand records in his book, *Penal Peninsula*, a favoured form of punishment in the early years of Port Arthur was the cat-o'-nine-tails lash, or a maddening stretch in solitary confinement in a small, darkened cell. According to Brand, in the first eleven months of 1833 alone, '165 men were flogged, receiving a total of 6197 lashes, an average of almost 38 each. In the same period, 161 men were sentenced to solitary confinement for a total of 1355 days, an average of over eight days each.'

If they escaped the lash or solitary confinement, disobedient prisoners might be ordered to walk the treadmill. This cumbersome structure, measuring 15 m in diameter and resembling an oversized mouse wheel, could hold up to 36 men who would spend the entire day 'walking' its steps, save for two meal breaks.

Runaways, being considered the worst offenders, could expect even harsher treatment. These men were shackled at the wrists, waist and ankles to a wooden, triangular frame and publicly lashed up to 100 times. Should a convict pass out during his punishment, he would be lowered into a salt bath that, upon the brine soaking into his raw wounds, would guarantee his revival.

Children were not exempt from barbaric punishment. The Point Puer juvenile prison lay on a small island across the water from the Port Arthur settlement and housed up to 730 'delinquent' boys, some of whom were only nine years of age when 'exported' from the United Kingdom. Just as with the adult prisoners, the boys began their sentences on labour gangs, before moving into a trade such as blacksmithing, carpentry or shoemaking. Bad behaviour was similarly punished according to the severity of the crime. According to Brand, in the twelve months between September 1844 and September 1845, 27 boys were whipped for an average of 34 strokes each. At the same time, an average of six boys a day were undergoing solitary confinement in cramped, dark cells for up to seven days each.

While such treatments were undoubtedly draconian, those convicts considered unbreakable were sentenced to an even worse fate. The Model, or Separate, Prison was built in 1849 within the Port Arthur complex to serve as a prison within a prison. As authors Alex Graeme-Evans and Michael Ross describe it in their guide to Port Arthur, the Model Prison introduced a form of psychological control designed to reform the most hardened convicts but which, more often than not, sent them insane:

On one hand, prisoners [in the Model Prison] were to be regularly exercised, attend church and [be] adequately occupied with an honest day's work. In their confined cells, they were fed an adequate diet, and physical abuse abolished. Yet, on the other side of the coin, major abuses of the mind were practised. In particular, the basic human desire to communicate with one's fellow beings was specifically denied. Extraordinary lengths were taken to secure anaesthetised isolation of the individual.

The Model Prison was a bizarre combination of Orwellian fantasy and interrogation techniques which, disturbingly, are still applied in parts of the Western world today. Inmates were confined to individual cells measuring 2 m by 3 m and forbidden at *all* times to communicate, by any means, with other prisoners. During their time in the separate prison, they were referred to by a number, not a name. The inmates were exercised individually, with hoods placed over their heads to prevent them from looking at each other as they passed, while special 'blinkered' pews were built in the chapel for the same purpose. Thick matting was placed on the floor of the prison to block out even the sound of a footfall. This was a maddeningly quiet, cold and desperately lonely place.

Life was also far from pleasant for the wardens patrolling the Model Prison, who were similarly confined to a rigidly silent world and communicated to each other by way of hand signals. The duty warden was also expected to show he had been fully attentive during his shift by 'punching' the pegs in a watch clock that could have been lifted from the pages of George Orwell's *1984*. Each peg had to be depressed at precisely fifteen-minute intervals during the night; any later and the peg would not slip into the slot. If any pegs remained out by morning, the warden could expect his wages to be docked.

A monetary fine, however, was light punishment compared to that which awaited a prisoner who broke any of the strict rules surrounding the Model Prison. Bad behaviour would see an inmate banished to a separate punishment cell for up to weeks at a time and fed nothing but bread and water. These cells were designed to block out all light and, once the heavy door was secured, the prisoner would be plunged into an impenetrable darkness. Visitors to the

Port Arthur site today can step inside one of the remaining isolation cells and experience a sample of what these convicts endured. Most tourists are hard-pressed to stay inside the darkened room for more than a few seconds before they fumble frantically for the latch.

For those convicts who did not survive their sentences in Port Arthur, a final humiliation awaited at what was then called Opossum Island, but is now known as the Isle of the Dead. The knob of land off Port Arthur, now part of a popular guided ferry tour, became the burial ground for convicts, military officials and their families, and the occasional free settler. While the graves of officers and soldiers were marked with often ornately carved headstones, more than 1500 convicts were laid to rest in unmarked graves. Photographs taken on the island after the closure of the Port Arthur prison reveal random mounds of dirt; the only sign of a life extinguished and, for the most part, forgotten.

The transportation of felons from the United Kingdom ended in 1853, but Port Arthur continued as a prison for another 24 years until September 1877, by which time about 12,000 convicts had served time there. As convict numbers dwindled, the last handful of inmates was relocated to Hobart to serve out their sentences and the reclamation of the Port Arthur site began in earnest. Several buildings were demolished immediately and brick walls were pulled down, cleaned and recycled for use in Hobart, together with furnishings and fittings retrieved from the government quarters.

By 1878, the entire area was divided into lots to be sold by the government, but, given its recent history as a barbaric prison, the sale attracted few takers. In a bid to shed the stigma of its past, the Port Arthur settlement was renamed Carnarvon in 1884 and began to develop a new identity as a town. Many of the former prison buildings were sold off at auction, with newspaper reports at the time recording the Model Prison and an adjacent superintendent's cottage sold for the total sum of 630 pounds. The penitentiary, meanwhile, was passed in at 800 pounds.

Nature also was to play its part in cleansing the site, with major bushfires sweeping through the area in 1895 and again in 1897, reducing many of the buildings to the ruins that remain today.

While curious sightseers began to visit Port Arthur almost from the day of its closure, it was not until the turn of the century that it began to harness its full tourism potential. The state government gradually began to buy up the most significant buildings to prevent them from falling into further disrepair and the Carnarvon people began to offer sightseeing tours.

While a convict in the family tree was still a source of shame, the early 1900s saw an increasing fascination with convict life in general. Critical to the rise in public interest was the 1926 filming at Port Arthur of a movie based on Marcus Clarke's classic 1874 novel, *For the Term of His Natural Life*. The filming of Clarke's fictional account of the life of convict Rufus Dawes attracted national and international attention and people suddenly wanted to know more about Tasmania's convict past and, in particular, the Tasman Peninsula. By 1927, Carnarvon had reverted back to the name of Port Arthur, which now had immense tourist appeal.

This same fascination with convict history, coupled with the modern trend of unearthing the family tree – convict skeletons and all – is what drives Port Arthur's tourism industry today. During the past 30 years in particular, millions of state and federal dollars have been poured into preserving the ruins and turning the Port Arthur Historic Site into Tasmania's most famous and popular tourist attraction.

Yet the balance between conserving Australia's most important historical site and still turning a tourist dollar has always been a delicate one. Relations between the site and the surrounding community became particularly tense during the late 1980s and early 1990s, when the management team was predominantly Hobart-based and under state government pressure to make a profit. Maintenance costs alone were up to $1.5 million a year by 1996. As a result, the 115 ha site was fully fenced, stopping any free access, and a toll booth erected at the top of Jetty Road to collect entry fees. There were also rising concerns that the site was at risk of degenerating into a convict theme park – with its ghost tours, plastic ball-and-chain trinkets and fancy dress photographs in felon uniforms – rather than a place deserving of quiet respect.

Just how distanced many had become from the bleak history of
Port Arthur, and indeed the history of white settlement in
Tasmania, was made clear after Martin Bryant pulled the trigger.
The reaction of complete and utter shock was not only at the scale
of Bryant's crimes, but because such violence happened in
Tasmania; a state that had successfully reinvented itself as a virginal
place of wide-eyed innocence. Australia appeared to have forgotten
that Tasmania, while still sparsely populated and wildly beautiful,
was built on the agony of those who were forced from their land
and those who were exported thousands of miles from their home
in sanctioned slave labour.

Bryant himself was keenly aware of the significance of Port
Arthur as the place to let loose his vengeance. While being interviewed for his defence by psychiatrist Professor Paul Mullen, Bryant
was asked why he chose the convict site. His answer was succinct:
'…a lot of violence has happened there. It must be the most violent place in Australia; it seemed the right place.'

15

SURFACING

Tasmania was struggling when Martin Bryant opened fire at Port Arthur. The beautiful island was widely loved for its convict history, its serenity and its wild places, but mainland Australians considered it a wonderful place to visit; not somewhere to live. It was too cold, too isolated, too conservative and, it was thought, too close-knit. There were the stale jokes about Tasmanians being two-headed, a disparaging reference to the fact that the bulk of the population was drawn from a small gene pool. The state was also an economic basket case, with astronomical debt, double-digit unemployment and a heavy reliance on old-fashioned industries such as logging and apple-growing. Young Tasmanians could enjoy Huckleberry-Finn childhoods full of fishing and running barefoot, yet turned their eyes to the lights of Melbourne across Bass Strait for a sense of their future. Tasmania had become a great place to bookend your life – to grow up in or to retire to – but to choose to live there in-between was considered quaint rather than bold.

For a place that was economically fragile, Martin Bryant delivered what should have been the knockout punch. In those few hours of unrestrained violence, Bryant not only destroyed the lives of his victims and many of their families, but mangled the confidence of an entire state. Tasmania was suddenly world news, for the worst possible reason. People were hearing about Tasmania, often for the first time, not because of its tranquillity and natural beauty, but for an act of bloodshed. Perhaps because of its isolation, Tasmania was always seen as safe. After 28 April 1996, that very isolation, particularly on the Tasman Peninsula, added to the sense of dread that maybe a copycat gunman could strike at any time.

Before her death in August 2005, English-born writer and poet Margaret Scott had lived permanently on the Nubeena end of the Tasman Peninsula since 1991 and, despite her status as a relative new arrival to the area compared to those of convict heritage, became a much-loved local. After the massacre, Margaret was entrusted with many of the stories of those who had endured the events of the day, upon which she based her 1997 book, *Port Arthur: A story of strength and courage.*

When we talked in 2003, Margaret recalled the terror that gripped the local community in the days and weeks after the shootings. It was a fear quite unlike that which might follow a natural disaster, such as the 1967 bushfires that ripped through the area.

'Our trauma was quite a different kind in that it had been perpetrated by a human being,' she said. 'The worst thing we had to come to terms with was that another human being could do what Martin Bryant had done. Our trust of people was gone. We had to deal with our fears of other people, with fears of going out and having a meal in a restaurant, or fears of walking down the street: would a gunman appear and shoot us? We had to cope with that sort of thing.'

If the locals were finding it hard to feel comfortable again in their own surrounds, the tourists were even more ill at ease. The Port Arthur Historic Site shifted from being Tasmania's top tourist attraction to a place to be avoided. As is so often the case after a tragedy in a particular location, the location itself becomes tainted. The thought of packing a picnic lunch for a day at Port Arthur was no longer the appealing prospect it had once been for thousands of tourists. As the visitors dried up, tourism ventures on the Tasman Peninsula began to suffer badly and many closed altogether. Others packed up and moved elsewhere, angered by what they considered to be a lack of state government support for their plight.

At the same time, tensions that existed before the massacre between the Port Arthur Historic Site, its staff and the wider community, further tightened. The site, despite being the major employer in the area, had long been seen as detached from the community. Its management team and board were seen as outsiders, or 'city people', who lived elsewhere and ran their own show without any input or feedback from the locals.

As Margaret explained, the animosity between the locals and the site – and between the site and its own staff – made sense when you looked at the convict history of the area. Many of those still living on the peninsula are direct descendants of the convicts who once toiled at Port Arthur and who, as free citizens, helped turn around the peninsula from a place of shame to the thriving town of Carnarvon, as it became known in 1884. Ex-convicts became storekeepers and farmers, bakers and butchers.

'So here you have a group of people who have taken over the place, who have made it their own and who have turned it around and it is like you have taken it away from them again,' Margaret said. 'I think that lies at the back of that bitterness, that one is being treated almost like a convict again and there are all those people "up on the hill" telling us what to do.'

Grief counsellors warned the local community that people who were once close as neighbours, friends and colleagues would most likely turn against each other once the initial shock of the massacre had settled down. It was all part of the grieving process; of wanting to lash out at someone, to blame someone for what had unfolded, particularly in light of Martin Bryant's complete lack of remorse. Of course the local community did not want to believe the warnings. Bound tightly together by shock and sorrow, the local residents could not do enough for each other in the first six months after the massacre. The event had drawn them closer together, not pushed them apart. Then, as Margaret explained, things began to change.

'There was a bad patch. There was a patch where those who had been very strong were unable to go on being strong. Some people had belated nervous breakdowns. Some people felt they had to get away. There were quite a lot of marriage break-ups, there were quarrels between old friends, there were disagreements between neighbours, there were a lot of arguments over compensation: people looking over each other's shoulders saying, "Well, you got more than me", that sort of thing.'

There was also only a belated recognition for the valiant efforts of the Port Arthur staff who had been thrown into an unimaginable situation and forced to cope as best they could. They helped save so many lives that day and, quite simply, nobody thought to say thank you. It was only after the 1997 Doyle report into the massacre that 31 workers finally received recognition through a series of bravery awards.

The large number of workers compensation claims also meant that individual claimants found themselves dealing with bureaucratic red tape that dragged on for years. By early 2004, almost 90 claims against the Port Arthur site had been finalised and still there were fresh claims being lodged, despite it being eight years since the shootings.

Yet for all the dire predictions that the Tasman community would implode and the Port Arthur Historic Site would never be the attraction it was, both have survived and, remarkably, are in many ways stronger than before. It has been a long and often arduous climb back, with a mix of change where it was needed, and stability where it was craved, pulling the peninsula back into the sunlight.

Many of those who lived on the peninsula at the time of the massacre, such as Walter Mikac, have moved on. Others, such as Keith Moulton, remained for several years, providing a highly visible symbol of courage, before returning to family on the mainland. The majority of staff at the Port Arthur site itself has also changed since the massacre, with the new staff members building on the work of those who went before them, while providing a renewed energy and vigour.

The entire management team and board of the Port Arthur Historic Site was also replaced within four years after the massacre and the new team immediately set about building stronger connections with the local community. Margaret Scott was one of six members of the board, headed by the widely respected former federal science minister, Dr Barry Jones.

'The board now takes an awful lot of pains to look at what is actually going on down at the site, to be here, to look at things and to find out about things. It doesn't just come down, come in and say hi, have a meeting and go away again,' Margaret explained. The locals are also invited to special events, lectures and community meetings held at the site and still enjoy free entry year-round.

Part of Margaret's brief when joining the board was to build bridges between the site and the wider community. 'I thought to myself, why am I here? One answer was that I am here to make sure that the community is considered in decisions the board makes and I am here to, as far as I can, give community views to the board.'

It is clear from the high regard in which Margaret was held by the wider community that they were delighted to have the diminutive former Pom batting for them around the boardroom table, a role she continued up until she lost a long battle against emphysema.

Margaret was also on the board of a new group formed after the massacre: the Tasman Institute of Conservation and Convict Studies. The group aims to create practical and theoretical courses on convict and colonial history, to further capture the special nature of the area. The idea is to attract students and scholars to Port Arthur to study its history, or to learn traditional skills such as lead-lighting or stonemasonry, which are fast becoming lost crafts in a manufactured world. On another level, the group represents the cooperation that has been forged in the past ten years between various bodies, including the state government, University of Tasmania, heritage groups and training organisations, and the Port Arthur region. The 'us and them' is moving towards a 'we'.

One of the most significant changes for the site came after a change of state government in 1998. The then newly elected Labor Premier Jim Bacon, who died of lung cancer in 2004, moved quickly to dispel ongoing fears that various commercial parts of the

Port Arthur site, such as the gift shop and café, would be privatised to help boost its financial return. Not only did the Port Arthur site keep control of all its assets, but in 2000 the Bacon Government set aside $10 million to be spent over the next five years on conserving and improving the site.

The funding guarantee meant the site no longer had to panic about where its next dollar was coming from and could budget one, three and five years ahead. The secure funding helped dissipate the friction around what was seen as an increasing commercialisation of Port Arthur in order to make a profit.

In late 1999, a $4.5 million visitor centre, paid for by the state and federal governments, was officially opened and created an impressive entrance to the site, redirecting visitors away from the Jetty Road and toll booth area. The following year, the memorial garden and reflective pool designed by Hobart landscape artist Torquil Canning were unveiled by the then Governor-General Sir William Deane in a moving ceremony that captured headlines across Australia. It was a ceremony that had been organised jointly by several of those directly affected by the shootings and the site management team.

The healing, it seemed, had begun.

The injection of cash and the changing of the guard at the site coincided with the Bacon Government's push to lure more tourists to Tasmania by improving access to the isolated state. Hundreds of millions of dollars were to be spent on two new ferries linking Melbourne and Devonport and, as of 2004, an ambitious new service between Sydney and Devonport.

Flights to Tasmania would also become more frequent and cheaper with the arrival of Virgin Blue and, later, Jetstar. Tasmania had never been more accessible. When the World Trade Center twin towers came down in the terrorist attacks on September 11, 2001, Tasmania found itself back on the radar as a tourist destination.

As terrorism fuelled mistrust of crowds and strangers, travelling to a quiet island in a politically stable country suddenly sounded very appealing. Australians were also happy to holiday closer to home and Tasmania once again felt very safe indeed.

By early 2000, people were starting to drift back. By late 2004, they were arriving in droves: turnover in the Tasmanian tourism industry was nudging an unprecedented $1 billion a year and visitors to the Port Arthur Historic Site had climbed from 190,000 in 1996 to a record 253,000. Another 60,000 people were turning up for the night ghost tours, which was almost double the amount in 1996 who were prepared to wander around the site after dark.

The tourism ventures which found themselves swept up in the massacre have also begun to regain their feet. The Fox and Hounds hotel, which harboured those injured by Bryant as he shot at passing vehicles, has since been bought by the Chancellor Hotel chain. The Tasmanian Devil Park, where police established their forward command station, has expanded to include a wine centre and on any given summer weekend is packed with motor homes and tourist buses. There are also restaurants and bed and breakfasts strung along the Arthur Highway, although the Seascape Cottage is not among them. The Martins' sons still own Seascape, which no longer offers the home-style accommodation that made Sally and David Martin so well loved, but still proudly bears its name on the property entrance. The pink-and-white colour scheme of the remaining buildings – a studio and a garage – mirrors that of the house that was lost in the flames and a tree has been planted where it once stood. Glenn Martin and his brother, Darren, decided not to recreate the property but instead leave a footprint of what once was. On the first anniversary of the massacre in 1997, Glenn told reporters that it was time to put the massacre in 'the background'. 'To screw yourself up and not to move on is not fair to the people you've lost. They've left you here to carry on. It's left to you to make the most of it,' he was quoted as saying.

The real estate investment boom and mainlanders in search of a lifestyle change have seen property prices on the peninsula skyrocket. Waterfront properties that had become out of reach on the mainland are still affordable in Tasmania and 'seachangers' are snapping them up by the handful. Against all expectations, the Tasman Peninsula has become in vogue.

To help the local economy recover, a regional marketing group was set up to promote not just the Port Arthur Historic Site, but businesses from across the peninsula. As of early 2004, there were 56 separate businesses involved, but all with the common aim of promoting the peninsula as a whole, rather than just individual ventures struggling in the shadow of the site itself.

Leading the charge at the Port Arthur site is Stephen Large, a tall, quietly charismatic man who, in 2000, took on what many would have thought was a poisoned chalice. Stephen had spent the previous eleven years working for the Department of State Development and it was in that role that he visited the site in the months immediately after the shootings. He was sent down in mid-1996 to meet with the Tasman Council to discuss business relief packages for those traders doing it tough.

Stephen remembers driving away from the peninsula at dusk with an enormous sense of relief at being able to escape the oppressive sadness that had enveloped the area. It felt cloistered and eerie. 'I got home and told my wife that it wouldn't worry me if I never, ever went back to the Port Arthur site again.'

Yet when he was asked in early 2000 if he would consider acting as chief executive of the Port Arthur site for six weeks, he grabbed the chance. It was, he said, a privilege to be asked to head such a historically important site and to work in and around the people of the peninsula.

'When I actually got down there and talked to some of the people and heard what they had been through, well, my thoughts and feelings just paled into insignificance. It became a challenge for me to work with them and help them make Port Arthur the place they wanted it to be.'

After he was appointed to the position permanently in July 2000, one of the first things Stephen did was sit down and talk one-on-one with each of the staff. With up to 155 staff on board, depending on the season, it was a time-consuming task, but invaluable. For many of the employees, it was the first time they had ever been inside the chief executive's office.

'I learnt so much about the place; the people, the problems, what needed to be done and what people would like to see happen.

While we haven't done everything, as a management team we have taken on board a lot of these suggestions and concerns and worked hard to address them.'

When we meet, Stephen tells of how managing staff and working with the wider community remain the most complex and delicate issues still faced by the site. At least twenty people still working at the site were employed at the time of the shootings and those who weren't must face daily reminders of what happened there.

'The effects of 1996 are still very much there. It is no good saying it has all gone away eight years later. I mean, what happened funda- mentally changed the whole human resource culture and that is something that remains a huge issue...it will be a long time before that goes and, you know, you need to compassionately and tenderly look after people while also getting the job done at the end of the day.'

For Stephen, that means being aware of how staff may react to certain triggers, such as media stories which inevitably link any event at Port Arthur with the 1996 massacre. Others remain upset by the conspiracy theories that continue to wash around Tasmania and beyond and, in some cases, are given credence through media coverage. There is also the stream of questions from tourists who, having once been deterred from visiting Port Arthur because of the killings, now want to know all about them in sometimes vivid detail. Stephen doesn't blame the visitors, especially as many of them only know about Port Arthur because of the massacre, not in spite of it. He agrees that Port Arthur's increased international pro- file after the massacre has been one of the positives, if it could ever be described that way, to come out of the disaster.

It can become difficult, though, to continually field questions about what happened on 28 April 1996, and then listen to stories about 'where I was when I heard about the massacre. Expectedly, you know, and it's not the fault of the visitors, because they are very interested in terms of how the place has recovered, what we've done and how it has affected people...they have got a genuine and profound interest,' Stephen says. 'Most of the visitor comments we receive are positive, but some are critical that we don't interpret what happened in 1996 enough.'

The guided tours of the site don't include details of the massacre. It is still too soon. Instead, visitors are invited to spend time
in the memorial garden and around the reflective pool, and most
do. It has the quiet, reverent atmosphere of what is a sacred site.
After walking in and around the shell of the Broad Arrow, words, it
seems, are no longer needed.

For some Tasmanians, their return to Port Arthur came through
two events held as part of the biennial 10 Days on the Island
Festival, first held in early 2001 and again in 2003. Festival director
Robyn Archer convinced Stephen and a sceptical Port Arthur management team that the site could be a successful part of the festival,
and she was right. The 2001 event attracted 2500 people, but even
this was surpassed in 2003 when more than 3000 people flooded
into the site for a mass choral spectacle. Choral Island saw almost
400 Tasmanian singers from across the state perform in and around
the Port Arthur ruins, their sweet voices resounding off the harsh
sandstone walls that had witnessed decades of brutality and pain.
Some visitors were moved to tears as the voices melted across
expanses of green where, just seven years earlier, gunshots had been
fired and people had fled for their lives. On this glorious autumn
Sunday, not unlike the blue skies of 28 April 1996, it was another
act of reclamation.

Tall, sandy-haired Guy Dobner is a livestock farmer and until mid
2005 was a member of the Tasman Council. He is also president of
the committee which runs the Tasman 97.7FM community radio
station from a former garage tucked in a shady corner of the Tasman
District School playground. The radio station is a small, but very
public, symbol of a community climbing back. When the Port
Arthur massacre exposed the poor communications across the
Tasman Peninsula, a community radio station was considered one
way of overcoming the isolation. It was an expensive idea, but one
which was met with an outpouring of generosity. Communications
giant Ericsson Australia donated $200,000 worth of studio equip-
ment, while ABC Radio chipped in with a free studio control panel.

Commercial station HO-FM, having upgraded to CDs, donated its entire cartridge collection. Local technicians put it all together.

When I first visited the studio in 2003, Guy took me on a short tour of the facilities, which include a recording studio for artists, and explained how the project was always going to be more than just a communication device to keep locals in touch. 'Through this catastrophic event, we were placed in a position where we had to do something positive, to bring the community together. Something like this is hugely important: it has led to a much greater sense of community, of being involved and a sense of working together.'

Through the work of Guy and others, the station came to life on 30 May 1999 as 89.3 Tasman FM and began broadcasting 24 hours a day to around 2000 people. By late 2003, the station had upgraded its transmitter and secured a permanent community licence, extending its coverage across the south-east of Tasmania to more than 20,000 people. A group of 25 volunteers create, produce and present the eclectic line-up that covers all tastes from country and western through to thrash. Others, such as Keith Moulton, had their own prerecorded shows, while the Port Arthur Historic Site offers a weekly update on its events.

Daphne Champion, for the most part, sells fresh fruit and vegetables to the Tasman Peninsula locals. Come Monday morning, however, and her throaty voice is back-announcing tracks in her weekly show, *Mixed Bag*. The studio phone rings almost constantly with listeners asking her to play this track or that. She loves the repartee. 'There is an enormous amount of pleasure in knowing people are enjoying it out there.'

Can a place ever really 'move on' after the enormity of an event such as the Port Arthur massacre? I asked Margaret Scott this question.

'I think it very much depends on how close you were to a victim. I mean, if it had been my daughter, or a niece or even my best friend's child who had been killed, then no. It is much too soon to be talking about moving on and perhaps we never will. But I was fortunate. I didn't really know any of the victims personally, so it was easy for me to talk about moving on.'

Indeed, it is impossible to capture the full breadth and depth of the impact of the Port Arthur massacre. Just as a stone is dropped into a millpond, the ripples from Martin Bryant's actions on 28 April spread through an entire community and well beyond. Everyone has a Port Arthur story, be it remembering exactly where they were when they heard about the massacre, knowing someone who was involved, or being directly involved themselves. In Tasmania, the ripples run wide. In researching this story, I stumbled across a newspaper clipping about a Tasmanian man, Kyle Spruce, who had just walked into the Port Arthur general store as Bryant approached Glenn Pears and Zoe Hall in their car. Kyle and his wife watched from the window as the full horror unfolded before them. Just a few weeks before reading this article, Kyle had been retiling my bathroom floor. He, although I never knew it, is part of the Port Arthur story.

So, too, is each of the Port Arthur staff who were rostered on that day or who lost colleagues. There are the more than 600 visitors who passed through the gates on 28 April and who, in their own way, were affected by what unfolded. There are also the hundreds of police officers and emergency service workers who responded to the crime, the more than 1000 witnesses who were interviewed, the dozens of doctors and nurses who attended to the wounded and the priests and counsellors who comforted those in grief. There is the former Tasmanian Director of Public Prosecutions Damian Bugg and his legal team, who pieced together the case against Bryant while remaining so sensitive to the victims and their families. There is the recovery team which was tasked with helping to rebuild the Tasman community; the Tasman Council; the politicians; the journalists and the lobbyists who pursued gun law reform. There is the family of Martin Bryant and their friends, none of whom could have foreseen what was to come of their son and brother. And there are the countless family, friends, neighbours and colleagues of the 35 people who were murdered that day. The ripples run wide.

I think about this on a November day in 2003 when I visit the Port Arthur Historic Site for the first time in many years. The husk of the Broad Arrow Café is busy. A steady stream of visitors, soaking up the afternoon sunshine, are wandering in and out of the stone remains, their feet crunching the pebbled floor. Some carry camcorders, muttering into the mouthpiece as they scan the scene with one eye pressed tightly against the lens. Others gather up their children for a photograph on the single wooden bench that is the only furnishing inside the remains of the building. Some walk in and stand for a moment, caught in their own thoughts.

Further up the hillside, about 100 m from the café, is the rugged cross of Huon pine. Its once rich honey colour has been washed grey by the weather and dusty cobwebs drift from its rough edges. Some of the tourists stand next to it, their heads beneath the crossbeam, as friends or relatives take their picture with disposable cameras. They then wander down to the wide, but shallow, granite pool that lies between the cross and the café. The gently rippling pool has the aura of a war memorial; formal and solemn with the penetrating words penned by Margaret Scott etched deep around its sides:

> May we who come to this garden cherish life for the sake of
> those who died
> Cherish compassion for the sake of those who gave aid
> Cherish peace for the sake of those in pain.

On this day, however, there is also another tribute.

A greeting card, bleached by sun, remains propped against one wall of the pool. It sits on a small bunch of daffodils that have been tied with a simple silk ribbon. They appear to have been bought for a young girl.

'Happy Trails', the card reads in embossed letters on its front, under an image of a girl on horseback: smiling and carefree. Inside, the card is addressed simply to 'Chicky Dee'.

Other words are hard to make out, the ink faded by time, but some of those who spend a moment to decipher the message take a step back, all at once moved and slightly embarrassed to be reading something so intensely personal. Through this simple card and faded flowers, the reality of what happened in this area on Sunday, 28 April 1996 is brought into sharp focus.

'Missing you every day,' part of the message reads.

My confidante and my reason for living.
Wherever you are, fly free angel.
Within my heart are memories of the perfect love you gave me
I remember.

THOSE WHO DIED AT
PORT ARTHUR
⤜ 28 APRIL 1996 ⤛

Winifred Aplin
Walter Bennett
Nicole Burgess
Sou Leng Chung
Elva Gaylard
Zoe Hall
Elizabeth Howard
Mary Howard
Mervyn Howard
Ron Jary
Tony Kistan
Dennis Lever
Sarah Loughton
David Martin
Noeline (Sally) Martin
Pauline Masters
Alannah Mikac
Madeline Mikac

Nanette Mikac
Andrew Mills
Peter Nash
Gwen Neander
Mo Yee (William) Ng
Anthony Nightingale
Mary Nixon
Glenn Pears
Russell (Jim) Pollard
Janet Quin
Helene Salzmann
Robert Salzmann
Kate Scott
Kevin Sharp
Ray Sharp
Royce Thompson
Jason Winter

NOTES

Chapter 1
Damian Bugg QC, address to Tasmanian Supreme Court at the hearing of Martin Bryant, *R v Martin Bryant*, 19 November 1996.

Tasmanian Chief Justice William Cox, sentencing remarks in the Tasmanian Supreme Court at the hearing of Martin Bryant, *R v Martin Bryant*, 22 November 1996.

Chapter 2
Walter Mikac with Lindsay Simpson, *To Have and to Hold: A modern-day love story cut short*, Pan Macmillan, Sydney, 1997.

Peter Samson, *Dunblane: Our year of tears*, Mainstream, Edinburgh, 1997.

The Honorable John Howard Prime Minister, foreword for *To Have and to Hold: A modern-day love story cut short*, Walter Mikac with Lindsay Simpson, Pan Macmillan, Sydney, 1997.

Walter Mikac, *The Circle of Life: Replacing hardship with love*, Pan Macmillan, Melbourne, 1999.

Walter Mikac and Kim Sporton (eds), *Reach for the Stars!: Uplifting messages from outstanding Australians*, Penguin Books Australia, 2000.

Walter Mikac, interview in *Woman's Day*, quoted in 'Mikac enjoying life again', *The Mercury*, 6 June 2000.

Chapter 3
Max Doyle, *Report of the Special Commissioner for Port Arthur Mr. Max Doyle into matters affecting the Port Arthur Historic Site and other associated matters*, Bellerive, Tasmania, tabled in Tasmanian Parliament, June 1997.

Chapter 4
Geoffrey Blainey, quoted in 'Massacre survivors reject slur on bravery', *The Advertiser*, 23 May 1996.

Chapter 5
Max Doyle, *Report of the Special Commissioner for Port Arthur Mr. Max Doyle into matters affecting the Port Arthur Historic Site and other associated matters*, Bellerive, Tasmania, tabled in Tasmanian Parliament, June 1997.

Memo from Port Arthur management to staff, 20 February 1997, reproduced as Attachment 9 in *Report of the Special Commissioner for Port Arthur
Mr. Max Doyle into matters affecting the Port Arthur Historic Site and other associated matters,* Bellerive, Tasmania, tabled in Tasmanian Parliament, June 1997.

Damian Bugg QC, *An inquiry by the Director of Public Prosecutions into the
door at Broad Arrow Café and related matters,* dated 23 July 1997, report for
the Joint Parliamentary Group on Port Arthur, tabled in Tasmanian
Parliament, July 1997.

Conspiracy theories
Joe Vialls, *Deadly Deception at Port Arthur,* self-published, Carine, Western
Australia, 1998.

Joe Vialls, website <http://vialls.net/portarthur/portarthurpart2.html>
[accessed July 2004]

Andrew MacGregor, *Deceit and Terrorism, Port Arthur,* CD-ROM, 2002.

Shooters Party website <www.shootersnews.addr.com> [accessed July
2004]

Chapter 6
Dr Kay Chung, *Going Public: Communicating in the public and private sectors,*
Hale & Iremonger, Sydney, 1999.

Celina Edmonds, in *Port Arthur Update,* newsletter produced by the
Department of Community and Health Services, Government of Tasmania,
Issue VII, 5 December 1996.

'News and Conflict', Across the Nation column, *AllNews,* in-house News
Limited staff publication, September 2005.

Chapter 7
Walter Mikac with Lindsay Simpson, *To Have and to Hold: A modern-day love
story cut short,* Pan Macmillan, Sydney, 1997.

Chapter 9
Dr Ian Sale, quoted in 'Managing Trauma', *Background Briefing,* ABC Radio
National, 18 January 2004.

Dr Julian Watchorn, 'Surviving Port Arthur: The role of dissociation in the
impact of psychological trauma and its implications for the process of
recovery', dissertation, University of Tasmania, October 2001.

Chapter 10
Superintendent Barry Bennett, quoted by Jenny Fleming in 'Forward Command at Port Arthur', Tasmanian Police Association newsletter, *Association News,* Vol I (2), December 1996.

Superintendent Bob Fielding, quoted by Jenny Fleming in 'Forward Command at Port Arthur', Tasmanian Police Association newsletter, *Association News,* Vol I (2), December 1996.

Chapter 12
'Stars of the 20th Century', *Australian Style,* Vol II, Issue 2, December 1999.

Professor Paul Mullen, psychiatric report on Martin Bryant for the defence, dated 12 November 1996, tendered to Tasmanian Supreme Court at the hearing of Martin Bryant, *R v Martin Bryant,* November 1996.

Dr Ian Sale, report on Martin Bryant for the Director of Public Prosecutions, 6 August 1996, tendered to Tasmanian Supreme Court at the hearing of Martin Bryant, *R v Martin Bryant,* November 1996.

Mike Bingham, *Suddenly One Sunday,* HarperCollins, Sydney, 1996.

Damian Bugg QC, address to Tasmanian Supreme Court at the hearing of Martin Bryant, *R v Martin Bryant,* November 1996.

Police interview of Martin Bryant, as quoted during evidence to the Tasmanian Supreme Court at the hearing of Martin Bryant, *R v Martin Bryant,* November 1996.

'Managing Martin: The jailing of Martin Bryant', *Background Briefing,* ABC Radio National, 16 March 1997.

Carol Altmann, 'Compassion for Forgotten Killer', interview with 'Rob', *The Weekend Australian,* 5 April 2003.

Carleen Bryant's message to the public on the first anniversary of the massacre, issued via defence lawyer John Avery, as reproduced by the *Herald Sun,* 25 April 1997.

Chapter 13
Simon Chapman, *Over Our Dead Bodies: Port Arthur and Australia's fight for gun control,* Pluto Press, Sydney, 1998.

Jenny Mouzos and Catherine Rushforth, 'Firearm Related Deaths in Australia 1991–2001', issues paper No. 269, *Trends and Issues in Crime and Criminal Justice,* Australian Institute of Criminology, November 2003.

Graduate Institute of International Studies, 'Small Arms Survey', Geneva, Switzerland, 2003. <www.smallarmssurvey.org/database> [accessed July 2003]

Chapter 14
Ian Brand, *Penal Peninsula: Port Arthur and its outstations, 1827–1898,* Jason Publications, West Moonah, Tasmania, 1978.

Alex Graeme-Evans and Michael Ross, *A Short History Guide to Port Arthur 1830–77,* Regal Publications, Hobart, Tasmania, 1993.

Chapter 15
Margaret Scott, *Port Arthur: A story of strength and courage,* Random House Australia, Sydney, 1997.

Stephen Large, *Victorian Tourism Conference Paper,* 23 March 2004.

Carol Altmann, 'Radio Helps Heal a Shattered Community', interview with Guy Dobner and Daphne Champion, *The Australian,* 21 August 2003.

Port Arthur Historic Site Management Authority Annual Report 2003.

PHOTOGRAPHIC CREDITS

Unless otherwise stated, photographs are from the author's collection.

Page 1: Photograph of Walter Mikac courtesy of Newspix

Page 2: Photograph of Brigid Cook by Kim Eiszele, reproduced courtesy of *The Mercury*

Page 4: Photograph of Ron and Gwen Neander courtesy of Ron Neander

Page 5: Photograph of Wendy Scurr and Brigid Cook courtesy of Newspix

Page 6: Photograph of Leigh Winburn by Sam Rosewarne

Page 9: Photograph of Bryan Walpole and Prime Minister Howard by Leigh Winburn, reproduced courtesy of *The Mercury*

Page 10: Photographs courtesy of Newspix

Page 11: Photograph of memorial garden courtesy of the Port Arthur Historic Site
Photograph of memorial cross courtesy of Newspix

Page 12: Photograph of Martin Bryant courtesy of Newspix

ACKNOWLEDGEMENTS

This book would not have been possible without the generosity and courage of those who were prepared to tell their stories. I thank all of those who entrusted me with some of their most personal experiences and, in many cases, also shared precious cards, letters, photos and documents: I feel immensely privileged to have been invited into your lives. I would also like to thank Richard Walsh ('Coach'), consultant publisher at Allen & Unwin, for approaching me to write his inspired idea for this book. Sue Hines for disproving all that I had been warned about editors and publishers: your enthusiasm and cheerful advice kept me going. Clare Emery and Karen Ward for their superb editing which transformed a manuscript into a book. Dr Julian Watchorn, for access to his research on critical incident stress debriefing and to the late Dr Margaret Scott for sharing her wisdom, her unerring support and healthy doses of humour over lunch: I want you to know we got there, Margaret. Claudette Wells, for teaching me so much about priorities and restoring my soul, Ainslie Davies for her lightning-fast transcription and positive feedback, Janet Weaving and Kerrie Denholm for their invaluable help in sorting out photographs and maps, and to each of my incredible and loving friends: all of the Adelaide girls (you know who you are), the inspirational members of the Tasmanian Swimmers' Club, the Girls of the Overland who are so strong in heart, mind and legs, Bev Evans for getting me this far, Michelle Watson for her beautiful friendship during the past 30-something years, and to Deb K for her belief and early encouragement. Finally, I acknowledge my three 'guardian angels' – Wally, Mildred and Ian – who have left this world, but not my side, and I especially thank my wonderful partner, Louie, for living and loving without reserve.